DEADLY
DECISIONS

DEADLY DECISIONS

HOW FALSE KNOWLEDGE

SANK THE *TITANIC*, BLEW UP THE SHUTTLE,

AND LED AMERICA INTO WAR

CHRISTOPHER BURNS

Prometheus Books

59 John Glenn Drive
Amherst, New York 14228–2119

Published 2008 by Prometheus Books

Inquiries should be addressed to
Prometheus Books
59 John Glenn Drive
Amherst, New York 14228–2119
VOICE: 716–691–0133, ext. 210
FAX: 716–691–0137
WWW.PROMETHEUSBOOKS.COM

12 11 10 09 08   5 4 3 2 1

Library of Congress Cataloging-in-Publication Data

Burns, Christopher, 1942–
    Deadly decisions : how false knowledge sank the *Titanic*, blew up the shuttle, and led America into war / Christopher Burns.
        p. cm.
    Includes bibliographical references and index.
    ISBN 978–1–59102–660–0 (alk. paper)
    1. Errors.

AZ999 .B89 2008
001.9/6 22

                                                                            2008030487

Printed in the United States of America on acid-free paper

For Owen and Gwydion Perry;
Ella and Oliver Copeland;
Emmanuel Tran;
Olivia and Parker Johnson;
Toby Seiji Sakata;
Robin and Henry Sinclair,
all now under five years old

CONTENTS

INTRODUCTION

I n the last weeks before the Iraq invasion, my wife and I went down to the center of our seaside town and joined a peace rally. We were just a small huddle of people drinking coffee and carrying signs, blowing on our hands and shifting from foot to foot on a cold March day at the edge of the water. Across the street I recognized a few men my age in old fatigue jackets and army hats, shouting that we were appeasers, traitors, and homosexuals, hooting at us as one by one we went up to the microphone and said how much we were opposed to the senseless bombing of Iraq.

I was going to say something, too. I understand that war is sometimes necessary and I was concerned that nuclear and biological weapons might fall into the hands of terrorists like those who attacked us on 9/11. But I thought the United States lacked the evidence to justify an attack on another country and I was afraid that we would be left once again with the terrible reality of war and no good reason for having started it. Years ago, as a US Army information officer in Vietnam, I had to find a quote to run in olive drab type across the title page of a report we were doing on the year's combat operations. We needed a simple, stirring statement that would capture our purpose for being there—something from LBJ or General Westmoreland that would work against a background of several dramatic photos we had of soldiers under fire. The information office at division headquarters was an open-sided hut with a dozen desks, two large fans, and a darkroom that flooded every afternoon when the rains came. We didn't have any books or reference materials and we hadn't been able to come up with the phrase we needed—not one we could print in an official army publication, anyway. So I sent a telex off to the public affairs office at the Pentagon and asked them for some suggestions. We got a reply back the following week: "Your request for a reason for the war has been forwarded." We never heard from them again.

We ended up running just the opening pages of pictures without any text, and it was even more dramatic that way: no words, no reasons, just the awful nobility of combat. The point I was going to make in my little speech was that war should not be accidental. When things get rough, it is important for the truth to be on our side and for our reasons to be clear and easy to prove if anyone asks. Because war is real, and its price is always heartbreaking.

I'm not afraid of public speaking, and my wife was elbowing me to get up there, but I didn't take my turn at the mike. In the end I thought my voice would make no difference. The news was full of political bluster and the clanging of alarms, and I knew that public opinion was sliding quickly toward war. We were on our way to invading Iraq, and there was nothing I could do about it. I felt profoundly defeated.

As a news executive and a consultant to both the government and the private sector, I had spent most of my career evaluating, researching, and designing information management systems for communities, businesses, government groups, and industries—not just the technology but the procedures, the organization, and the economics as well. My work has focused on ways to make the existing information infrastructure better, which is to say, more truthful, more timely, more relevant, and more agile in responding to external events. So I knew an information malfunction when I saw it. That afternoon, in the last days before going to war in the Middle East, it seemed to me that the United States was helplessly tangled in propaganda. Our democracy was not working properly, and the outcome was likely to be a repeat of the many disasters in recent years: a plane gets shot down for the wrong reason, a nuclear power plant spews radiation into the air, a major business fails at great cost because the people making the decisions had fooled themselves with false information. It was a question of truth, and I didn't think there was much I could do about it. But I decided that with a little research I might find the bones of the problem. Perhaps these mistakes could be avoided in the future.

In *The Meaning of Truth* (1909), William James, that patrician philosopher from Boston, looked at this question through his thoroughly American eyes and saw a can-do, down-to-earth solution that put the dusty European philosophers in their place: "How will the truth be realized? What, in short, is the truth's cash value in experimental terms? The moment pragmatism asks this question, it seeks the answer: True Ideas are those that we can assimilate, validate, corroborate and verify. False ideas are those that we cannot. That is the practical difference it makes to us to have true ideas; that therefore is the meaning of truth, for it is all that truth is known as."[1]

If this was the modern view of truth, it seemed to me to be wrong in two important ways. First, it is often extremely difficult to validate, corroborate, or verify the information we are dealing with, except by comparing it to the other information we are dealing with. And often the whole system is contaminated by misunderstanding, bad data, and false assumptions that are hard to spot. The truth test rarely works. And second, the real issue of truth is not whether you or I should believe this or that, it is what we believe together. The truth that matters is group truth, and where we get into trouble is when a whole organization—a company, a community, a nation—starts to act on information that has been gathered from many sources and processed by many people but that has come to contain significant elements that are false.

The more I learn about major disasters and the decisions that led to them, the more it seems to me that the Information Age, for all its promise, is drawing us into danger. We live in a world where many of the things we believe cannot be confirmed, and some of them are simply not true. Truth is a temporary description of reality that is accurate enough to guide the intended action, and it is affected by how the brain selects, blurs, imagines, and remembers the information it receives. Truth is affected by how people in groups clarify and distort, exaggerate and suppress the news they share. Truth is affected by the media, by propaganda, by advertising, and by public advocacy. But although great strides have been made in cognitive and communications science, we don't know enough about how individuals and groups assemble and maintain large information constructs such as medicine, aviation, computer systems, and government on which our lives and fortunes depend. And, based on recent evidence, we often get it wrong.

The purpose of this book is to clarify these failures in detail so the pattern of error can be spotted when it begins again. The biology of the brain, the behavior of groups, and the structure of society provide surprising clues as to why individuals and groups succumb to wishful thinking, information overload, and the unintentional twisting of facts. With a better understanding of our own information handling behavior, we might learn to make more successful decisions.

The story here is not 9/11 or how we got into the Iraq War. It isn't just Three Mile Island or the space shuttle *Challenger* or the USS *Vincennes*, or the medical errors and the business failures and the engineering mistakes and the endless, pathological mendacity of politicians scuttling for power. The story is about the Information Age and how it challenges us to be more truthful in our daily work and public discourse. It is not a story about somebody else; it is about you and me, about the dangerous behavior we have fallen into, and about the miracles that information can bring if we are willing to struggle honestly with the facts.

I am grateful to Ben Spencer, Bob Ross, Chester Kerr, Mark Carroll, Jan Carlson and my friends at the *Massachusetts Review* who long ago gave me shelter and encouragement when it seemed unreasonable to do so. We rarely get a chance to publicly discharge such debts of gratitude. I am grateful to my wise and generous clients over thirty years, from whom I have learned so much. Leland Schwartz turned his laser eye to the text and, with a gentler mien than mine, caught many errors of fact and phrasing. And I am thankful to my friends and colleagues who urged me to undertake this project and then coached me along the way: John Woolley, Paul Zurkowski, Pat Martin, Maggie Perry, Julia Copeland, Fran Collin, Linda Regan, and especially Bill Johnson, who has listened to these arguments for so many, many years. Thank you.

1

FALSE KNOWLEDGE

I t was nearly midnight on April 14, 1912, when the White Star liner *Titanic*, racing along on its maiden voyage across the North Atlantic, struck an iceberg many times larger than the ship itself. We now know from extraordinary new photographs that the seam along the starboard hull was ripped open by the impact. The ocean poured in, breaching the double hull, flooding the mail room, the squash court, and the third-class berths. It spilled over the "water-tight" bulkheads to snuff out the giant steam boilers and pull the ship down in one of the greatest disasters of modern times.

In the wake of this tragedy, the British government ordered that ice patrols commence along the major shipping lanes to guard against another disaster. They should have called for truth patrols instead.

TITANIC: UNSINKABLE

There was nothing surprising about icebergs in the North Atlantic. All day the *Titanic* had received detailed information about the ice ahead, delivered directly to Captain Edward Smith and to other officers on the bridge. Two hours before the incident, the *Mesaba* sent the *Titanic* a warning of icebergs at 42° 25'N 50° 14'W, almost precisely where the accident later occurred. At least one report was given to Bruce Ismay, president of the White Star Line. Eager to set a new record for transatlantic crossing, Ismay calmly stuffed the note in his pocket. In spite of frequent and specific warnings, he made the decision to let the ship race ahead at full speed.

Ismay believed three things to be true: first, he knew from his own experience with other ships that the lookout would give him actual sightings of any iceberg in time to steer around it. Second, his team of engineers assured him that even if the *Titanic* struck an iceberg submerged or otherwise difficult to see, the ship would not sink. And third, if there should be an accident of any kind, there was a tight and mutually supportive community of ships nearby that would come to his aid. A truth patrol would have noted that he was wrong on all counts.

The night was not dark and stormy, but clear, cloudless, and spangled with stars; conditions for timely warning seemed excellent. But the lookout actually assigned to watch for ice couldn't see that well. Frederick Fleet had not been given an eye exam in five years[1] and, in spite of his frequent requests, had not been provided binoculars. More important, the unprecedented size and speed of the *Titanic* were so great that, unlike other ships in Ismay's experience, this one could not be stopped or significantly turned in less than a mile with engines full astern. Even a lookout with excellent vision could not have spotted the iceberg at that distance.

Nor was it unsinkable. The *Titanic* was built to remain afloat even with its first four watertight compartments flooded, but the new design had not been tested. Ismay even overruled the worried engineers who built the ship, cutting the number of lifeboats from thirty-two to sixteen, the minimum required by the British Board of Trade. He later observed that the reason the *Titanic* carried any lifeboats at all was so they could rescue passengers and crew from other ships.[2]

And finally, the *Titanic* was for all practical purposes alone. Ten miles away, the Leyland liner *Californian* had slowed down in the dangerous ice field when third officer Charles Victor Groves saw the lights from a large passenger liner racing up from the east. As he watched, the liner seemed to stop as if in trouble. He went to the radio room, found that the operator had gone to bed, and tried to operate the radio himself but was unable to make contact.[3]

For the next two hours, Groves and his fellow officers studied the strange behavior of the *Titanic*. She seemed to float awkwardly on the sea, firing white rockets normally considered a signal of distress. When they reported this to Stanley Lord, captain of the *Californian*, he told them to try to make contact by Morse lamp, but this proved unsuccessful. Finally, when it seemed that the lights of the nearby ship were beginning to disappear, the officers went again to Captain Lord, who was lying down in his cabin. "Were they all white rockets?" he asked. And hearing that they were, he went back to sleep.

At the conclusion of the British inquiry, Lord Mersey, chairman of the inquiry committee, wrote: "When she first saw the rockets, the *Californian* could have pushed through the ice to the open water without any serious risk and so have come to the assistance of the *Titanic*. Had she done so, she might have saved many if not all of the lives that were lost."[4]

Why didn't Lord take the distress signals seriously? He testified later that he believed the *Titanic* was "unsinkable," that the distress signals seemed ambiguous, and that he was in a dangerous ice field himself. His officers concluded from the same evidence that they were witnessing a disaster of unprecedented proportions, but they stood at the rail and kept their silence.

It is part of the *Titanic* legend that Robert Sarnoff, the twenty-one-year-old employee of Marconi Wireless Telegraph Company, stayed at his primitive radio for seventy-two hours, receiving and passing on the names of those lost at sea; the first major demonstration of the revolutionary new wireless telegraphy. It seems ironic that we should find there, at the birth of the technology that epitomizes our age, the specter of an ancient and enduring problem. The *Titanic* sank because of multiple failures to manage information correctly: failure by Captain Smith to heed warnings, failure by Bruce Ismay to credit evidence that was contrary to his ambitions, failure by Captain Lord of the *Californian* to act in the face of doubt. The *Titanic* sank because of false knowledge.

The errors that surrounded the sinking of the *Titanic* are not unusual. A number of recent disasters on a comparable scale indicate that the problem may be growing worse. Early warnings are often brushed aside by men and women in the thrall of their own dreams. Critical information is frequently delayed or lost in organizations blundering through a crisis. And at the last moment, when the situation could be saved, communication systems fail and dissenters often fall silent.

Every new age begins with a drum roll of novel disasters and ends in a fog of nostalgia. One of the unexpected problems of the Industrial Age, for example, was finding low-cost labor to come in from the farms and cottages to tend the mills, a task that precipitated bloody riots and decades of dissent. Now, with the onset of the Information Age, our information systems seem to offer new power over a complex world, but then those systems fail us. The warning is late, the message is confusing, the signal never gets through. Failures are attributed to some cause over which we can comfortably claim no control: equipment malfunction, system complexity, inadequate training, bad weather. Even our new disasters are understood in terms of old conditions.

It is customary in business management literature to say that, in such cases, the decision system failed. The one responsible for the final evaluation of alternatives was distracted, deluded, indecisive, unable to handle all the data, or emotionally ill-equipped for the stress. And when none of these conditions can be confirmed with certainty, those who rake through the ruins of an accident say he made the best decision he could, given the information available to him at the time. No one is to blame. The solution is to build more decision support systems, get more data, make better presentations, order extra computer checks.

But the reality is otherwise. Some of the information, though wrong, looks right. It fits neatly with the rest of the data. It comes from a trusted source. It has been reviewed and approved by several hierarchies of analysts. The danger is that we live in a world where the evidence and analysis always makes sense, but where, through personal and social processes we scarcely understand, the information gathered by the organization has come to include false knowledge. Everyone is to blame.

Our ability to determine the accuracy of information is increasingly inadequate. Smart men and women in the best organizations, surrounded by data, make the wrong decisions. We race ahead like Ismay on the bridge, charmed by the possibilities but betrayed by the facts. We are vaguely aware of the need for speedy and relevant information but insensitive to the limits of cognition and almost entirely ignorant about how information is distorted as it travels through an organization. We cling to the idea that a reasonable man in a position of authority should make these complex decisions alone, and we ignore the fact that the whole community—the engineers, the lookout, the signalman, the radio operator, the officers on the deck of the *Californian*—have already narrowed his choices and set the future in motion. We are trying to manage communities, businesses, and nations on the basis of garbled reports and unreliable message systems without having achieved the ability to test for truth—not as some philosophical matter, but as the basis for action in a complex world.

Even direct observation can often be misleading. Beyond a certain speed and level of complexity, the world we observe is a false one. The *Titanic* was effectively traveling blind: by the time Fleet spotted the iceberg, it was already too late to turn the ship. The collision had occurred downstream in time and nothing in his power could then undo it. Until that moment, a man's ability to observe nature had been approximately equal to his power to react. He could run from a volcano, dodge a screaming artillery shell, and steer a ship through a storm. But new technology has changed the rules. Some armies in history have marched faster than their supply trains and starved to death on the eve of victory. Fighter pilots joke that beyond the speed of sound there is no point looking out the window: all you see is the past. At Mach 2 another fighter coming directly at you appears as a speck a mile away, but within one second—faster than many pilots can react—the planes have passed each other or collided.

A hundred years ago, the truth was easier to establish. One could visit the mills, go to the market, see the laboratory, and reach a conclusion based on personal experience. Information was a record of market transactions, a notebook of observations from the mill, or a report of distant events. It could be confirmed by personal observation. But now, as organizations expand to undertake broader and more specialized tasks, financial trading systems have become the marketplace, software development is the mill floor, reports are the events. And the decision center of an organization is often too far from the relevant reality to check for accuracy. The real world we need to observe is deep in the reactor core, in the night sky on the other side of the world, or in the purchasing behavior of millions who will buy the product. We discover too late that our observations are not timely enough, or complete enough, or accurate enough to be relied upon. We design products for consumers we have never met. We prescribe medicine we have not tested ourselves for patients we scarcely know to treat illnesses diagnosed by others. We aim our missiles at nations whose language we cannot read or speak and we are betting our future health and productivity on genetic devices and nanotechnology we can no longer see or feel.

MEDICINE, MONEY, AND WAR: UNTHINKABLE

How shall we test the quality of complex information? How was Ismay to decide the truth of the message "There are icebergs ahead?" In the middle of a modern management situation, it is rarely possible to consult some long-standing authority. Events change quickly, and authority has a habit of hiding in generalities. Nor can we always measure the truth of a message by comparing it rationally to other information available. Too often the other information comes from the same source. The liar's art, after all, is to weave from ambiguous and dissonant data a "reasonable tale." It was certainly contrary to Ismay's style—and to the style of his times—to gather his officers together and evaluate the problem. And if he had, what good would it have done? The officers might have been more cautious but they were not better informed.

Consider three fields where information is the primary reality—medicine, finance, and international relations.

In the field of medicine, the inability to see errors in the patient's diagnosis or treatment has led to a startling increase in patient deaths. In 2000, the *Journal of the American Medical Association* published the results of a study showing 225,000 deaths a year as a result of medical error: 12,000 from unnecessary surgery, 7,000 from medication errors in the hospital, 20,000 from other hospital errors, and 80,000 from infections occurring while the patient was hospitalized. One hundred and six thousand deaths resulted from "non-error" negative effects of drugs.[5] The total number of deaths caused by medical error in the United States is roughly equal to the number of casualties from two jumbo jets crashing every day.

It is possible that doctors are trained to be more attentive to the problems of false knowledge than engineers, lawyers, financial analysts and intelligence professionals—as we shall see. In modern medicine, truth is their life's work. But the mistakes they make are more visible, and the results more personal. A study published in 2008 by the New England Healthcare Institute concluded that 8.8 percent of hospital patients in a sample of eight Massachusetts hospitals suffered from "preventable adverse drug reactions," ranging from a change in respiratory rate to a fever or a seizure to anaphylactic shock. "Conservative estimates show that nationwide, adverse drug events result in more than 770,000 hospital injuries and deaths each year."[6]

And that's in the hospital, where a team of professionals works within the discipline of protocol, where outcomes are measured, and where insurance companies have a special interest in preventing mistakes. This doesn't take into account the errors committed by individual physicians treating patients in their own offices. Dr. Vincent DeVita, director of the National Cancer Institute at the US National Institutes of Health, said that of the 462,000 cancer deaths in the United States that year, at least 20 percent occurred because the doctor didn't have—or wouldn't use—information that was immediately available to him or her. In each case, the doctor reached a conclusion based on experience and prescribed the indicated therapy. In each case, the patient died. DeVita went further: the number of deaths "could be cut by as much as 50 percent" if doctors would (or could) take the time to look beyond their desktop for prevention and treatment knowledge already available.[7] Although the information can be found in journals, textbooks, online databases, and university research departments, many doctors cannot or will not use it. Instead they rely on their own memory and judgment, heavily influenced by the desire to heal, and reluctant to use diagnostic tools that might define the disease in terms they don't recognize.

According to a study at the Harvard School of Public Health, 20,000 heart attack deaths a year could have been prevented over the last decade if doctors had accepted research findings when they were first published.[8] Simple discoveries such as the value of aspirin in preventing second heart attacks were ignored for a decade because they were published in a statistics journal doctors don't read. It isn't that they couldn't get access to the journals;

access is easy. The doctors couldn't come to grips with information that seemed foreign and contradictory, information that challenged their competence or caused confusion, information of unknown and indeterminable quality.

Herbert Simon, the Nobel economist, writing about how decisions are made, suggested that there are limits to reason. Individuals tend to identify a new situation as representative of a class of conditions they are familiar with. And as they decide how to respond, they remember successful or vivid responses in the past. People do what has worked before. But when the information is incomplete, people have to imagine what might be missing. When the experience is insufficient to explain what is going on, people have to search for other less familiar responses and make judgments about the efficacy of each one. Usually, Simon says, they choose the first combination of situation and remedy that seems to fit the facts. Not the best one, just the one that is, in Simon's language, most "available."[9] In other words, they guess.

From 1996 through the summer of 2001, the executives of Enron engaged in fraud and asset manipulation to raise the price of its stock from $20 to $90 per share. By the second quarter of 2001, the company claimed that sales in the trailing twelve-month period had jumped from $52 billion to $171 billion. During this astonishing rise, financial analysts, accountants, and the media cheered them on, believing that the company's executive talent and the so-called new economy were the reasons for such success and the herald of happy days to come. According to "independent" analysts at many investment banks, Enron was a brilliant example of the executive's art that cast its glow on other financial schemes being offered by the sales side of the same firm. If you missed out on Enron, my colleague has something just as good. Even in the last month of trading, fifteen of the eighteen investment analysts covering the company rated it a "buy." Senior executives with years of experience couldn't see the crash coming:

I have been asked how I viewed the August 14, 2001 resignation of Enron's then-CEO Jeffrey Skilling. At the time, we viewed Kenneth Lay's return as CEO to be a positive development given his promise of openness and a commitment that Enron would shed non-core assets and focus upon its core business lines. Upon learning of Skilling's departure, I and my colleagues immediately arranged for a meeting with Lay, which was held in Alliance Capital's Minneapolis offices on August 21, 2001. At that meeting, we had a very detailed discussion about Enron's business, and our questions appeared to have been answered in a complete and satisfactory manner. (*Alfred Harrison, vice chairman, Alliance Capital, in testimony to the US Senate Committee on Commerce, Science and Transportation*)[10]

But months before the meeting with Harrison, Lay, and colleagues, Bethany McLean, a thirty-one-year-old English major from Hibbing, Minnesota, wrote an article in *Forbes* calling the whole scheme into doubt. She said she couldn't understand how the business worked. Suddenly others began to notice the same financial reporting tricks, and within nine months the company had filed for bankruptcy, the largest in United States history. Shareholders lost $60 billion, much of it from the personal retirement funds of Enron employees.

On February 6, 2003, Secretary of State Colin Powell stood before the United Nations Security Council and presented the case for the invasion of Iraq. Based on months of research and analysis by the CIA, the State Department, and the Department of Defense, Secretary Powell used satellite photographs, audiotapes, official documents, and captured material to show that Iraq had already developed biological weapons of mass destruction and was in the process of building nuclear weapons. He made three key points: first, the United States had seized precision-ground aluminum tubes on their way to Iraq, tubes whose only purpose could be as part of a centrifuge for the enrichment of weapons-grade uranium. Second, he said that the United States had actual documents showing Iraq's effort to buy yellowcake uranium from Niger—the only ingredient needed to complete its nuclear bombs. And third, Iraq had built mobile systems for producing nerve gas, anthrax, and other forms of biological and chemical warfare. "Our conservative estimate is that Iraq today has a stockpile of between 100 and 500 tons of chemical-weapons agent."

"My colleagues," Secretary Powell said, "every statement I make today is backed up by sources, solid sources. These are not assertions. What we are giving you are facts and conclusions based on solid intelligence."[11]

The heartfelt and articulate arguments from a man as honored and honorable as Powell seemed difficult to doubt, but they were known to be false in every case. The "suspected chemical weapons site" had been visited by the UN inspection team and was determined at the time to be an old ammunition storage area often frequented by Iraqi trucks.[12] The mobile production labs, shown in artist drawings, were just what the Iraqis said they were: facilities for the production of hydrogen gas to fill weather balloons.[13] The "decontamination vehicles" shown in the satellite photographs were really just fire trucks. The VX nerve gas Powell cited had already been destroyed, and the destruction had been confirmed by the UN. The existence of five hundred tons of chemical and biological warfare material had already been denied by a United States Defense Intelligence Agency report. The audiotape seeming to show that Osama bin Laden was in partnership with Saddam Hussein, when correctly translated, indicated that bin Laden was appealing to the Iraqi *people* and actually wanted Saddam Hussein dead.[14]

The documents that showed that Iraq was buying yellowcake uranium from Niger had been declared forgeries by Secretary Powell's own State Department weeks before; an investigation by the Italian parliament later concluded that they had been forged in Washington by Michael Ledeen, Dewey Clarridge, Francis

Brooke, and Defense Department consultant Ahmed Chalabi.[15] The aluminum tubes had been a controversial issue for months, and as early as January, the *Washington Post* had reported that UN weapons inspectors were "confident" that the tubes were not part of any nuclear weapons program.[16]

Years later, Powell said that he was merely reporting the truth as he and everyone around him understood it:

> Do you feel responsible for giving the UN flawed intelligence?
>
> I didn't know it was flawed. Everybody was using it. The CIA was saying the same thing for two years. I gave perhaps the most accurate presentation of the intelligence as we knew it— without any of the "Mushroom clouds are going to show up tomorrow morning" and all the rest of that stuff. But the fact of the matter is that a good part of it was wrong, and I am sorry that it was wrong.[17]

What defense do we have against a complex description of reality that includes false information? What hope is there when the financial press is almost entirely, spectacularly wrong about the most dramatic business failure in history? Whom can we trust when hospitals—not just individual physicians—get the diagnosis and treatment so wrong that in 2000 medical error killed four times more people than motor vehicle accidents, and fifteen times more people than AIDS? How do we survive in a complex world when the entire $40-billion-a-year engine of American espionage, diplomacy, and defense intelligence cannot tell whether another country is or is not preparing weapons against us?

It is not enough to say that people lied. We must also admit that we *believed*. The doctors certainly believed that they were doing the right thing. The investment managers and accountants put their own money down on Enron. Secretary Powell believed he was reporting the facts. But we live in a world of virtual truth where the information is so complex, so internally consistent, and presented in such a persuasive way that the false knowledge cannot be detected. The traditional tests for truth are all positive: the description is defended by men and women of authority and experience, the proffered evidence seems unimpeachable, and broad consensus supports the conclusions. But we pay too little attention to how easily an individual can distort the report. Wishful thinking colors the facts, new knowledge is twisted into old shapes, and self-interest beckons us toward a false conclusion through cognitive processes we have only recently begun to identify. And when the information is processed by a group, these errors are compounded by social forces we know too little about. Each individual in the chain adds his or her own misconceptions. Uncertainty is removed, and additional information is added to make a more "reasonable" story. Members of a group try hard to agree with each other even when they don't, and those who disagree are punished or fall silent. New information is subtly altered to be more consistent with the prevailing view of the world and slowly, inexorably, the description takes a turn for the logical, the complete, the flattering, and the persuasive. Somebody makes the slides. Somebody else sets up the chairs. Truth is lost. Virtual truth has taken its place—a full, articulated, and flawed description of the real world, leading us into disaster.

Years ago, on a rainy evening, a World Airways cargo plane on its way from California to the Philippines was forced to approach the Cold Bay, Alaska, airport on instruments alone. Captain John Weininger consulted his charts and set the plane on the correct course, heading cautiously toward the runway. Thirty-five miles out, he asked the flight engineer for a position, but none could be determined electronically. "What kind of terrain are we flying over?" the engineer asked. "Mountains everywhere," said the captain. The crew decided to climb a little to four thousand feet, and the altimeter needle suddenly started to jump around. The first officer called out, "Hey, John. We're off course . . . four hundred feet from something." Six seconds later, according to the aircraft accident report, "the aircraft struck rising terrain." The three crew members and three passengers were killed.[18]

According to the accident report, the fault lay with the captain, who deviated from approved approach procedures and descended into an area of "unreliable navigation signals and obstructing terrain." Pilot error. But a lawsuit filed by the family of one the crew members showed that the navigation chart Captain Weininger used was wrong. The altitude data gathered and distributed by the federal government had left out a mountain, and Jeppesen, the publisher that made the maps, hadn't checked the new version against the old.[19] The entire community of pilots, aircraft controllers, and government officials accepted these maps as "accurate," but in fact there was no way to confirm the truth of the information on which they had been taught to risk their lives.

We are all in Captain Weininger's chair. We take the medicine, we buy the stock, we cast our votes, and we send our sons and daughters into war. We place our faith in the truth of the information that others have provided without an adequate understanding of how our modern systems can distort and belie reality. We have wandered into a world of virtual truth where much is simulated, where information and ideas pretend to be each other, where logic and consistency are man-made. The markings on the compass fade; the needle starts to jump.

2

VIRTUAL TRUTH

I n the past, when mistakes were made, organizations focused on whether the facts were true or not, whether the decision was flawed, or whether someone in the group told a lie. But the greatest danger we face in the coming Information Age is virtual truth—vast, internally consistent, and detailed representations of reality that have grown to include false knowledge. If we are to have maps we can bet our lives on, medicines that heal, and navigation systems that bring us safely home, they will not come from turning a message over and over in our hands at the last minute trying to decide whether or not it is "true," whether or not the messenger is "honorable," or whether the information is "logical." They will come only from a more careful understanding of how virtual truth is assembled, how it works, and how it fails. Two examples, sadder and more complicated than the *Titanic*, help us see the pattern of how early warnings were discounted or ignored. Critical communications systems proved unreliable. Misinformation led to misjudgment, and the errors were covered up. Complex organizations thought to be the best in the world failed to manage successfully information on which many lives depended. They let it happen, they got it wrong, and they wrote it off.

THREE MILE ISLAND: THE OPPOSITE IS TRUE

On November 1, 1977, Joseph Kelley and Bert Dunn, two engineers for Babcock and Wilcox, one of the world's leading nuclear engineering firms, sent a formal memorandum to seven officials within their company. They warned that, in the nuclear power plants they were building, the valve controlling the water that covered the reactor sometimes stuck open, causing the water to drain out. Under those circumstances, the memo said, operators often misunderstood the event and shut down the emergency water supply pumps, which only made matters worse. Dunn, manager of the company's safety analysis division, wanted the company to warn operators about the sticky valves.

Disasters, however grim a text, allow a detailed examination of the decision-making process. Because the cost in these cases was high, the search continues for years to determine who did what and why. Public disasters, in particular, present the opportunity for an impartial analysis, as if fixed in amber, and by looking at them together we can see patterns of failure that might be avoided in the future. In the major disasters of the last twenty years, four major elements have been usually present: warnings are ignored, internal systems designed to identify risk often fail, communications break down in a crisis, and when it is over, officials deny that any serious error occurred.

Take, for example, Three Mile Island in Harrisburg, Pennsylvania. The memo written by Kelley and Dunn cited several occurrences of the sticky valve problem, most recently at the Davis-Bessie nuclear plant in Ohio in September 1977. In a sequence of events strikingly like those that would occur at Three Mile Island two years later, the valves stuck open. The Davis-Bessie operators were confused and unable to detect the cause of the problem for twenty-two minutes while water drained out of the reactor's cooling system. Kelley and Dunn urged the company to recognize this issue and warn their client plants. None of the officials responded.[1]

Three months later they sent a second memo to ten more company officials, including James Taylor, manager of the company's licensing section, who was required by law to inform the Nuclear Regulatory Commission of any substantial safety problem at an operating nuclear power plant. According to Daniel Ford, author of *Three Mile Island: Thirty Minutes to Meltdown*, Taylor never responded. He later claimed that the warning memo had been sent to the wrong department because it was "on the wrong form."[2]

In the same year, Aerospace Corporation reported to the NRC that, from a human-factors standpoint, the control room at Three Mile Island was very poorly engineered. Examiners pointed out that this would be a severe handicap if a crisis were ever to occur. This report was stamped "for future resolution" and then forgotten.[3] The decision was made to do nothing.

May 1978. The shift supervisor at Three Mile Island sent a strongly worded memo to his superiors saying that the feedwater system that regulated the pressure inside the reactor was subject to failure that might precipitate "very significant damage." He suggested remedies and urged immediate action, but this memo, too, was apparently ignored.[4]

Wednesday, March 28, 1979, at about 4:00 a.m. One of the valves that regulated the feedwater system inside the Three Mile Island reactor stuck open, and water began to drain out of the reactor at the rate of 220 gallons a minute. Within a few minutes, fifty alarms, lights, and gauges began to warn that the nuclear reactor was no longer functioning normally. In the next five minutes, eight hundred more alarms were triggered, but it was hard for the operators to identify the cause since there were more than six thousand gauges, meters, lights, and alarms on a floor-to-ceiling panel that ran for ninety feet around the room.

A computer had been installed to give the operators further information about each alarm, but four seconds were required to print each message, and with the sudden rush of failures to report, the system quickly fell behind. After an hour, the printer jammed, by which time there were more than two hours of emergency messages backed up.

The operators in the room were, by their own description, "bouncing around from panel to panel." "I saw a lot of alarms," said one operator, "but so much was happening there wasn't time to figure out what caused it."[5] After fifteen minutes, they decided they had the problem under control and began an orderly shutdown of the reactor, which, had they been successful, would have pumped the remaining water—now highly radioactive—out into the Susquehanna River.

But they couldn't get the reactor cooled down. Instead, the temperature was rising rapidly, and the pipes were beginning to shake. The information on the control panel told the operators that the water level was rising inside the reactor, when in reality it was draining rapidly away. The emergency pumps kept kicking on, pouring water into the reactor while the operators—just as Kelley and Dunn had warned—kept overriding the system and turning the pumps off. After a while, just to be sure, they opened some emergency drains.

Inside the reactor the water level fell below the safety level, exposing the nuclear core. The metal tubes holding the uranium fuel began to crack and rupture, and the temperature soared from 600°F (which is normal) past 2,000°F, at which point the reaction begins to perpetuate itself, and on to 4,000°F.

There was a thermocouple mounted above the reactor correctly monitoring the temperature the whole time, but the computer system that interpreted this signal had been programmed to report data only in the normal range, and after the temperature went above 700°F the system simply printed question marks.

6:00 a.m. The plant manager held a conference call with the engineers from Babcock and Wilcox, as well as with executives from the power company, and while this was going on, there was a second critical event. The oncoming shift supervisor arrived an hour early, looked at the control panel, and, guessing that the valve might be stuck open, took steps to close off the drain at another point.[6]

At that moment, the plant manager, who was on the conference call, sent a messenger into the control room to check the status of the pipe control valve. He was told that it was closed but not that it had *just* been closed. The manager returned to the phone baffled, and for hours more, everyone assumed that the reactor was full of water. The supervisor's action had slowed the mounting crisis but not averted it, and in leaving out an important piece of information, he had unwittingly made the problem even more difficult to diagnose. No one could see into the reactor chamber.

7:00 a.m. Radiation alarms were starting to sound. With nearly all of the fifty on-duty employees now crowded into the control room, the station manager declared a site emergency. He began to go down the list of agencies to be called: state police, civil defense, and others, including the insurance agency. He also called the NRC, responsible by law for the safe operation of all nuclear facilities in the United States. But he got a recorded message saying that no one was available to take the call and to please leave a message at the tone.

When the NRC finally got the report, the commissioners treated it as a routine alert on a minor problem, and that, to some extent, was the impression the Three Mile Island managers had intended to convey. Later, when the reports indicated that the radiation level inside the reactor was fifty times higher than the lethal dose, the commission dismissed the data. "It was so inconsistent with the original report that it must be wrong."[7]

1:40 p.m. The technical staff assigned to monitor accidents assured the commissioners that everything was under control. There was no mention of boiling in the reactor core, and no one suggested that the nuclear fuel had been uncovered. Only one engineer suspected the truth, and his view was overruled.[8] The commission issued a press release that misstated the technical situation and encouraged a generally rosy view. But the media had grown suspicious and, supported by experts, they began to paint a very different, darker, and, as it turned out, more accurate picture.

In the commission's defense, it should be noted that during most of the crisis the telephone lines between headquarters in Washington and the control room at Three Mile Island were unavailable or simply out of service, and information had to be relayed through a regional office in Philadelphia. Moreover, the commission was seen by the Three Mile Island staff as simply a bureaucratic pest. Rather than provide a full briefing, they assigned a junior executive to the task of keeping the federal agency off the power company's back.

6:00 p.m. As a result of its own preconceptions, a decision to ignore critical data, a technical failure of the most rudimentary kind, and a conspiracy to keep them out of the way, the NRC was led far astray from what was really happening. When it reported to the White House, the commission staff explained that there was not and never had been any danger.

In fact, the nuclear reactor at Three Mile Island was out of control. The managers tried everything that came to mind—without a theory, without leadership, without proper engineering drawings, and without correct data. Subsequent studies suggested that on two occasions they came perilously close to blowing up the plant as they turned the dials first one way and then the other.[9]

Meanwhile, back at the contractor's office, Babcock and Wilcox had mounted a major engineering diagnosis that was moving steadily toward the hypothesis that there was too little water in the reactor, not too much. But a telephone failure prevented the firm from discussing this idea with Three Mile Island managers until early evening when, after sixteen hours, the pumps were finally turned on in a brief test. The temperature dropped. The pumping was increased and the temperature dropped some more. With thirty minutes to go, nuclear meltdown was averted.

The following morning, the NRC commissioners told Congress that the whole event had been a normal procedure: "a deliberately slow process of cooling the plant down."[10] Joseph Hendrie, chairman of the commission, went further, dismissing the high radiation readings as "oddball instrument error," denying any serious ongoing problem, and claiming that the reactor had never been anywhere near a meltdown.

By then, of course, the nuclear reactor had been fundamentally destroyed. Staggering along the brink of a hydrogen explosion on one hand and meltdown on the other, the Three Mile Island incident had endangered the lives of hundreds of thousands of citizens. (Nuclear energy engineers have told me they don't like to use the phrase "hydrogen explosion" when describing what might have occurred. When all of a sudden there is a loud noise, a cloud of smoke, and a big hole in the reactor wall, they prefer to call it a "prompt critical fission excursion.") Even in a dormant state, the reactor harbored radioactive steam, water, and materials that could not be safely removed for years.

And yet the confusion continued.

Friday, 8 a.m. Two days after the accident began, the crew at Three Mile Island tried to transfer some of the radioactive steam out of the reactor into a storage tank, but each time they tried, a little of the steam escaped into the atmosphere. A helicopter monitoring radiation levels began to report readings of twelve hundred millirems per hour. Unaware that this jump in the levels occurred only when a burst of steam was escaping from the relief stack below, the technicians concluded that the whole neighborhood was in danger.

They tried to contact the Pennsylvania Emergency Management Agency but couldn't get through, so they called the local civil defense office and asked them to pass on the message that evacuation might become necessary. Telephone trouble or not, it didn't take long for that message to reach the governor, or for him to get to the NRC and ask for a confirmation of the radiation readings.

At the same time, Three Mile Island officials had sent a message to the commission through the regional office that they were releasing radioactive steam into a storage tank. The message was garbled as it was relayed to Washington, and the commission thought steam was being released directly into the air. When the governor's call arrived, the commission staff mistakenly thought he was confirming the earlier report of radioactive emissions, and six minutes later—before checking with Three Mile Island or anyone else—the commission recommended an evacuation of the surrounding area.[11]

The governor was called, the civil defense agency was called, and a local radio station went on the air with the story: "The Nuclear Regulatory Commission is expected to shortly call for a major evacuation of the Harrisburg area . . . details at ten."

Later, this story was revised to say that only children and pregnant women needed to leave the area, but that distinction was lost on a population now running for its cars.

And then the White House got into the act. Zbigniew Brzezinski and the National Security Council briefed President Carter, who ordered the Signal Corps to get a telephone line cleared between Washington and Harrisburg. The Army was mobilized to fly the commission staff to Three Mile Island and support them as they set up a command center in a neighbor's living room.[12] Chairman Hendrie briefed the Department of Energy (which, until this point, had been uninformed), while Gerald Rafshoon, the president's media adviser, began arranging television appearances for each member of the commission. A special effort went into crafting a press release that would be reassuring, but by then, more than one hundred and forty thousand people had abandoned their homes and were well out of hearing.

Not everyone has come home again. Reactor Two at Three Mile was permanently closed, and after nearly $1 billion in cleanup costs, the radioactivity still cannot be removed from the concrete. Many of the outstanding orders for new Babcock and Wilcox reactors were cancelled, and the promise of nuclear power in the United States fell under a cloud of doubt. Like the *Titanic*, Three Mile Island is referred to as an "accident"—another testament to the risk and complexity of high technology. Not much is said about the information management failures that occurred, the memos that were ignored, the phones that failed, the alarms left with answering machines, the deliberate effort by the plant to mislead the NRC, by the NRC to mislead the White House, and by the White House to mislead the public. More operator training was ordered, more computers were installed, more regulations were written to define more tightly what constitutes a "reportable incident."

Although Three Mile Island presents a rich display of information management failure in many forms, one aspect of the incident is particularly instructive. Information was repeatedly mishandled whenever it was unflattering or contrary to self-interest. Information is processed by people who subscribe to value systems, who have intentions, who bring varying levels of knowledge and experience to the task, who are subject to insights, group pressure, and individual failures of reason, who respond to emotions and hunches, but who, above all, have ideas about the information they are processing. At Three Mile Island, even when the information was right, the wrong decision was reached, and vice versa.

Earnest and authoritative warnings from the engineering staff were repeatedly ignored and suppressed in spite of substantive evidence and a real incident. In its early reports to the NRC, the plant managers minimized the situation and misled the NRC. In informing the families around Harrisburg about the incident itself, the NRC withheld information about the potential threat to health and safety, and even when the incident was over; both the White House and the NRC understated the seriousness of the event to the media and the public.

IGNORE, DENY, FORGET

Warnings Are Ignored. People are by nature optimistic, and any warning evokes a feeling not only of fear but of inadequacy. In every major information disaster there is a trail of such warnings leading back into the past. Reports of icebergs in the North Atlantic were timely and accurate. Warnings about Enron were frequent and frequently ignored. The persistent memos from Joseph Kelley and Bert Dunn developed into a ghoulish clanging of the alarm, although the warning itself was written in language only an engineer could love:

> This memo addresses a serious concern within ECCS Analysis about the potential for operator action to terminate high pressure injection following the initial stage of a LOCA [loss-of-coolant accident]. Successful ECCS operation during small breaks depends on the accumulated reactor coolant system inventory as well as the ECCS injection rate. As such, it is mandatory that full injection flow be maintained from the point of emergency safety features actuation system (ESFAS) actuation until the high pressure injection rate can fully compensate for the reactor heat load. As the injection rate depends on the reactor coolant system pressure, the time at which a compensating match-up occurs is variable and cannot be specified as a fixed number. It is quite possible, for example, that the high pressure injection may successfully match up with all heat sources at time t and that due to system pressurization be inadequate at some later time t2.[13]

If ever a disaster was caused by bad writing, it is this one. Bear this in mind when you have a warning to send: Be Stark.

What does the mind do when it encounters information that is contrary to its existing concept of the world? First, as both communications scientists and psychologists observe, it experiences stress and discomfort. Any alternative is often better than the task of revising a fundamental portion of one's world model, and such a project may take hours—or, in traumatic circumstances, a lifetime. When the contrary fact strikes deep at a person's faith, love, or sense of personal worth, then the task is nearly impossible. It must be denied or deferred through a complex dance of self-delusion.

The first response of a manager struggling to avoid concept revision is to ignore the evidence. Lose it. Place it deep in the queue. Avoid meetings where the matter is discussed and stay away from people who keep bringing the subject up. Pretend to be occupied by some other task or claim that the message is hard to understand. As Captain Lord did on the *Californian*, roll over in your cot and go back to sleep.

When the warning cannot be ignored, it is denied. Say it isn't so. Demand more proof. Challenge the semantics. Call for a second opinion. Create a committee to study the problem. When the readings around the Three Mile Island nuclear plant showed high radiation levels, the data was attributed to error. Even after the scope of the accident was clear, the NRC reported to Congress that the accident had been followed by a "deliberately slow process of cooling the plant down." The denial quickly becomes a concept of its own—not only immunizing the mind against further evidence but serving to impeach the source. The warning is a threat to the shared beliefs of the group that, once acknowledged, might spread, corrupting as it goes, toppling first one well-loved idea and then another, until all that remain are the jagged shards of a bombed-out philosophy.

When information cannot be ignored or denied, it is forgotten—the last refuge of the tidy mind. Rise above the details. Throw the memo away; if it is important, it will be reissued. Turn to more important projects. Delegate. Even after Babcock and Wilcox agreed to change the operations guidelines for its nuclear reactors, the firm never did it.[14]

The company has forgotten the whole incident. Two thousand

personal injury lawsuits were filed on behalf of the people who lived nearby, but after fifteen years of litigation, all the claims were rejected by the courts for lack of evidence. Subsequent lawsuits based on the company's use of asbestos, however, drove Babcock and Wilcox to seek shelter in bankruptcy, from which it emerged in 2006, stronger than ever.

In his classic work on how the mind functions—written before the current connectionist view emerged—F. C. Bartlett wrote that memories are not recalled, they are reconstructed from the separate memory components and linked concepts into which the mind originally parsed the experience. And in the process, dissonant and ambiguous bits are discarded. "Thus what is reconstructed during recall or reproduction comes to contain not only omissions and abbreviations but elaborations and distortions. On each occasion of recall, further modifications are made. The more often it is recalled, the more 'familiar' and comfortable we become with it, until the actual experience recedes into a weak, distant pattern soon to be forgotten. 'He told the story so many times he came to believe it.'"[15]

Systems Lie. Throughout the Three Mile Island story are examples of system safeguards that turned out to block or disguise real data, making the crisis worse. The program designed to report reactor temperatures above normal did not anticipate how abnormal things could get. Beyond the range that the designers could imagine, the program stopped reporting. Systems designed to alert the operator to a dangerous condition were switched off by the weary operator after a few days of responding to false alarms. The reactor at Three Mile Island was programmed so that when the water level fell too low, the pumps would automatically turn on to cover the reactor core. But when the crisis began, the operators thought the water was too high. Every time the emergency system kicked in, the operators turned it off, and they finally turned off the warning system entirely.[16] This pattern of silencing the alarms occurs in many information disasters: after the Russians shot down

Korean Airliner KAL 007 in 1983, for example, an examination of the disaster revealed that on takeoff the pilot had typed the wrong coordinates into the airline's onboard computer, and when the alarm system began to sound, he just switched it off.[17] The emblem of how such systems lie—and the ultimate example of virtual truth—was that at Three Mile Island a special light had been installed to indicate whether the sticky valve was open or closed. It was the brightest light on the panel. But the light had been wired to the switch, not to the valve, and it indicated whether the switch had been thrown, not the valve's real position. It was "true" because the operator wanted it to be true, but it ignored the sticky condition of the real world.

Communications Break Down. Communications systems, too, often fail in a crisis. At Three Mile Island, the call to the NRC emergency center was taken by an answering machine. The telephone line between Washington and Harrisburg went down in the middle of the accident. In 1988, when the USS *Vincennes* mistakenly identified a commercial Iranian airliner and began to fire on it, the radio system connecting the essential members of the tactical response team kept failing, so they all had to periodically jump to another frequency. During the terrorist attack on the World Trade Center in 2001, the secure line from the White House to Air Force One failed. The line from the White House to the mayor's command center in New York failed. The radio network connecting the firefighters to their commander failed. Videoconferences set up by the White House, the FAA, and the Pentagon were not successfully connected to each other. Technology failure might not be a natural law, but it often happens. And it is almost never anticipated by those who imagine an emergency response scenario in our virtual world.

The Cover-Up. With grim predictability, every disaster ends in denial. No errors occurred. Everyone made the best decision possible given the information available at the time. Officials claim that the situation was never as dire as the media painted it. As a result, the conditions that contributed to the disaster remain in place. Executives pretend that the decision was reasonable under the circumstances, the public is taught to doubt the media, and everyone continues to ignore the problem of determining the accuracy of information.

SHUTTLE *CHALLENGER*: NO ONE IS TO BLAME

Ten years later, all of these errors were repeated in the explosion of the space shuttle *Challenger*. Space travel captures our imagination the way the great iron steamers did at the turn of the century, and NASA, like nuclear engineering, has been synonymous with modern management of complex technology. So when the shuttle exploded in January 1986, the cost went beyond the lives of the seven crew members and the billion-dollar shuttle. America's space program was brought to a halt, and confidence in our ability to proceed was profoundly shaken.

Monday, January 27, 1986. 4:00 p.m. Allan McDonald, Morton Thiokol's director of the Solid Rocket Motor Project, was in Florida preparing for the following morning's launch of the shuttle *Challenger*—the twenty-fifth in a series of shuttle launches begun in 1981. He received a call from Bob Ebeling, his colleague in Utah. Ebeling's message was that the temperature at the Cape Kennedy launch site was forecast to drop to 18°F that night, a record low. The engineers in Utah were seriously concerned about the shuttle's O-rings.

The solid rocket motor around which NASA had designed the shuttle program was a series of steel tubular sections twelve feet in diameter, stacked on top of each other to form a rocket one hundred and fifty feet tall. Two of these rockets were designed to provide 80 percent of the thrust necessary at liftoff. Then they would fall back into the Atlantic twenty-four miles downrange, leaving the *Challenger* to ride up into space, clinging to the belly of the giant external fuel tank until that, too, broke away. The space shuttle design was complex and seriously criticized from the outset, but by employing these reusable rocket motors, the program promised great savings.

Where the sections of the solid rocket motor were joined, two rubber O-rings rested in grooves to seal what was called the "clevis joint." As the pressure inside the rocket increased during launch, these O-rings would be forced even more tightly into their grooves, preventing the hot gasses being generated inside the rocket from blasting out between the sections to ignite the external fuel tank. But the O-rings were trouble from the start.

Nine years before, in a September 2, 1977, memorandum, Glenn Eudy, chief engineer of the Solid Rocket Motor Division at NASA's Marshall Space Flight Center, summarized a long investigation by concluding that the O-ring was unreliable: "I personally believe that our first choice should be to correct the design in a way that eliminates the possibility of O-ring clearance. Since this is a very critical . . . issue, it is requested that the assignment results be compiled in such a manner as to permit review at the S&E Director's level as well as the project manager."[18]

Other memoranda followed, urging Thiokol to correct the problem. On January 19, 1979, the Marshall Center executives wrote to Thiokol: "We find the Thiokol position regarding design adequacy of the clevis joint to be completely unacceptable." While NASA was tough on its suppliers, it took the opposite stance when discussing the problem with the public. In 1980 NASA's Space Shuttle Certification Committee studied the worthiness of the entire system and urged NASA to verify the joint integrity with more serious testing, but NASA replied that this was not necessary. The joints had been "sufficiently verified" in earlier lab experiments.[19]

Once the shuttle started to fly, evidence began to accumulate that showed that the O-rings often failed to seal the joint completely, in spite of several modifications made throughout 1982. As a result, in early March 1983, the O-rings were reclassified as "Criticality-1," which meant that there was no redundancy. If either ring failed, it would risk, in NASA's words, "loss of mission, vehicle and crew due to metal erosion, burn through, and probable case burst resulting in fire and deflagration."[20]

By February 1985, it was obvious to Thiokol that the probability of O-ring failure was greatly increased by low temperatures. A review of the April 1985 flight of the *Challenger* spacelab mission showed clearly that gasses had burned through the primary ring and badly scorched the secondary ring. Larry Mulloy, director of the Marshall Center's Solid Rocket program, was obliged to place a "launch constraint" on all subsequent shuttle flights. Over the next six months, Mulloy made five exceptions to this "constraint," one for each scheduled shuttle flight, but neither Thiokol nor its Marshall Center managers notified NASA headquarters of the situation.

And then they forgot about it. Confronted with information that contradicts existing beliefs or self-interest, people follow a classic pattern of ignoring, denying, and forgetting. And nowhere in the recent history of information failures do we get a clearer example of that behavior than in this tragic case. In December 1985, a NASA administrator told Thiokol that the director of engineering wanted to "close out" any remaining technical issues that had gone unresolved for six months or more. Thiokol responded, suggesting that the O-ring problem be taken off the list of current issues, since it "will not be fully resolved for some time." This request was relayed to Larry Mulloy's office at NASA, where a quality assurance administrator noted "contractor closure received" on all the Shuttle Problem reports. The O-rings were thus removed entirely as a launch constraint on the flight-readiness review of January 15, 1986. Five days before the launch, a NASA administrator marked the Problem Reports "problem is considered closed."[21] But as Richard Cook, a NASA auditor, later said: "[T]hey held their breath every time the shuttle took off."[22]

The O-rings weren't the only example of NASA bending its

own rules to fit the situation. Guidelines prohibited launch if the temperature on the nose cone of the external fuel tank fell below 45°F because ice might form on vents and prevent the gaseous oxygen from boiling off. Moreover, sensors in the nose cone, designed to measure pressure building up inside the tank, were not certified to operate reliably below that temperature. But as a different kind of pressure built up on NASA to keep this shuttle program on schedule, Mulloy again waived the rules, lowering the minimum temperature requirement with each new weather report. In fact, on the morning of the launch, much of the shuttle *Challenger* was shrouded in ice.

When the call came from his Utah colleagues, Allan McDonald, who knew better than many what cold temperatures might do, quickly scheduled a telephone conference to review the situation. It was clear that Thiokol was getting ready to recommend against a launch.

8:15 p.m. That evening, three groups joined in the conference, each from a room equipped with speaker phones. At Cape Kennedy, Larry Mulloy and four others representing the Marshall Space Flight Center (NASA) gathered at one end of a conference room equipped for thirty people; at the far end of the room sat McDonald and Jack Buchanan, manager of Thiokol operations at Cape Kennedy. At the Marshall Center in Huntsville, Alabama, fifteen others were gathered in a similar room, including George Hardy, deputy director for science and engineering, and Jud Lovingood, head of the shuttle project. Finally, in Utah, fourteen Thiokol executives had assembled, including Roger Boisjoly, an engineer on the Thiokol O-ring task force, and Arnold Thompson, Thiokol's supervisor of the rocket motor casing.[23]

Now at last the government (NASA/Marshall) and its contractor (Thiokol) were meeting face-to-face over a problem each had recognized for years but done little about, and it was the worst possible time to resolve the matter. Launch of the shuttle *Challenger* had been postponed twice in the last few days because of weather. If they postponed it again, NASA feared that the whole year's schedule would slip, provoking more criticism from Congress and jeopardizing long-term budgets.

Thiokol, too, had a great deal at stake. In 1973, in a process that some felt had been questionable and unfair, the then small Utah chemical company won an exclusive contract to provide solid rocket motors for the shuttle.[24] Business was booming; Morton Thiokol made nearly $100 million a year in profit from space operations, mostly from providing solid rocket motors for the shuttle. Now a new billion-dollar contract was about to be awarded for the next one hundred and twenty rockets, and Thiokol's exclusive position was being seriously challenged by other aerospace companies.[25] Cancellation of the launch because of problems with the Thiokol rocket could well cost the company its NASA contract and send the executives into a twilight of collapsing revenues, massive layoffs, and corporate losses.

Malcolm McConnell's excellent book *Challenger* went on the bookstands with a cover design claiming in fiery letters that this was a "true story of politics, greed, and the wrong stuff." While that may fit our concept of how businesses operate, it seems anything but true in this case. All the evidence suggests that the men who joined in that decisive conference were professionals intent on evaluating the information fairly and reaching the right conclusion. As the teleconference began, we can imagine how White Star Line's Bruce Ismay and his engineers must have argued over lifeboats, and how, decades later, the engineers at Babcock and Wilcox must have pleaded their case with management.

The meeting started with a detailed presentation by Thiokol engineers in Utah, showing the history of the O-rings failing to seat at low temperatures. In spite of the passionate concern of Roger Boisjoly, who had done the failure analysis, Thiokol's vice president of engineering Bob Lund presented his conclusions in an appropriately analytical manner. Although low temperature was not the only cause of O-ring failure, it was obviously a major contributor. The recommendation was that launch should be delayed until the temperature of the O-ring seals was at least 53°F.

From Cape Kennedy, Marshall Center's Larry Mulloy responded angrily that the Thiokol data was inconclusive, and that the recommendation, if followed, would have the effect of delaying the launch for months.[26]

Boisjoly responded that the evidence was solid, and McDonald joined in from Cape Kennedy to say that Boisjoly's evidence was more reliable than the lab tests. Mulloy then challenged Thiokol's management, asking vice president Joseph Kilminster for his opinion. But Kilminster also sided with the engineers and said he could not recommend a launch below 53°. The NASA executives were angry, not only because the data was inconclusive but also because of the eleventh-hour nature of the recommendation. George Hardy said he was "appalled," but he added that they wouldn't fly without Thiokol's recommendation. Thiokol asked for some time to discuss the problem once more among themselves.

In their subsequent testimony before the national commission created to investigate the disaster, Jerry Mason, senior vice president in charge of Thiokol's shuttle business, and Roger Boisjoly, the engineer, both described the Utah conference. As soon as the Thiokol men were alone, Mason said quietly: "We have to make a management decision." They all agreed that the O-ring was less likely to seat properly in cold temperatures, but they also agreed that a little burn-through might not necessarily mean that hot gasses would escape. While that seemed an innocent and logical inference, it directly contradicted the major 1983 finding that the seals were not redundant.

Still, Mason knew they were in a bad spot. NASA clearly wanted to launch, and Thiokol management wanted very much to please its client. In the past, the company had been required to constantly prove that the shuttle was ready. Could they now prove that it wasn't? They couldn't, of course.

Boisjoly later told how he and his colleague Arnold Thompson argued vigorously on behalf of their engineering concerns, but the more they fought, the more they seemed to be excluded from the discussion until only Thiokol's business managers were involved in the analysis:

> Arnie actually got up from his position which was down the table and put a [graph paper] pad down . . . in front of the management folks and tried to sketch out once again what his concern was with the joint, and when he realized he wasn't getting through he just stopped. I tried one more time with the photos. I grabbed the photos and I went up and discussed the photos once again and tried to make the point that it was my opinion from actual observations that temperature was indeed a discriminator and we should not ignore the physical evidence.
>
> I also stopped when it was apparent that I couldn't get anyone to listen. There was no point in me doing anything further than I had already attempted to do.[27]

As McConnell points out in his book, the NASA officials were not aware that Mason and Calvin Wiggins—both senior nonengineering executives—were participating in the conversation. In a conference call, the normal rule is that everyone identifies himself at the beginning, but Mason and Wiggins had remained silent.[28] When the call was stopped for half an hour to let the Thiokol people talk among themselves, Mason led the discussion and turned it into a management decision, but when the call resumed, the conclusion was falsely reframed by Bob Lund as an engineering decision, which gave it much greater weight in the NASA culture. The fears and protests of Boisjoly and Thompson were not only voted down but effectively stripped from the report, and management's view of the solution was presented in their place.[29]

The denial of the O-ring issue continued. When Stanley Reinartz, manager of the shuttle project, met that evening with Dr. William Lucas, his boss at the Marshall Space Flight Center, Reinartz essentially dismissed the O-ring issue as a concern about the "weather." Reinartz later explained this remarkable failure to address so serious a problem by saying that he had no hard data to present Lucas and knew that his boss would be harshly critical of information based on "concerns and projections" instead of facts.[30]

And the false status report continued. When Larry Mulloy briefed Arnold Aldrich, deputy administrator of NASA, late that night, he made the decision not to mention the O-ring problem at all, even though it had occupied the last six hours of his day. The launch would proceed. In his testimony to the Rogers Commission, Mulloy explained the system they had developed for handling detailed information like this and emphasized that the system had been faithfully adhered to. The O-ring issue was a "Level III that had been resolved."

"There was no violation of Launch Commit Criteria. There was no waiver required in my judgment at that time and still today."[31]

Later, even under close questioning, they forgot the problem:

CHAIRMAN [WILLIAM P.] ROGERS: Would you please tell the Commission when you first heard about the problem of the O-rings and the seals, insofar as it involves launch 51-L?

DR. LUCAS: Yes sir. It was on the early evening of the 27th, I think about 7:00 p.m., when I was in my motel room along with Mr. [James] Kingsbury. And about that time, Mr. Reinartz and Mr. Mulloy came to my room and told me that they had heard that some members of Thiokol had raised a concern about the performance of the Solid Rocket Boosters in the low temperature that was anticipated for the next day, specifically on the seals, and that they were going out to the Kennedy Space Center to engage in a telecon with the appropriate engineers back at Marshall Space Flight Center in Huntsville and with corresponding people back at the Wasatch division of Thiokol in Utah. And we discussed it a few moments and I said, fine, keep me informed, let me know what happens.

CHAIRMAN ROGERS: And when was the next time you heard something about that?

DR. LUCAS: The next time was about 5:00 a.m. on the following morning, when I went out to the Kennedy Space Center and went to the launch control center. I immediately saw Mr. Reinartz and Mr. Mulloy and asked them how the matter of the previous evening was dispositioned.

CHAIRMAN ROGERS: You had heard nothing at all in between?

DR. LUCAS: No, Sir.

CHAIRMAN ROGERS: So from 8:00 that evening until 5:00 in the morning you had not heard a thing?

DR. LUCAS: It was about 7:00, I believe, sir. But for that period of time, I heard nothing in the interim . . .

CHAIRMAN ROGERS: . . . And you heard Mr. Reinartz say he didn't think he had to notify you, or did he notify you?

DR. LUCAS: He told me, as I testified, when I went into the control room, that an issue had been resolved, that there were some people at Thiokol who had a concern about the weather, that that had been discussed very thoroughly by the Thiokol people and by the Marshall Space Flight Center people, and it had been concluded agreeably that there was no problem, that he had a recommendation by Thiokol to launch and our most knowledgeable people and engineering talent agreed with that. So from my perspective, I didn't have—I didn't see that as an issue.

CHAIRMAN ROGERS: And if you had known that Thiokol engineers almost to a man opposed the flight, would that have changed your view?

DR. LUCAS: I'm certain that it would.

CHAIRMAN ROGERS: In view of the fact that you were running tests to improve the joint, didn't the fact that the weather was so bad and Reinartz had told you about the questions that had been raised by Thiokol, at least, didn't that cause you serious concern?

DR. LUCAS: I would have been concerned if Thiokol had come in and said, we don't think you should launch because we've got bad weather.

CHAIRMAN ROGERS: Well, that's what they did, of course, first. That is exactly what they did. You didn't know that?

DR. LUCAS: I knew that I was told on the morning of the launch that the initial position of some members of Thiokol—and I don't know who it was—had recommended that one not launch with the temperature less than 53 degrees Fahrenheit.

CHAIRMAN ROGERS: And that didn't cause you enough concern so you passed that information on to either Mr. Moore or Mr. Aldrich?

DR. LUCAS: No, sir, because I was shown a document signed by Mr. Kilminster that indicated that would not be significant, that the temperature would not be—that it would be that much lower, as I recall it.[32]

When information travels through an organization, each person involved in the process has an opportunity to judge its accuracy, to translate, to contribute, to emphasize, and to suppress details. The result is a system that tends to reinforce what is expected rather than reveal what is new. The information is normalized; dissenting views and contradictory data are trimmed out and discouraged. Prevailing concepts are thus strengthened not dispelled, and when the information affects the power structure within the group, the danger of corruption is doubly great. Accuracy is lost even as knowledge spreads, and just at the moment when the information is gathered for the final decision, its truth is most dangerously weakened.

The truth system in operation at NASA that night was a cobble of arrogance and self-interest. Following the famous "pilot's checklist," these men had devised a process for decision making that aggressively discounted intuition and consistently placed the truth assessment task in the hands of the person least interested in disturbing the schedule. There was no apparent concern—at least none voiced—for the lives of the astronauts themselves. For all its vaunted "accountability," NASA doesn't seem to have assigned the O-ring decision to anyone in particular, and no one has since come forward to acknowledge responsibility.

CHAIRMAN ROGERS: By way of a question, could I ask, did any of your gentlemen prior to launch know about the objections of Thiokol to the launch?

MR. SMITH [KENNEDY SPACE CENTER DIRECTOR]: I did not.

MR. THOMAS [LAUNCH DIRECTOR]: No, sir.

MR. ALDRICH [SHUTTLE PROGRAM DIRECTOR]: I did not.

MR. MOORE [ASSOCIATE NASA ADMINISTRATOR FOR SPACE FLIGHT]: I did not.[33]

A CONSPIRACY OF SILENCE

In retrospect, it seems astonishing that Boisjoly, Thompson, McDonald, Lund, Mason, Mulloy, and Reinartz, each of whom had at one time or another expressed serious doubt about the O-ring, should now join in silence, keeping their secret from NASA and from the astronauts as well. Why didn't they scream? They could have broken ranks with a phone call and stopped the project cold. They could have taken their story to the press, which by then was flocking south to Cape Kennedy in large numbers. Instead, they fell silent.

Albert O. Hirshman has proposed an explanation for how people respond to failure and decline in the organizations to which they belong. In *Exit, Voice and Loyalty*, Hirshman wrote that when people have been born into a group, or become committed to it in such a way that they can neither leave nor be expelled, they speak freely and often about what is wrong. What's the risk? But when the cost of joining has been very high, criticism of the group means criticism of one's own investment. For the builders of the *Titanic*, for the nuclear engineers at Three Mile Island, and for Roger Boisjoly, pressing the attack meant premeditated injury to the organization—even the profession—that had given meaning to their lives. After all, the *Titanic* was the greatest ship ever built, nuclear engineering was the pinnacle of applied science, and NASA stood for the finest management systems in the world. Having joined the elite, these men couldn't leave and couldn't bear expulsion. Most people would rather belong than tell the truth.

In organizations that impose severe initiation tests or harshly punish those who defect, individuals develop a powerful sense of loyalty that keeps them in line no matter what happens. As dissonant information and criticism builds up around them, the members begin to engage together in various forms of self-deception: they develop an inordinate interest in trivial details about the organization that outsiders would find irrelevant or boring.[34] They come to hold views about the rest of society that are wrong but that help to explain away a problem the organization is having. "They just don't understand us" or "These attacks on us are just motivated by politics and greed." They narrow their range of activity in order to minimize contact with the "normal" world and all of its conflicting evidence. They pounce ferociously on doubters in the ranks and in time they lose both sensitivity and perspective.

There is a second explanation for the silence. Information accuracy is too often seen as a function of intelligence and honor, and any person who presents false evidence must therefore be stupid, dishonest, or disloyal. A challenge to the facts deteriorates into faintly veiled accusations of misrepresentation or gullibility. Moreover, without an acceptable vocabulary for discussing ambiguity and information management failure, the group lurches recklessly toward arguments over authority, reaching for more primitive verbal and political weapons until someone suggests that the group divide or take a break. Most disagreements over information accuracy are not resolved, they are only silenced.

Boisjoly did tell someone. He said later that he went home that night, exhausted and afraid. When his wife asked him what was wrong, he told her, "Oh, nothing, honey. I had a great day. We're going to launch tomorrow and kill the astronauts. That's all."[35]

Larry Mulloy, who made the decision to launch the *Challenger*, resigned from NASA six months after the tragedy, at the age of fifty-two. He said the accident had not been the fault of the individuals involved; it was a systems failure. "Given the information I had at the time, I can't say that anything different would have been done," he said.[36]

But because the underlying problem of handling dissent was never acknowledged and addressed, it remained in place. In February 2003, the space shuttle *Columbia* exploded on reentry, killing all seven members of the crew. An investigation later determined that pieces of insulating foam had separated from the front of the spacecraft and punctured the wing, piercing the thermal protection skin and exposing the underlying structure to a blast of 3,000°F gasses. Like the O-ring problem, the "foam shedding" problem had been recognized as an unresolved issue for several years, and for several years the constraints were adjusted for every launch. Warnings were ignored, memoranda about the issue went astray, and even the engineers who knew the risk remained silent. The report of the *Columbia* investigation concluded:

> Cultural traits and organizational practices detrimental to safety were allowed to develop, including: reliance on past success as a substitute for sound engineering practices (such as testing to understand why systems were not performing in accordance with requirements); organizational barriers that prevented effective communication of critical safety information and stifled professional differences of opinion; lack of integrated management across program elements; and the evolution of an informal chain of command and decision-making processes that operated outside the organization's rules.[37]

It is my purpose to show that the quality of information (truth) is a responsibility shared by all members of the group and that we can learn to manage it more thoughtfully and directly. By examining the details of major information catastrophes, independently reported, we can come to recognize the pattern of error when it appears in our own lives. We can be more demanding of truth in our colleagues, our leaders, and the media. We can reduce the scale and frequency of disasters in the future.

On the *Titanic*, at Three Mile Island, and in the conference rooms of NASA, the intelligence and judgment of these men and women had been overpowered by personal bias and defeated by faulty truth systems. Over a long period of time, they had been taught that all facts are equally true and that the quality of reason automatically increases with rank and accountability. But the truth of a message cannot be tested alone, not even in the context of other information available at the time. Bruce Ismay should have slowed the *Titanic* down. Babcock and Wilcox should have sent out a memo about the sticky valves. Larry Mulloy should have stopped the launch. But our traditional ideas of finding truth in a final moment of insight, analysis, or consensus just don't work anymore. Truth is not a product; it is a process. It is the result of information quality management practices and standards adopted by the group and followed over time. We must look at the biology of the brain and how the mind handles, and sometimes mishandles, information. We must look at the behavior of groups: how organizations pass the news along, altering it as they do. And we must look at the structure of organizations: who decides what is true, and how? We need to understand these issues better or learn to live with the failures that result:

At 11:38 a.m., January 28, 1986, the shuttle *Challenger* was launched. Because of the cold temperature, the O-rings failed to seat, the hot gasses generated inside the solid rocket motor blasted through the seal a quarter of the way around the circumference. Like a torch, they burned away the skin of the nearby external fuel tank and ignited the 790 tons of liquid hydrogen and liquid oxygen stored within. One minute and fourteen seconds after launch, the tank exploded, destroying the shuttle and pitching the crew— some still alive—ten miles down into the sea.

3

MEMBERS OF THE MIND

How do these decisions go wrong? How is it that men and women up and down the organization, at very different levels of skill and accountability, all make the same mistakes? Part of the answer is that information is an elaborate tapestry of real and imaginary facts woven from gritty experience and organizing illusions, a panorama built up from childhood to reflect the world as we believe it to exist. But the matter is more complicated. The mind itself is not a single coherent organ but a combination of several contentious entities with competing goals and complex tactics, much more inclined to reduce confusion than to find the right answer. To achieve a workable focus and a narrative structure, it aggressively discards unnecessary data, distorts the remaining information, and occasionally washes reason away in a tantrum of self-preservation and desire. Clear thinking is often achieved at the expense of truth.

To the earliest scientists and philosophers, it wasn't obvious that there was a mind or that it had any specific location. Everyone had direct personal experience with thinking but no working notion of how or where it was achieved. For most, the mind was an integrator of sensations received, a rather simple mechanism compared to the emotions that rumbled mysteriously elsewhere among the body's organs. Homer believed that thought, sensations, and emotions might be located together in the lungs. Even the word *psyche* originally meant not to think but to breathe.

Poets later relocated the center of man's rational and emotional processes to the heart and, after flirting for a while with the gastrointestinal tract, popular consensus placed the center of man's thinking just behind the eyes. *Noos*, the Greek word for mind or reason, means "to see." And after a while the Greeks came to think seriously about thinking. Man began to "see" himself.

Today we understand that the brain is far more complex. It consists of several major components: the two halves of the cortex, the cerebellum, the reticular formation, and the several tiny structures that make up the limbic system. To understand how deci-

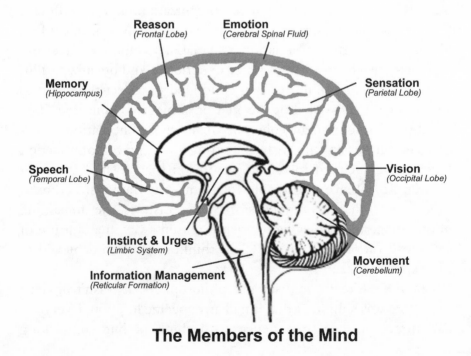

The Members of the Mind

sions are made, and how information and ideas—both true and false—contribute to our understanding of reality, we have to search for clues in the biology of the brain itself.[1]

THE TRUTHFUL BRAIN

The cortex, which accounts for most of the brain's volume and nearly all of what we call "thinking," is a mat of gray nerve cells about one-eighth of an inch thick and comparable in area to an average dish towel, deeply folded inside the skull.[2] The outer surface of this cortical mat faces into the cranial cavity, where every square centimeter is washed constantly by a bath of cerebral spinal fluid. The inner surface faces down toward the center of the head and is profoundly interconnected by billions of nerve cells, like the back of a telephone switchboard.

Over the last fifty years, scientists have made considerable progress in understanding which areas of the cortex seem to govern the mind's major functions. It now appears that the frontmost portion lying behind the forehead seems to perform those most human of the brain's activities: moderating emotional response, planning and decision making, adapting to new situations, and drawing inferences from experience.[3] Across the middle of the head from ear to ear are the areas that interpret sensations coming in from the body, devoting relatively greater cortex area to the hands, the lips, and the tongue.[4]

On either side of the head, behind the ears, lie the two temporal lobes that handle hearing, speech, and the sense of time. Electrical stimulation of these lobes can jumble or disassociate memories, creating a feeling of déjà vu or making familiar things seem strange.[5] Finally, at the back of the head lies the occipital lobe, the portion of the brain that manages and interprets visual information.

Our ability to remember, calculate, draw, speak, create music, or manipulate concepts in time and space seems to be closely related to these specific structures. Memory, mathematical aptitude, artistic ability, facility with language, or hand-eye coordination may be features we associate with high general intelligence, but they also appear in people who have low reasoning power, low receptivity to new ideas, or low analytical skill. The human sense of time and space, the ability to conceive of history, to create music, and to realize complex drawings are faculties associated with particular functional organs, members of the mind that may be uncoordinated and extravagantly disproportionate in strength or activity.

Marvin Minsky, a pioneer in building computer programs to mimic the functions of the mind, has for years tried to parse problem-solving behavior into rational units that could be replicated by computers: a combination of subroutines under the general control of a conscious problem-solving strategist.[6] Part of the mind drives the car to work while another part of the mind absorbs music on the radio, all while a third agent is struggling to resolve a difficult political problem that needs to be faced within a few hours.

Dr. Michael Gazzaniga, who did some of the earliest experimentation on the different roles played by the left and right lobes of the brain, also suggests that the brain may have many "mental units [that] can exist, can have memories, values, and emotions.[7] But what puzzles them both is the mystery of "consciousness." If we are surrounded by this noisy family of exuberant, unequal, unfaithful, and inscrutable members—memory, emotions, instincts, sensations—how are we able to think?

The dominant characteristic of consciousness seems to be the sequential processing of information in a series of questions and conclusions. While we may occasionally hear dissident "voices," we consider experience, project our own concepts onto the evidence, and resolve the task in a manner that best satisfies the demands of day-to-day living. But if there are several sides to be considered in every decision, then the mind must have a way to organize these conflicting voices in order of importance so that only one is heard by the conscious mind. Or, at least only one at a time.

By what process does the mind reconcile such conflicting information? School children are taught that if they think about a problem logically, the answer will come to them, but logical adults constantly fail to chart the right course through complex information. The operator on duty in the control room at Three Mile Island certainly had no chance of finding the right answer through logic. No chance at all. To the analysts covering Enron, the information available was totally logical but false and incomplete. Deferring for a moment the question of how teams work effectively toward truthful conclusions, how does the individual mind cope with a constant flood of dissonant and diverse stimuli?

The answer seems to lie in three very different subsystems that participate in coordinating consciousness. *Thresholds* operate throughout the body to select and regulate the volume of information received. Within that stabilized information stream, the *reticular formation* controls signals arriving up the spinal cord, directing each one to the appropriate processing center. At the same time, the *limbic system* balances the body's chemistry, setting primitive priorities. Without actually predetermining the outcome of reason, each of these mechanisms seems to dampen the volume of conflicting information and suppress data at any given moment so that only one melody is heard. In a manner very similar to the way groups function, the mechanisms that permit the mind to work also ignore experience, reroute signals, reorganize priorities, and occasionally flood the whole system with powerful and distracting messages of an entirely different sort.

Thresholds. Consider first the extraordinary ability of the mind to selectively fail at its data-gathering job. Throughout the body's nervous system, and particularly in the brain, are threshold mechanisms that rise and fall to block information or let it pass, to process data or suppress it. Thresholds exist at our fingertips to admit more or less sensory information. They exist in the central nervous system to monitor movement more carefully or to utterly deny the signals, and they exist in the mind, permitting us to focus on an issue or ignore it.

Unfortunately for the pursuit of truth, the mind has a tendency to please itself. Experiments indicate that people are more sensitive to information that is pleasant or alarming and less sensitive to information that is unpleasant or boring. On detecting attractive or specifically threatening odors, for example, the nostrils will involuntarily expand until the mind becomes accustomed to them. A lovely smell will dominate all other messages.[8] The pupils of the eye actually expand in response to a pleasant sight.[9]

In a military experiment, navy recruits were told that as a test of their ability to recognize images in low light, they should try to identify three objects projected on the screen before them. The screen actually showed only random patterns of gray. Subjects who had eaten within the last hour reported an average of 2.14 edible objects on the screen. Those who had not eaten for sixteen hours reported nearly twice as many. According to David Katz, "a hungry animal divides the environment into edible and inedible things. An animal in flight sees [only] roads of escape and hiding places."[10] As information becomes ambiguous or hard to understand, people unconsciously choose the interpretations that are most likely to relieve stress. This is not personal, it's biological. Through habituation, thresholds are constantly adjusted to allow the person to receive a meaningful range of signals. After walking into a dimly lighted area, for example, the senses will adjust to detect minor variations of gray, just as the trained Indian ear can enjoy a raga played on a dozen semitones within the range of two or three of our Western notes. Blind people have learned to understand Morse code at the rate of fifty characters a minute, received through minor electrical stimulation of the skin that most of us would dismiss as an itch.[11]

The process of focusing, on the other hand, is a conscious raising or lowering of these thresholds in order to pick out information that up to that point had been suppressed. It is uncanny, really, how a person in a noisy room can block out irrelevant conversations all around and yet still hear his or her name mentioned twenty feet away. Especially if it is whispered.

We aren't even aware of information arriving at the edge of our perception to secretly alter our calculations, and if that isn't enough to challenge our confidence, the mind will make up false signals when none are received, just to keep the sensory pipeline full. According to James Grier Miller, depriving a person of normal sensory input can cause subjective experiences that resemble hallucinations, impair the reasoning processes, and make the person more susceptible to propaganda.[12]

The members of the mind, like a well-organized group, are thus coordinated in part by a process that seeks to steady the flow of information, constantly adjusting its analysis to the most meaningful range of variation. The process has a bias for the pleasant over the not so pleasant, the interesting over the boring, the relevant over the irrelevant. And then, without further consultation, it throws the rest of the information away.

Reticular Formation. Although these sensory thresholds are distributed throughout the body, the Great Regulator is clearly the reticular formation, a thick cable of neurons that rises from the neck to become a tight bundle at the base of the brain. This is the second device for regulating information flow, and it transports the most important sensory messages up to their respective processing centers selectively. The reticular formation regulates the volume of information by ignoring or suppressing certain messages deemed "uninteresting" and it can shut down altogether as a result of chemical imbalance, injury, or sleep, causing the person to "lose consciousness."

Limbic System. The third system coordinating the many functions of the mind is a cluster of small structures called the limbic system that moderate mood and memory, note punishments and rewards, control the body's autonomic nervous system and frame the context for decisions. Crouching like a troll under the bridge of the brain, this is the primitive portion of our intelligence inherited from our oldest ancestors. The thalamus regulates communications within the brain; the hypothalamus regulates pleasure, hunger, sleep and the basic body functions; the amygdala gland regulates rage and fear; and the septum pelucidum seems to govern pain. Here are the basic instincts of our species—the rules for primal group behavior and the drive for survival being dictated relentlessly from a dark pulpit well beyond reach of the conscious mind.

The limbic system processes information and issues commands, though usually at a more rudimentary level. It certainly analyzes sensations, reaches conclusions, and signals a course of action. But when these appetites and urges conflict with the results of reason, how is the conflict resolved? Most observers seem satisfied that the cortex and the limbic system divide their jurisdictions in an amiable fashion, but no one who has struggled to make a decision in anger or follow reason against instinct can accept so simple a view. For the operators at Three Mile Island, all the available evidence—the dials, the lights, the gauges—showed that the water level in the reactor was rising. To look at this data and believe the *opposite* required them to trust their imagination and to swallow their fears.

There is growing evidence that emotional messages from the limbic system can even force a decision in ways that are hard for the conscious mind to detect. Dr. Richard Restak recounts the experience of one young man who, while babysitting his girlfriend's two-year-old daughter, "flew into a rage, then beat and choked the child until she was unconscious." The man blamed his anger on the child's "constant crying," but in reality he had become increasingly aware of occasional, inexplicable outbursts of anger. After this episode, he sought the help of a neurologist, who found a large lesion in the area of the amygdala. When it was removed, the violent behavior ceased.[13]

The sensations of fear without a face, persistent and unmanageable lust, and waves of rage that sweep all reason away are often experienced but rarely understood; and in many cases the mind, ever the tidy one, responds by inventing rational causes. If the heart is beating faster, if the muscles are growing tense, if adrenaline is pounding through your system, then you must be angry at something. And that something must be this! Emotion—which has always seemed the result of thought—secretly becomes the cause.

The notion that the mind is a single, integrated information processor, largely under conscious control, is, unfortunately, a romantic image from the nineteenth century and not the best expression of current knowledge. If evidence, memory, and logic are experienced as messages being processed by the cortex, then emotions must be experienced as conditions under which that processing takes place. They are not elements to be reconciled in a rational analysis so much as they are an environment that changes the way that decision is made. They set the rules by which the speakers are permitted to present their case and they determine the weight to be given to arguments of different types. One "thinks" about an issue in the context of how one "feels" about it, and a change in that feeling can alter the outcome of the decision. It is as if the members of the mind were a committee working on a difficult problem when suddenly the lights flicker, the room tilts, and papers begin sliding onto the floor. Strictly speaking, the information before them has not been altered; there is no new speaker on the scene. And yet the outcome is surely changed. The course of discussion shifts and the team begins to reach conclusions that are hard to explain later when only the incoming data is available. Fear, anger, desire, pain, and fatigue affect our decisions, but we don't know precisely how.

Cerebral Spinal Fluid. It may be that there is a fourth mechanism that regulates consciousness. The cerebral spinal fluid that surrounds the cortex might do more than simply cushion and cool the brain. In the last few years, experiments have suggested that the changes in the chemical composition of the fluid seem to be correlated with a person's mental state.[14] Generated at the center of the brain, right around the area of the limbic system where the primitive regulators of fear, appetite, and pecking order all reside, the fluid floods up through the fissures and over the whole cortex to be reabsorbed at the top of the cranial cavity. The current is normally slow—no faster than a dripping faucet—and the fluid is completely replaced every five or six hours. But in moments of stress, this rate of flow can be dramatically increased, forcing the fluid to move more quickly through the deepest fissures. A few drops from the hypothalamus, introduced at the base of the brain, will change the solution everywhere within a few seconds.

Perhaps in the future when we can monitor the changes in the fluid from minute to minute, we will find that this is a chemical message network connecting the limbic system to the surface of the cortex, delivering primitive emotional signals even as more rational information arrives from the nervous system beneath. Since it doesn't depend on the synaptic networks to deliver its signal, the cerebral spinal fluid can broadcast messages even to a young, injured, or untrained mind—as primitive emotions do. And the message can well up quickly, creating a powerful but inarticulate voice that overwhelms doubt in the best of times or washes all reason away. The complex folds and fissures of the cortex offer the advantage of placing nearly every vertical neuron in direct contact with the cerebral spinal fluid, while keeping the volume of the fluid—and therefore its speed as a message system—at a minimum. Even predawn dreams of fear, hunger, and arousal may be merely the uncoordinated awakening of the limbic system, momentarily out of balance, being rationalized by a sleepy mind.

We have scarcely begun to understand the role played by each of these regulating entities: thresholds, the reticular formation, the limbic system, and cerebral spinal fluid. They are not the dragons of an earlier existence, but they might be the merry wizards of our own personal cave, whose magic is not entirely under our control.

SOME THINGS MUST BE BELIEVED TO BE SEEN

We are gaining greater knowledge about the several organs of the brain and the roles they play, but we know little about how ideas exist and change, or how new information is evaluated, stored, and retrieved. All of this activity seems confined to that thin gray mat of neural cells whose inscrutable uniformity has puzzled science for so long.

In 1872 the Italian anatomist Camillo Golgi discovered that staining brain tissue with silver chromate turned the neurons black, permitting him for the first time to see their detailed structure clearly through a microscope. A decade later, Santiago Ramón y Cajal, a young Spanish scientist, improved on Golgi's stain and then dedicated the rest of his career to diagramming the nervous system and ridiculing Golgi's theories. They were awarded the Nobel Prize, together, in 1906.

The picture given us by Golgi and Cajal is a network of interconnected nerve cells that have essentially two orientations: vertical cells like the trunks of trees run from the surface of the cortex down through it and out the bottom to connect with points elsewhere on the underside of the cortex, to other components of the brain, or down the spinal column to the rest of the body. Horizontal cells, like tree branches, interconnect these vertical cells in six layers within the cortex, creating a complex network of extraordinary flexibility and potential.

The six layers of interconnecting horizontal cells develop sequentially during the first few years of life, with the lowest layer emerging first and the layer closest to the surface emerging last. Again, little seems to be known about how these layers differentiate themselves. But there is some indication that the lowest level of the network—and the earliest one to begin functioning—handles simple and direct communications, while the last and highest level handles more abstract and conceptual information.

Although thirty billion neurons are in place at birth, the network continues to form slowly through childhood and adolescence. During the first few years of life, these neurons expand their information-gathering dendrites exuberantly in all directions. The tiny tendrils reach out, possibly responding to a chemical beacon, possibly following a genetic code. And by the teenage years, when each neuron has generated about ten thousand potential connectors, neuron growth comes essentially to a halt.

Do the dendrites and the axons automatically connect to form a network? Yes, said Golgi. The cortex is a genetically prewired system that stores information and experience in the form of circuits established by nature; its structure is coded in the DNA. Not necessarily, said Cajal. The dendrites poke and probe toward their axon targets from their earliest embryonic beginnings, but it takes the stimulation of experience to create the connection.

If Golgi was right, then one can say that we inherit "ideas." The structure of the brain imposes relationships on experience, predefined for our species. But if the purpose of this predefined network is only to create the potential for perception, then the nervous system does not give us ideas, only the ability to have them. It endows us with the power to think in time and space. It gives us a sense of social order—when to argue and when to submit—and it instills in us a simple morality—a love of family, an aversion to shame, loyalty to the group. For the Morton Thiokol engineers, debating the fate of the *Challenger* in their conference room in Utah, the decision to recommend a launch was consistent with the most primitive ideas about pride and survival of the immediate group. To cancel the launch was supported by weaker, perhaps genetically newer ideas about long-term safety and the common good.

Researchers currently believe that nature creates the potential for knowledge by placing the neurons in appropriate proximity, but experience causes the synapses to form, "stabilizing" both the knowledge and the rational mechanism. But learning must happen when we are young. If the connection is not made within a reasonable time, the dendrite will wither and future opportunities for that particular connection are foreclosed. Thus the individual is permitted to develop in a variety of ways within the broad envelope of genetic possibility, though not all variations are equally easy. In the language of current science, an experience can be "resonant" if it is easily recorded in the natural structure of dendrites and axons, or if it requires only a minor expansion of an existing "neuronal assembly." The experience can be "dissonant" if it is not easily recorded by the neuron structure one has inherited. It may be true that some thoughts are easier to think than others, some memories easier to save, some kinds of decisions easier to make. And there may be a natural mechanism that encourages similarity of thought processes within a species.[15]

How does information travel across this network, and how is it stored? The secret seems to lie with two tiny "learning" devices: the synapse, which forms the connection between two neurons, and a protein molecule in the body of the neural cell. The synapse is the basic connecting mechanism. Once an electrical signal jumps the gap between two neurons, both sides of the synapse modify their surfaces to become more sensitive to future transmissions. If this happens frequently, the two surfaces become deeply joined in a manner that will not decay over the years. Once through the synapse, the signal is gathered by the dendrite to the center of the next neuron, where we find the second secret device: a protein molecule that decides whether the signal should be sent on. Depending on parameters that are stored as proteins in the cell body, the "decider" molecule determines whether the signal is coming repeatedly from the same source or being combined with signals from certain other dendrites. If the parameters are met, the new signal moves out indefatigably along the axon to the next synapse, bearing no more information than the fact of its own existence.

Complex circuits can be "triggered." Signals rush across a previously traced pattern of synapses, exciting certain nerve cells and stimulating what we experience as "thought." And they seem to fire in waves—big thoughts, strong feelings, goose bumps— ultimately prevented by some unknown mechanism from sweeping across the brain in a confusion of electrical activity.

Within the last few years, though, a vital new modification has been discovered to this widely accepted description. Some dendrites—or maybe some synapses—are negative. A signal received on one of these paths will cause the neuron to shut down instead of sending the message on. The activity of one neuron can thus directly inhibit the activity of another, temporarily silencing it without destroying it. In this way a memory, an experience, or an idea can be "repressed" by another memory, experience, or idea through the simple expedient of inhibiting the action of a key neuron, though how the synapse or dendrite is turned negative is still a mystery.[16]

What the synapse does not do well is record a maybe. It is difficult for a person to remember what is uncertain, and that biological handicap is repeated in the behavior of groups. An analyst may be careful to note ambiguities, but they almost always get lost once the message is delivered. Uncertainty is difficult to remember, and hunches often harden into fact.

These details of neurology may have been obscured until recently, but teachers, advertisers, and propagandists for two hundred years have known that students are more likely to understand and remember information if it is associated with something they already believe or care about. They know that to teach the student or persuade the listener they have to "awaken" a related interest and exercise the new knowledge in the context of the student's own conceptual, emotional experience. If this connection is not made, the new knowledge will be "forgotten." The information might be stored, the synaptic connections might be recorded (however weakly), but the circuit will be rarely if ever be used. It is not associated with the main currents of that person's thought, its activity is being inhibited by another experience, or it has become weak through disuse. Facts are ignored or denied because they are irrelevant, disturbing, unpleasant, or contradictory—and this is the most common problem we have in gathering accurate information about the world.

If our current understanding is accurate, then strongly held ideas and experiences make it more difficult to learn contradictory facts. Some people are less tolerant of disagreement than others. Sometimes the evidence just can't be seen. Experience that is contrary to existing belief is stored in circuits less sensitive to stimulation or more remote. It is hard to remember what you don't understand. In one of the most notorious examples of false knowledge, Johannes Kepler, the Renaissance astronomer and mathematician, plotted the positions of the planets as they orbited the sun, and each time he did it the data showed the path to be elliptical. But for ten years Kepler dismissed his data as false, since he knew perfectly well that orbits could only be circular. "I was almost driven to madness in considering and calculating this matter," he wrote later. "I could not find out why the planet would rather go on an elliptical orbit [than a circular one]. Oh, ridiculous me."[17] Making a change in so fundamental a scientific concept was profoundly difficult, but exhausted and humbled by his failure, Kepler fell back in his chair, looked out the window, and entertained for the first time the possibility that the evidence might be correct.

If knowledge is stored as a pattern of synapses, then how can that pattern be undone? How is false knowledge removed? People find it difficult to forget a vivid experience or discard an explanation with a long and useful past. Those associations have been established, and the mechanism for changing them is not very good. The mind is wired for learning, not unlearning.

To change a concept, stimulate the neurons. Carefully explore the ambiguities and contradictions that are inherent in the existing concept and then offer additional information or an alternative thesis that resolves these problems. Like good advertising, a good argument always begins by accepting the belief that exists and then adds the information, step by step, that will lead the listener to a new conclusion.

People not only start from different beliefs, but they have different truth systems—different standards and procedures for determining truth. They can be intuitive, rational, or realistic, and an argument that works effectively for one person might be counterproductive for another. At the UN, where diplomacy and consensus are honored to a fault, beating the podium with your shoe or shouting "my way or the highway" are behaviors unlikely to persuade. To modify strongly held ideas, it is usually necessary to enter the person's truth system, accepting both the reality of his beliefs and the legitimacy of the truth-testing process he prefers. This is difficult. Most people would rather fire away at opposing opinions from a safe and self-righteous distance. But a resourceful leader who really wants to change the listener's views will empathize, study his listener's truth system, seek out the inconsistencies, and start building there.

Information is dangerous, and dissonant information is particularly so because it brings the threat of confusion. The truth may make men free, but it's certitude that makes them happy. Under a barrage of new information, the old knowledge that once empowered us now threatens to collapse with nothing to take its place except the nauseating prospect of disorientation and paralysis.[18]

With substantial "thinking" going on in many different structures, the mind is more collegial than hierarchical. Experiences are contributed to consciousness from many corners; there are several centers of motivation and dozens of threshold systems operating in an uncoordinated way to enhance or suppress the flow of information.

This is an information system with a bias for order, not truth. Details disappear because they are unrelated, trivial, or contrary to a strongly held idea or experience. We remember only what makes sense—as we may have altered it, rehearsed it, and aligned it with desire. Thus ideas supplant reality, and "experiences" come to exist that never were but are nonetheless both vivid and "true" for the believer. Maybe we are coming to the end of the paradigm that has nurtured us for so long: the idea of the rational man. This assumption no longer conforms to the physical reality of the brain and is certainly not supported by the psychology of behavior. On the contrary, like all great paradigms, this lovely concept that has served so well for four hundred years is now under attack from the very science it spawned, and we are challenged to turn bravely toward the still incomplete, still contradictory outlines of a new view.

The function of reason, alone cannot be relied upon to detect the truth. In fact, many of the processes that make the mind so powerful are not logical. The ability to learn springs in part from the mind's willingness to abandon an old fact for a new notion. The ability to conceptualize is the ability to blur detail. The brain is hardly an engine designed for the reliable processing of information.

Nor does the brain have an organizational hierarchy. Instead it has a broad, generous, and redundant network connecting processing centers adept at handling certain kinds of information. Where we see powerful centers of control such as the reticular formation or the thalamus, we find that they are devoted to communications and relatively insensitive to content. Where we find memory, judgment, and unique processing skill—the special areas of the cortex—we find no control. There is no devil, no evil instinct, no heart of gold, but there is memory and there are concepts of the world that vary in their accuracy. There are faculties of differing strength such as language, pattern recognition, and computational skill. And there are emotional forces such as rage, fear, pain, and desire that seem to operate their own message network, changing the conditions under which the mind processes experience. The mind has many voices, prattling and panting, dictating, raging, whimpering and whispering, compromising, interjecting, and talking everlastingly. And from time to time it comes to a decision that is dead wrong.

USS *VINCENNES*: THE SYSTEM WORKED FINE

In the summer of 1988, the Persian Gulf conflict was heating up. Iraq was running air strikes against Iranian oil facilities and ships. Iran was responding by stepping up naval and air attacks, choosing in the process to move several F-14 fighters from Bushehr to the Bandar Abbas airfield, which supported both military and civilian operations. That in turn put US forces in the region on alert for "more aggressive behavior."

One of the causes for this increasing tension was a harassing campaign waged by the Iranian Revolutionary Guard, irregulars who ventured out into the narrow Straits of Hormuz in open boats equipped with rocket launchers and rifles. Their purpose was to frustrate the passage of tankers and supply ships up the Gulf to Iraq. The United States, then on the side of Iraq, had agreed to provide escort to some of these ships and had stationed the USS *Vincennes* in the region for this purpose.

On the morning of July 3, several Iranian gunboats were reported approaching a German merchant vessel, circling around it and challenging it to turn back. The *Vincennes* sent a helicopter to monitor the action and then began heading toward the scene itself. While still at least four nautical miles away, the helicopter reported the sound of gunfire below, and Captain Will Rogers, commander of the *Vincennes*, chose to interpret this as a hostile act. He quickly ordered the giant battleship to close in at flank speed, prepared (many observers said he was itching) for battle.[19] The boats, still miles away, could not actually be seen in the low morning haze, nor could the reason for gunfire be determined. And as this video game nightmare began, the boats appeared to the *Vincennes* commander merely as symbols moving about on his computer screen. Worrying that the boats might turn toward the *Vincennes*, Rogers contacted fleet headquarters in Bahrain, five hundred miles away, and requested permission to fire. Permission was granted, radar locked onto its target, and the five-inch guns began to blast away.

9:37 a.m. Iran Air Flight 655 took off from Bandar Abbas a few minutes behind schedule, headed to Dubai, 123 nautical miles southwest across the Straits of Hormuz. Visibility was eight to ten miles with low, scattered patches of haze; a typical Sunday morning on the Gulf. Like all aircraft, Flight 655 was equipped with an automatic transmitter that broadcast its identity as "Mode III"—a commercial airliner. The signal was correctly received and recognized by the *Vincennes*'s Aegis command and control computer, a $400 million system that was designed to track as many as two hundred ships in the open ocean, to rank them according to potential threat, and to even take over targeting and missile control. The plane's identifying signal was confirmed by several other navy ships in the area as well.

9:48 a.m. In spite of this, the Iran Air flight was erroneously tagged as hostile. From the US Navy's own investigation, and from subsequent reporting by ABC's *Nightline*[20] and *Newsweek* magazine,[21] it is clear that at this point two enlisted men in the *Vincennes* command center made the first in a series of small information processing errors that multiplied into a full-scale disaster. Petty officer second-class Andrew Anderson was assigned to determine the identity of any aircraft in range—it was his only task. And when his computer screen showed an unidentified plane leaving the Bandar Abbas airfield, he searched his current schedule of commercial flights to see who it might be. But in the flickering light of the command center, with the warship firing at the gunboats, he couldn't find any departures scheduled at that time. There was a commercial flight scheduled for 9:59, but it seemed unlikely that it would be leaving early. This was an error: in the Gulf region there are four time zones, and the Bandar Abbas airfield was thirty minutes ahead. Correctly framed, 9:59 was in the past, not the future, and the plane was a little late taking off, not twenty minutes early. But all this was lost on the nervous and inexperienced seaman.

He turned to petty officer second-class John Leach at the console next to him. Could it be an F-14 fighter instead? There was no other information. Until he could resolve the issue, Anderson tagged the flight on his computer screen as "hostile," and this action was reported by his supervisor, Lt. Clay Zocher, up to his supervisor, Lt. Cmdr. Scott Lustig.

Unfortunately, Lustig was not fully qualified to perform the tasks of an anti–air warfare officer. He was there because Captain Rogers trusted his advice on other matters. According to the official Report of Investigation (the "Fogarty Report," named after Rear Admiral William M. Fogarty, who led the investigation), Rogers "did not as a practice deal with his CRO [computer screen], relying rather on the information from operators . . . who were better trained."[22] Rogers knew Lustig well and wanted him at his right hand, even though Lustig had not completed the formal training necessary to become "position qualified." Lustig was also unfamiliar with the computer displays in front of him and, because of the way the room was designed, he had his back to the specialists who were gathering the data.

9:49 a.m. In the next two minutes the problem grew dramatically more serious. The *Vincennes* was still firing at the launches, turning sharply at high speed in order to keep the maneuverable little boats within range. But every time the guns went off, the lights in the command center dimmed and the noise reverberated around the room, much more like the experience of being fired upon than of firing. This was the first trial of the Aegis system in real combat, and even though the enemy was little more than a group of Boston Whalers, the crew in the command center was struggling under entirely unexpected conditions to work complex computer consoles that many of the men simply didn't understand.

9:50 a.m. Nor did the communications system help. The commander, tactical operations officer, and other key managers were linked together on a radio network called Net 15. But many seamen onboard had learned that this signal could be picked up on their Walkman radios, and as more of them tuned into the channel, the signal grew weaker and more noisy. To correct for this, according to *Newsweek*, the officers using Net 15 would periodically shout "shift" as a signal to the others to go to the alternate frequency, Net 16, which they would use until the rest of the ship was tuned into that one; and then they would shout "shift" again.[23] In the midst of all this, someone—Anderson or Leach—yelled "Possible Astro!" The incoming plane might be an F-14.

Anderson checked again to see what signal the plane was transmitting, but in the process he made another error. Still focusing on the Bandar Abbas airport, he mistakenly picked up the transmission of a different plane that had just landed. This time the signal said "military cargo." In spite of the fact that the Aegis system continued thereafter to recognize the plane correctly as an innocent commercial airliner, the image had now formed in Anderson's anxious mind and in Leach's of an F-14 bearing down on them about thirty nautical miles away; they decided to become much more aggressive. They both later testified that they thought Zocher and Lustig were weak and inexperienced and that the commanders had become "sidetracked" by the gunboats, "forgetting about the guy coming in." So the two seamen began to shout over the intercom at every opportunity. The Fogarty Report says: "Even though the tone of these reports must have seemed increasingly hysterical (yelling and shouting) . . . [Lustig] made no attempt to confirm the reports on his own. Quick reference to the [computer screen] in front of him would have immediately shown increasing, not decreasing altitude."[24]

9:51 a.m. Captain Rogers continued to fire obsessively on the gunboats until the main gun jammed and he was forced to swing the giant warship hard to starboard to bring a second gun to bear. As he did so, the floor tilted thirty degrees, the lights in the command center began to flicker, and all the papers, notebooks, and equipment started sliding onto the floor. Although the *Vincennes* had not been fired on at all—they were not even within range of a hostile vessel—the scene must have resembled every sailor's nightmare about a terrible battle at sea, and truth was an early casualty.

Anderson and Leach, having tagged the incoming flight as hostile, now took the tag as truth, and from that moment on they began to count down the miles between them and the incoming "enemy" craft. At some point, they also started to report that the plane was descending toward them and accelerating, though there was no information at all to support this. The Aegis system clearly showed that the flight was climbing through its normal takeoff pattern and that it was still transmitting the identity of a commercial airliner. Other navy ships in the area reached the same conclusion. Although the flight had originated at an airfield that supported both military and commercial flights, this was obviously just another shuttle to Dubai. Even the console in front of Lt. Cmdr. Lustig showed that the plane was continuing to climb away from them, but as he later testified: "That data to me doesn't mean anything, because I reacted to people that . . . I had operated with that were reliable . . . and when they reported at short range they had a decreasing altitude, increasing speed, I had no reason to doubt them. I had to make a split-second recommendation to the Commanding Officer, and I did."[25]

Behind him, Captain Rogers heard another officer conclude the opposite: that it was obviously a commercial flight; but *Newsweek* speculates that Rogers may have been swayed by the case of the USS *Stark*, which failed to defend itself against an incoming Iraqi fighter and was nearly sunk. Rogers directed the crew to continue the radio challenges to the pilot over the international military warning frequency, and if no response was received by the time it came within twenty nautical miles, he would shoot it down.

Even the language of the warning was misleading: "You are standing into danger and may be subject to USN defensive measures." Standing? To the pilot of a commercial Iranian airliner, this arcane usage must have been difficult to translate. Defensive measures? Under the circumstances, this euphemism for "attack" served no useful purpose.[26]

9:54 a.m. Leach and Anderson continued to shout imaginary altitudes—ten thousand feet, nine thousand feet, seventy-eight hundred feet. (When confronted with the difference between what the computer screens showed and what the seamen thought they saw, Admiral Fogarty later dismissed the disparity as "scenario fulfillment, . . . an unconscious attempt to make available evidence fit a preconceived scenario.")[27] In the darkened, noisy room still reeling from the last starboard turn, all the men faced away from each other with earphones clapped on, trying to communicate over a network that periodically failed. The designers of Aegis had placed greater faith in their intercom system and computer screens than they did in the people. And they didn't just subordinate the judgment of one colleague looking into the face of another—they made that judgment impossible. At this point the elaborate decision support system was being operated by inadequately trained managers in an environment of unexpected stress. It began to lock in on a narrow set of data, rigidly trimmed and reframed to exclude the nuances of human doubt and dissent.

There had been early warnings of such technological tunnel vision. In the original tests of the system, named Aegis for the shield of Zeus, the US Navy experienced several situations in which the crew failed to interpret correctly the data being presented. Examiners found that unless the crew members were tipped off to the kind of problem they were trying to solve, they usually made the wrong decision. Critics of the system complained that this was a fundamental flaw in the Aegis design and that the Navy's practice of coaching the crew through the test was a form of cheating. But the systems contractor responded that the fault lay simply with inadequate training. The system was fine; it was the people who were flawed.[28]

Thus Captain Rogers faced the problem of truth. In a manner exactly as predicted in the original warnings about the Aegis system, the men misinterpreted the information presented to them on their screens. Small misunderstandings were compounded by poor communications, and by the time the critical information had reached the man responsible for the decision, the errors were already in place. With his own adrenaline pumping and the command center rocking to the sound of guns, Rogers was a poor judge of the situation. He couldn't phone headquarters this time. He couldn't look out a window. He didn't know how to interpret the data on the screens, and he didn't trust the men around him. According to the Fogarty Report, many of those who observed the situation said he was predisposed to see everything in a hostile light. Unexplained gunshots from miles away had alone been sufficient for him to bring the full power of the *Vincennes* to bear on a few open boats. In the end, he fell back to procedure: challenge the pilot over the radio, and if he doesn't answer promptly he must be an enemy. Simple, fast, rational, unambiguous.

Taking the word of two hysterical seamen whose judgment he couldn't evaluate, based on data he didn't confirm, Rogers made the decision to fire on a plane that he couldn't see full of people he didn't know. He gave the order, the firing key was turned, but the rattled Lt. Zocher tried twenty-three times to hit the right key before finally launching two missiles off the deck to strike the Iranian airliner eight nautical miles away. At the time it was still climbing routinely at thirteen thousand feet with its two hundred and ninety innocent passengers who had entrusted their lives to the system.

The commanding officer of the nearby USS *Montgomery* watched from the bridge as the airliner exploded, and he knew immediately that a terrible error had occurred. Aboard the USS *Sides*, nineteen miles away, the captain was told by his radarman that the plane was obviously a commercial airliner and he said he almost vomited. Back on the *Vincennes*, amid cheering and shouts of "Kick Butt!" a lookout came into the command center and told the executive officer that the plane falling in pieces from the sky seemed to be a lot bigger than an F-14. Something was wrong. This was the first indication the officers had that their information was false. The Aegis command center was designed without windows—direct observation having been determined to be irrelevant—and at no time had any of the officers actually seen either the gunboats they were firing on or the Iran airliner they had just destroyed. Now the video game was over, and it seemed that they had not done well.

Or had they?

In the aftermath of the *Vincennes* incident, the official investigation headed by Admiral Fogarty reached three conclusions:

1. The mistaken decision to fire on the commercial airline was the result of "psychological stress" among the members of the command center crew. This didn't seem to be anyone's fault, but in the future the panel suggested that such crews be selected more carefully: "It is recommended that [the Chief of Naval Operations] direct further study . . . [of] stress factors impacting on personnel in modern warships with highly sophisticated command control communications and intelligence systems such as Aegis. This study should address the possibility of establishing a psychological profile for personnel who must function in this environment."[29]

2. The system worked fine. The review panel thought the Aegis displays should be augmented to indicate the altitude of aircraft on the screen and suggested that in the future it would be easier on the commanders if all the "crucial" information was collected onto a single screen. They didn't suggest, though, how to decide what was "crucial." Otherwise, the technology got a blue ribbon: "The Aegis Combat System's performance was excellent—it functioned as designed. Had the CO USS *Vincennes* used the information generated by his [computer] system as the sole source of his tactical information, the CO might not have engaged the [aircraft]."[30]

3. The men of *Vincennes* were all awarded combat-action ribbons, and Commander Lustig received the Navy Commendation Medal for "heroic achievement." The award cited his "ability to maintain his poise and confidence under fire," which enabled him to "quickly and precisely complete the firing procedure." Even a Navy recom-

mendation to censure one of the participants was disapproved by the Joint Chiefs of Staff on the grounds that it might be more embarrassing than instructive. And with regard to Captain Rogers, it was concluded that he had made no mistakes. "Based on the information used . . . in making his decision, the short time frame available to him . . . and his personal belief that his ship was being threatened, he acted in a prudent manner." The shooting down of the Iranian airliner was "not the result of any negligent or culpable conduct by any US Navy personnel associated with the incident."[31]

In the rich tradition of ignore, deny, and forget, Captain Rogers later denied any culpability. After retiring from the US Navy three years later, the man who made the decision to shoot down the airliner wrote his own book, *Storm Center: The USS* Vincennes *and Iran Air Flight 655: A Personal Account of Tragedy and Terrorism.*[32] In it he said that the *Vincennes* was being attacked at the time he shot the Iranian airliner down, a claim disproved by independent investigations. He admitted that there was confusion over the identification of the airliner, but he said that the Iranian pilot was the one at fault for disregarding the Navy's warning and flying into the middle of a gunfight.[33]

We cannot be so generous in our assessment. For all the millions invested in technology and training, the Aegis system failed exactly as had been predicted. It may be true that no one individual was directly responsible for the error, but their romantic understanding of the hierarchical decision process was wrong. Everyone in that room pulled the trigger; everyone was to blame. In many ways the behavior of those men exactly mimicked the biology of the brain. In gathering, evaluating, and summarizing the information they handled, the men on the *Vincennes* suppressed unpleasant evidence, removed ambiguity, enhanced the aspects of the data they found alarming, and framed their conclusions as fact so that the "virtual truth" of their situation seemed clear, rational, and compelling, even when important elements of it were false. Their decisions were made while the room was rocked with con-

{ 84 }

ditions identical to combat. The floor was steeply tilted as the ship turned in pursuit of the Iranian boats, with the heavy guns pounding away. Feelings of fear and aggression flooded the room as men shouted to each other over the din. And when the decision came to fire, it was made by a man some said was predisposed to war, unfamiliar with the data being shown on the screens, and distrustful of the men around him. This was not a rational process.

FASTER THAN THE SPEED OF THOUGHT

One of the failures that occurred in the control room of the *Vincennes* was simply information overload. There are limits to the amount of information the mind can effectively process, and in the last few decades, research has demonstrated that beyond those limits, additional information causes the quality of the decision to decline. The mind can generate information at about twenty symbols per second—the top speed of typists and piano players—but can only receive at about sixteen symbols per second—the best rate of readers and listeners.[34] Training can achieve slight improvements, but the constraint on information processing speed is biological.

There is also a limit on the number of alternatives the mind can consider at the same time. In his well-known essay "The Magical Number Seven Plus or Minus Two,"[35] George A. Miller observed that while people can easily bear five or six choices in mind, they experience a marked reduction in processing ability when the number goes beyond seven. Individuals pick five or six radio or television stations they turn to regularly, even when there are many more on the dial. Executives generally manage five or six subordinates well, but not more than that.[36] Computer systems that present a menu of up to seven choices are easy to use, but those that go beyond that limit seem to be much more difficult. Together, these experiences hint at another biological limitation that, like processing speed, is difficult to overcome.

What happens when these limits are exceeded? The most comprehensive survey of research in this area is presented in James Grier Miller's book *Living Systems*,[37] which reaches an incontrovertible conclusion: as information flow increases, the quality of the decision gets better, up to a point. Then, as the rate of symbols per second continues to increase beyond the individual's limit, the quality of the decision turns sharply down again. Doctors make mistakes. Jet pilots lose their orientation. Analysts fail to discriminate correctly between choices. Although the individual thinks the decisions are still getting better, he or she gets confused. The decisions have now started to become rapidly worse.

Two conditions in particular seem to aggravate the problem. First, when the important information is mixed with irrelevant data or is delivered in a jumbled sequence, the quality of the decision collapses even more rapidly than normal. Second, when the information is of many different types (statistics, images, text, blinking lights, maps) or is presented rapidly in many different ways (on a computer screen, over the phone, a message held up on the other side of the room), the mind apparently loses time switching from one vocabulary to another and gets disoriented. Executives who work with high volumes of information know this instinctively and often reject the advice of a knowledgeable expert using an arcane vocabulary in favor of a less qualified person whose style is more familiar. Captain Rogers of the *Vincennes* wanted Lieutenant Commander Lustig at his side, even though neither of them had been completely trained on the use of the new technology. Truth is traded in for less stressful communications. One measure of an executive's information management skills is the range of styles and voices to which he or she can become comfortably attuned.

Another method for getting lots of information across without triggering an overload reaction is, as psychologist George A. Miller points out, to increase the meaning of the symbols being processed.[38] Let a word, an acronym, or a graphic symbol stand for a concept, an event, or an object, and the trained person can greatly increase the net information processing speed. An air traffic controller, a trader in the stock market, or the technical director in a television studio, for example, uses codes and acronyms that can be quickly communicated. The number of symbols has not been increased, but the meaning the symbols convey has. Air traffic controllers use a terse language that allows them to move multiple planes around the sky, but there is no room for hi-how're-you-doin'. A typical communication would be:

Delta one-twenty-three slow to one-seventy-eight and descend to three thousand, make a hard left turn heading two-niner-zero. Continental seven-eight-niner you have traffic at your three o'clock, fly south heading one-eight-zero and verify visual contact.

For a person unfamiliar with the language, the message may be difficult to understand. In the hands of the skilled information worker, though, such special vocabulary and syntax is a powerful tool for rapid exchange of complex information, permitting members to process large blocks of meaning with a normal level of intellectual effort. By contrast, beware the earnest, articulate person who has nothing to say and will not stop saying it.

Training with the message system helps reduce the stress of overload, but the risk associated with using codes, acronyms, and high-value words is that the decision might become more abstract and mechanical. And there is always the chance that the person you are trying to communicate with has no idea what these terms mean.

Psychologists who study group communications have identified four common ways to bring the volume of information under control and keep the quality of the decision high: chunking, source selection, queuing, and questioning. And these strategies can be used together. A person scans the environment, sampling the information available for indications of change or abnormality. As attention begins to focus on a particular issue, the person selects the sources that are most relevant and spends less time with others. Within this narrowed stream of incoming information, the experienced information manager focuses on critical data, putting the rest of the information in a queue to be examined as time permits. Finally the person turns to a questioning mode in which specific answers are sought out of the data at hand. Each of these strategies permits the person to work with only as much information as he or she can understand at the moment, deliberately discarding the rest according to judgments and procedures already in place.

Chunking. The most successful information managers monitor many sources but actually use only a little of what is delivered. One "browses" a magazine, "skims" a book, "looks at" a memo, or "keeps in touch" with a colleague, deliberately limiting the time spent with each source, gambling on one's own ability to spot the significant trend and on everyone else's tendency to be redundant. The more informed the "chunker" is, the more likely he or she is to detect significant changes quickly.

Source Selection. As events ripen into an issue that requires diagnosis, the best coping mechanism shifts to source selection. Now the decider must ignore some of the incoming data in order to listen more closely to a few trusted and relevant indicators. A source that is ambiguous or noisy requires too much time to process; we tend to avoid advisers who bury their good suggestions in a drone of irrelevant or pompous prattle. A source that has proven wrong in the past is too risky in a pinch. A source that lacks concreteness or uses unfamiliar language is ignored—even though the information may be both critical and true. In each case, information is discarded without evaluation because the benefit of working with the source has proven in the past to be unequal to the cost.

James Grier Miller cites an illustration from Bertram M. Gross in which a clear warning of the impending attack on Pearl Harbor was ignored:

Two days before the Japanese attack on Pearl Harbor, three intelligence officers interpreted intercepted Japanese codes as indicating an attack on an American installation in the Pacific by One P.M. on December 7, 1941. But their efforts [to warn headquarters] were unsuccessful because of the poor repute associated with Intelligence, inferior rank and the providence of the specialist or longhair. General [Leonard T.] Gerow, head of the Army's War Plans Division, for example, felt that "enemy information of such grave moment would be brought to my attention by the Assistant Chief of Staff, G-2, and not by a Signal Corps Officer."[39]

Some years ago I was asked by a client to identify the conventional methods for placing value on information. How do people decide what information is worth? If information has higher value in one place than it has in another, and moving it there has a cost, when does the cost exceed the value? In the process of the research, I interviewed detectives, investment analysts, weather forecasters, purchasing officers, and gamblers, and I found an unconventional but consistent pattern, best exemplified by a Chicago cop who tried to explain how he figured what to pay a tipster. "I don't buy the tip," he said, "I buy the guy." Whenever an informer offered to provide a little inside news, the detective would consider the information this source had brought him in the past and then pay what it took to keep him coming back. "Sometimes I paid the guy for !&$#*. Sometimes I got a break. Most of the time I had no real way of knowing." The trouble with a great deal of information is that you can't kick the tires. One subscribes to an information source without knowing precisely what information will be delivered or what value it will have, believing that over time the cost of subscribing will be justified by episodes of real benefit.

It is important to maintain redundant sources, as well. Given the errors that can occur in evaluating and expressing information, having more than one source for all critical types of information is not inefficient, it is good practice. Slightly different descriptions of an event help to capture its ambiguity and meaning, and no one source has to be "right" or "wrong." Chances are there is much truth in each account.

Queuing. The third of the four most popular coping mechanisms is the ultimate weapon of a bureaucracy. When overload begins to occur and the quality of work is threatened, the right answer is sometimes to place all incoming information in a queue that is organized by some system of priority. The information is then processed at a rate that permits good decisions. But even the best-organized queues can go wrong: the Nuclear Regulatory Commission arranged its resources so that no one could reach anyone else except during office hours.

For someone scanning the horizon and chunking data that he finds most interesting, it is easy to ignore an unpleasant fact or filter out a source that is irrelevant or inefficient. But a queue is wonderfully procedural and easy to express in standard, impersonal guidelines. When new information conflicts with old knowledge, the information can be deferred with the promise that it will be heard in turn, even though its turn may never come. The engineers at Babcock and Wilcox wrote memos about the sticky valve at Three Mile Island for at least two years before the accident occurred. The company did not respond to any of them. The last and most urgent memo was returned because it was on the wrong form, and when it was resubmitted it was marked for "later action" and consigned to the queue. Queuing is a simple mechanism that permits the organization to replace individual myopia and unpredictable bias with a consistent level of planned ignorance.

Questions. The last of the four popular strategies for managing overload is to regulate the volume of incoming data by asking specific questions, the most precise and powerful method for avoiding information overload. But questions are entirely under the control of the decider and they tend to elicit only the information that he or she is predisposed to hear. As the primary method for controlling information flow, questioning alone is a narrow approach that often leads to trouble.

At NASA, the practice of asking the right questions had been raised to a formal system, but as the launch of the shuttle *Challenger* drew near, questions about the O-ring kept producing the wrong answers. So they changed the questions, modified the tests, and overruled the procedures until the answers became more palatable.

What communications scientists have been trying to explain for several decades now is that making decisions under stress is not a matter of "executive style" or "personal philosophy." It is a difficult task. Some deciders are better at "chunking" or asking the right question, while others are masters of the art of team information processing, and they carefully cultivate and train their sources. Like it or not, the Information Age has drawn us into a world where the whimsical or intuitive procedure for analysis is no longer adequate. Managing information is not a function of general intelligence but a skill to be learned and practiced.

It is curious how much the group's information-handling behavior resembles the biology of the brain. The volume of information a group can handle has limits, and when those limits are exceeded, information is indiscriminately ignored, just as the thresholds in the nervous system rise to prevent an overflow of sensations. In the process, groups tend to listen to information that is attractive or alarming, just as the brain does. Boredom is the sin that neither can abide. Group information systems, like the brain, have great difficulty with "maybe's." Uncertainty is removed, ambiguity is clarified, the synapse is closed, and messages are forwarded in simple yes/no terms. The brain sorts incoming information and directs it to specialized processing centers—images, smells, feelings, language, muscle movement—just as groups tend to break work down and assign it to specialists. And some brains, like some groups, are better at processing one kind of information than another. These specialized functions then seem to proceed in parallel, contributing their results, and sometimes their failures, to produce (this is the mystery) conscious thought. And all of this takes place in an emotional context that can radically alter the outcome. Groups fail the same way the brain does, from confusion. The results of the specialized processing functions don't fit together again. The conclusions reached by the eye are inconsistent with the whispers in the ear. The men on deck see what the captain up in the windowless command center does not.

4

CHALLENGING TRUTH

At the age of thirty-nine, with two small daughters at home, Betsy Lehman, prize-winning health columnist for the *Boston Globe*, checked into the Dana-Farber Cancer Institute for a series of four chemotherapy treatments intended to arrest the growth of her breast cancer. The medical team there seemed to have a detailed understanding of the disease and an extraordinary record of innovation at the forefront of science. And although the recommended therapy was difficult and risky, she and her husband, who worked there, believed it offered her the best chance for life. They were wrong.

For centuries, philosophers have argued about how an individual can determine which descriptions of the natural world to believe. When your own experience says one thing and educated authorities tell you another, how should you decide? It is an interesting problem, but frankly speaking, it is not something people think much about. As individuals, we believe what we believe and we muddle on. But in the last several decades we have found ourselves together in offices, on teams, and in complex information networks. We work in technology, finance, medicine, science, government—all based on information, all gathered by and shared with others. There the important problem is not what one of us believes is true but what all of us believe is true. When the knowledge we are all acting on begins to ring false, how do we challenge it without attacking the team, the community or the profession to which we belong? Without being attacked ourselves? Is contradictory evidence a sufficient basis for questioning the leader's decision? Is reason enough? Is consensus necessary? Can we simply say that the group's conclusion on a matter is immoral, that it is unpatriotic, or that it feels wrong? The real motive behind the old philosophical debate over truth has always been to justify or condemn the impudence of a few individuals who want to overturn established views, and this is not an abstract issue. Sometimes, as in the case of Betsy Lehman, challenging the group's virtual truth is a matter of life and death.

BETSY LEHMAN: TRUTH TO POWER

Her first treatment began on November 14, 1994, and it was, in the language of the medical community, "aggressive." Some of her blood would be drawn and held in safety while she was given a dose of cyclophosphamide (Cytoxan) intended to kill all the cancer cells in her body. Then the stem cells extracted from her saved blood would be reinjected into her bloodstream to form new blood cells and replenish the immune system. The first two treatments seemed normal. The Cytoxan made her sick but not much sicker than was expected. By the third treatment, though, it was clear that there were problems. The protocol that prescribed how each treatment should be administered was a twenty-page document developed by the research team, and the summary page—which is apparently all that anyone read—said that the patient should receive: "cyclophosphamide dose 4 grams/square meter over 4 days."

Dr. James Foran, a second-year oncology research fellow, was responsible for interpreting the protocol. According to the *Boston Globe*, he decided that it meant four grams per square meter of body surface, every day for four days. Given her body weight, that would be 6,520 milligrams a day. The pharmacist, Caroline Harvey, was surprised. As subsequently reported in the *Boston Globe*,[1] she questioned the high dosage. Anything over one thousand milligrams a day was unusual, and this was six times that. But the doctor recalculated the body weight, adjusted the dosage slightly, and assured her that it was correct. A second pharmacist questioned the dosage as well, but with five physicians signing off, the doctor made the decision to continue the treatment.

As the days went on, Lehman became violently ill. She vomited intensely. Her blood tests showed abnormal readings. Her electrocardiogram had the classic indications of Cytoxan damage to the heart and it had been marked "abnormal," an indication to doctors to consider "drug effects." On the morning of December 3, Lehman was alarmed. "Am I going to die from vomiting?" A nurse described her as "weepy, anxious this a.m. regarding discharge home before she is ready."[2] Her husband asked the staff to check the dosage; her reaction was far worse than anything they had been told to expect. But the doctors assured him that it was normal in cases of bone marrow or stem cell transplant.

Betsy Lehman grew worse. "She was vomiting sheets of tissue," said her husband later, and the doctors admitted that it was the worst example of side effects they had ever seen. Lehman called her friends, pleading for help. In one message, left on the answering machine of one of her closest colleagues, she said, "I'm calling because I am feeling very frightened, very upset. I don't know what's wrong, but something is wrong." The physician responsible for Lehman's treatment looked over the lab results and reviewed them with her superiors. According to her lawyer, "She saw nothing that indicated there was a red flag."

The staff decided to make no change in the treatment program.

According to their understanding of the therapy, this was the way things were supposed to be. In the last forty-five minutes of Lehman's life, no one even went into her room. Betsy Lehman died alone.

Two days later, the head of the medical team who had cared for Lehman sent a memo to the chairman of the "human protection committee." "At this point," she wrote, "I do not know the cause of death. It is extremely uncommon for patients undergoing bone marrow or cell transplants to experience a 'sudden death' phenomenon."

The pathologist who did the autopsy found no traces of a Cytoxan overdose, but he noted that at least the cancer was gone.

The Board of Registration in Medicine, which issues medical licenses in Massachusetts, and the Division of Registry, which grants licenses to nurses and pharmacists, were told nothing about the accident. (They would first learn about it when they read the morning paper.) There was apparently no review of the patient's death. No errors were identified, no one was reprimanded. Medicine is risky business.

But ten weeks later, in routine processing of patient records, one of the hospital clerks discovered that the dosage was wrong. Instead of four grams per square meter every day for four days, page 11 of the protocol actually specified a total of four grams per square meter *over four days*. Lehman had been given four times the prescribed dose. A month later, the hospital filed a "serious incident report" with the state health officials. According to Richard Knox, the *Boston Globe* reporter who broke the story, "National experts in cancer chemotherapy say confusion in protocol language between daily and cumulative doses is a leading cause of medication error that has led to dozens, if not hundreds of deaths."[3] And in retrospect, the error surprised no one. According to Knox, daily and cumulative doses are often confused; look-alike and sound-alike drugs are confused (Adria and Aredia); abbreviations are misunderstood (MTX can be one of three cancer drugs or a nitrogen mustard); decimal points are overlooked or misplaced, especially in prescriptions for children; handwriting is illegible and transcriptions are garbled.

"We can't get oncologists to standardize the way they give drugs and write orders," said one pharmacist from Walter Reed Hospital. "We wind up seeing a lot of confusion among nurses and doctors on how to mix and administer these drugs."[4] "We call it the tombstone mentality," said Michael Cohen of the Institute for Safe Medication Practices. "Everyone waits for someone to die before they do something about it."[5] Death is the early warning signal.

These errors were not even rare. According to Knox, one Dana-Farber source said the pharmacy staff there had "caught many, many errors. If you had access to the record, you would see that between October and February, physicians made eight or nine errors in writing orders, including four or five mistakes that might have been quite deadly if they had not been caught by the pharmacists."[6]

And the errors continue. In 1999 a day-old baby at a Denver hospital was diagnosed with congenital syphilis, and the pharmacist, more familiar with treating adult forms of the disease, mistakenly prepared a dosage that was ten times larger than doctor specified. Some nurses questioned the numbers and others worried about how to administer so much medicine to such a tiny child. In the end they decided on an intravenous injection, failing to notice the manufacturer's warning poorly printed on the drug's packaging. The baby died almost immediately. An autopsy revealed that the diagnosis of syphilis had been incorrect.[7]

In late 2003 a two-year-old cancer patient died at Johns Hopkins Children's Center after receiving a botched prescription that contained four to five times the amount of potassium called for. The parents said it was not the mistake of a single individual but a "cascade of failures" in a system without enough safeguards.[8] No one was to blame.

To help prevent rejection of a newly transplanted kidney, twenty-nine-year-old Tiffany Phillips was given a prescription for Prednisone, but when she went to her local pharmacy they didn't have enough, so they phoned a nearby CVS store and passed the prescription information on. Somehow the original dosage, 250 milligrams a day, was mistakenly transcribed as 1,250 milligrams a day. According to WCNC-TV in Charlotte, North Carolina, the CVS pharmacist put a label on the bottle, automatically produced by her dispensing computer, which said "Take 62.5 tablets a day." (Try shaking 62.5 aspirin tablets into the palm of your hand.) Strange? Yes, but if the system says so, it must be right. In fact, the computer's high dose alert went off, but the pharmacist said later that she ignored it. As she passed the bottle over the counter to Ms. Phillips, she said, "This is a lot of medicine. You won't eat, you won't sleep." Later in court, the pharmacist was asked why she didn't call the prescribing physician to make sure the dosage was correct, and according to Phillips's lawyer she said it was too late. "I was getting off at 9."[9] Phillips lost the new kidney, but she survived. The person who originally called the CVS pharmacy and conveyed the prescription was never publicly identified.

A new study of extraordinary death rates associated with radiation treatments in French hospitals suggests that between 1989 and 2006, hundreds of cancer patients were burned and injured from excessive radiation doses. At least five are now known to have died as a result. The first question raised by the investigating team was why the radiation equipment instruction manuals were available only in English.[10]

There are many dimensions to the Betsy Lehman tragedy. The lack of respect paid to the pharmacist's doubt is certainly consistent with the notorious disregard for nurses, pharmacists, and the staff by many doctors, even young ones. In most hospitals, the doctor is always right. And Dana-Farber was also a research facility, focused on testing and calibrating new cancer treatments as well as caring for patients. But from an information management perspective, Dana-Farber's inability to determine whether the prescription was right or wrong is a case study in how virtual truth goes unchallenged.[11]

The dosage was correct because the doctor said it was correct, and in the truth system in place the doctor was the final arbiter, even though there was evidence to the contrary all around. The blood levels, the electrocardiogram, and the patient's adverse reaction all seemed to indicate an error. Several of the people involved, including the pharmacists, the EKG technician, the husband, and even the patient were concerned. But there was apparently no acceptable mechanism for questioning the prescription without insulting the doctor and running the risk of looking hysterical. A recent review of medical errors in Massachusetts hospitals showed that while many have implemented preventive procedures— counting sponges, marking the arm or leg where the surgery should be done, labeling the X-rays left or right—the errors continue. Surgical instruments are still left in the patient; doctors still remove the wrong kidney; the operation is still done on the wrong patient. Surgeons still ignore the procedures, and nurses are still afraid to confront them. "The culture piece is huge," said Diane Rydrych, assistant director of health policy for the Minnesota Department of Health. "Hierarchy is a huge presence in hospitals, especially in ORs. A surgeon can come in and say, 'I'm going to do it my way.' We have heard that very, very often. And hospital analyses reveal that someone knew something was wrong but didn't speak up."[12]

THE TRUTHFUL TEAM

How does the team tell the doctor he is wrong? The question of why some groups tolerate open discussion of truth and others do not has been investigated by the Dutch psychologist Geert Hofstede, who studied team decision making in many different cultures and found five dimensions to the behavior. In Hofstede's language, a team may have a high "Power Distance Index" when everyone agrees that the team leader will make the important decisions. A team can have a high "Individualism Index" when the members are able to act more independently of the group. In teams with a low "Individualism Index," Hofstede says that members often embrace extended families and lifelong work groups that offer support and protection in return for unquestioned loyalty. A "Masculinity Index" measures the extent to which the leader is assertive (which Hofstede calls masculine) or supportive and caring (feminine). An "Uncertainty Avoidance Index" measures the degree to which the members of the group can tolerate operating in a situation where the rules are not clear and the facts are not certain. And finally Hofstede has measured a "Long-Term Orientation Index," which indicates the extent to which the team adheres to such virtues as thrift and perseverance instead of the shorter-term values of saving face or accommodating political realities.[13]

Hofstede believes that these indexes vary greatly by national culture, but in the United States at least, such a simplification is hard to defend. NASA's culture and the culture at Dana-Farber both placed great emphasis on the group's goals and on the power of the team leader to make decisions. But America's freewheeling tradition of innovation in high technology, art, and business just as strongly supports individualism. Nonetheless, these insightful indexes help us to measure the willingness of a team to engage in a candid discussion of truth. And what we can measure, we can change.

As psychologists came to realize that different groups have different decision-making styles, the airline industry, among others, began to look more closely at the authoritarian way pilots have traditionally treated their crews. After the crash of a United Airlines plane in 1977,[14] the National Transportation Safety Board began to focus on pilot/crew communications as a potential source of error— particularly the often observed problem that members of the crew knew something was wrong but were afraid to speak up. Over the next few years United Airlines trained their crews to be more frank and assertive toward the pilot, and pilots to be more considerate of other opinions. Crew Resource Management (CRM) training has since become standard for major airlines around the world, teaching crews how disagreements should be voiced:

Get the team leader's attention. Speak specifically to the person in charge. Don't just talk among yourselves.

Identify the problem. Explain your concern without emotion or insult. Focus the conversation on the decision being made.

Describe the issue clearly. Expand on your concern, laying out the facts and projections on which your view is based.

State the solution. Recommend the specific action you think is necessary to fix or further diagnose the problem.

Obtain agreement. Try to find a course of action acceptable to you both.[15]

Dr. Gerald B. Healy, president of the American College of Surgeons, has been a longtime advocate of bringing this new openness into the hospital:

> Operating rooms suffer from the same flaw that once plagued cockpits: Just as crew members had feared questioning their captains, many surgical team members still fear questioning surgeons. Many medical errors could have been avoided if a nurse, resident, or anesthesiologist had felt free to speak up.
>
> At my department at Children's Hospital of Boston, our medical error rates have dropped to zero after airline pilots taught us team training, and team training resulted in lower death rates, and more satisfied patients in the cardiac surgery program at another New England hospital.[16]

Patients can challenge the doctors as well. Hamilton Jordan, President Jimmy Carter's chief of staff who fought four different forms of cancer over twenty-four years, advised patients to take information management seriously. In his book, *No Such Thing as a Bad Day*,[17] he tells patients to take an active role in both the diagnosis and treatment. Don't take no answer for an answer:

> *Be an active partner in the medical decisions.* Don't be passive. Learn about your disease, and participate in the decisions that are

made. For example with my lymphoma, if I would have accepted the first treatment offered, I'd be dead today. It was assumed that I only had a mass in my chest. I later learned that the lymphoma was all through my body.

Seek the truth about your illness, and prognosis. If you don't have the facts, and don't know the truth, you won't make good decisions. It takes courage to ask questions about statistics and your prognosis.

Get a second opinion. We wouldn't buy the first computer or cell phone we looked at. Shop around when your life is at stake. I got second opinions on all of my cancers.

Determine your physicians' experience. If you have something that your doctor says, "I've never seen this before," get another doctor. You want your doctor to be very familiar with your disease.[17]

INSPIRATION, REASON, AND CONSENSUS

How should groups decide what is true? Families, teams, companies, communities, and societies have different methods, but over the course of history three general standards have been offered: inspiration, reason, and consensus. Thousands of years ago, whenever information or ideas grew so complex and ambiguous that their truth could not be determined, villages relied on inspiration, communed with the gods or attended to the revelations of a prophet. The Church guided the way they ate, married, settled their disagreements, and went to war. As long as the source remained unimpeachable or charismatic, the pronouncements were accepted as true, whether or not they were particularly consistent or in accord with the evidence. Priests and prelates, oracles and emperors multiplied, rising in a splendid hierarchy of increasing infallibility that reached all the way to God.

But as people began to write down these revelations, inconsistencies became apparent and reason suggested a better set of rules. With reason, a man could participate in government and practice medicine, measure the seasons and the tides, and divine the intentions of an opponent on his own. The truth of any new or ambiguous statement could be tested by comparing it logically to other statements that were known to be accurate. Finally, after several centuries of torture and deception, mystics receded into the distance and those whose office it was to interpret the new rules mounted to power, wielding reason like a sword.

The age of science has offered a third test for truth: consensus. A statement is true if it explains most (but not necessarily all) of the evidence. A theory is true within the context of a current paradigm, although it may not be true tomorrow when the paradigm shifts. An idea is true, according to William James, if it provides a successful basis for action.[18] Even in physics, where laws once seemed immutable, we now measure the "probability" of a molecular description being true at any given moment, although the uncertainty principle says that moment is brief. In government we vote: truth is whatever the majority says is true. In economics, the year is "bountiful" when our pooled investments grow slightly faster than inflation. And we have begun to measure the truth of our medical knowledge in terms of how many were healed compared to the cost of healing and the severity of the illness. This is not just a triumph of complexity over common sense; consensus is a genuinely new standard for truth.

But in each regime, authority took charge. The priests, the professors, and the politicians stabilized the system and ran the process in a manner that allowed the group to act successfully in the real world while, not incidentally, keeping themselves in power. Serious challenges have always been discouraged.

In the sixth century BCE, Lao Tzu, curator of the Royal Library of Choui, suffered so acutely from the contrast between his own experience and what the political authorities were saying that he renounced his court position, turned away from the disputatious and conniving ways of "bookish young persons, inventors and lawyers," and led his friends and students into a new way of life based on principles of simplicity and peace. Life without anguish, he said, comes to those who retreat from false knowledge, who yield to the authority of nature alone, and follow calmly in its path.[19] This may be a philosophy for old men, but it found a powerful disciple in Confucius, who urged on his students and followers a veneration of orderliness to the point of ritual. His own interpretation of ancient literature suggested a model for management and a standard by which the difficult questions of science could be resolved. Like Plato, who was practically his contemporary, Confucius dreamed of a government that would have more knowledge and purer motives than its people, but that didn't happen. Within three hundred years, China was reduced to a cruel military dictatorship and all books were burned. As the fires of political warfare raged, the hopeful words of Confucius and the book of Tao were consigned to memory and their ideas were buried in the soul of China.[20]

The standard of inspiration reasserted itself in the writings of Plato. Even though we can't see them, the Greek philosopher said, the true ideas can be sensed. They transcend the evidence and provide men with a standard for judging truth, beauty, and the virtue of action. In retrospect, we have to allow for the fact that the language of philosophy was new and wobbly. By "ideas," Plato may have meant not intellectual concepts as we think of them today but natural laws, a sense of orderliness and instinct that one comes to recognize through study. In "Meno," for example, Socrates shows how a boy can be prompted to discover fundamental geometric laws without ever receiving instruction because, says Socrates, such laws exist all around us.[21]

If we are willing to say "most ideas" instead of "all ideas," then it isn't difficult to agree with Plato that they are embodied in nature and are discovered, not invented. But Plato went further, arguing that unfortunately these ideas are so difficult to understand and apply in the real world that people ought to simply trust a few philosophers. Those who greeted the philosopher's vision with enthusiasm were themselves candidates for enlightenment, given discipline and time. But those who objected to what the philosophers said were, by definition, beyond hope and must remain slaves. It was a cunning remedy for handling dissent, still widely practiced today.

As Plato grew old, he grew mean-spirited, and his opinions of man were even more fully revealed. He came to believe that human nature was bad, if not evil, and that government should exercise tight controls over education, the arts, and public opinion. Endorsed by the state, the official truth was to be questioned only at one's peril, and the facts might beat upon it without effect. Anaxagoras, for example, had declared that the sun was not a god but a flaming stone. (He was condemned to death for this but escaped to die an old man on the Hellespont.) Empedocles suggested that man had evolved from lower forms of life and threw himself into a volcano to convince his fellow villagers that he would ascend to a higher form himself. (He did not.) Hippocrates announced that all diseases have natural causes and were not necessarily the afflictions of an angry god, and Alcmaeon had already determined that the brain, not the chest, was the seat of consciousness and thought. "Through it we think, see, hear and distinguish the ugly from the beautiful, the bad from the good."[22]

The first glimmer of an alternate standard for truth came from Aristotle, Plato's most devoted student. More than anything, Aristotle was the father of reason who sent his students out every morning to gather all forms of biological data so they could classify it together and learn how the world worked. Instead of starting from ideas about order and beauty, he struggled toward them. Instead of teaching the wisdom of history, Aristotle encouraged systematic questioning, classification, and deduction. Unlike Plato, he seems to suggest that men can logically arrive at new ideas that are as valid as the old ones. But like Socrates, his questions made him unpopular, and his lessons were increasingly contrary to the truth of the state. At the age of sixty-three, condemned to death by the government of Athens, he was smuggled out of the city to die a few months later at his mother's family home in Chalcis. The government of classical Greece, paragon of public wisdom, was not about to be questioned.

Nor, during the Renaissance, was the Church. Giordano Bruno, an Italian playwright, was fond of wild, earthy comedies. Brilliant, compulsively irreverent, possessing a photographic memory and an incandescent intellect, he charmed kings and cardinals throughout Europe—and then infuriated them. Like a precocious child toying with the elements, Bruno brought the arguments of science to bear on the Church's truth and laughed as the sparks flew. If other planets were inhabited, he asked, did Christ die for their sins, too? If infinity existed in the world of science, and if God was also infinity, then were there two infinities? He struggled toward the idea that God must be a universal force present in all things, and not some external, judging Mind. But there were difficulties here. Though he loved the Church, he could not keep from confronting it with his audacious questions, and in time the Inquisition arrested him. On account of these heresies he was imprisoned and tortured for eight years, whereupon in due course, on the order of nine cardinals and the pope, they tied his tongue, strapped him naked to an iron stake, and burned him alive.[23]

The prospect of challenging authority has always been a discouraging one. But as the writings of Aristotle reemerged, circulating secretly among sixteenth-century scholars, the call to "reason"—truth based on evidence—became irresistible. Francis Bacon was an ambitious lawyer who advanced through the ranks of the English court, became a member of Parliament, and after several political setbacks, came to be Queen Elizabeth's learned and level-headed counsel. His contemporaries thought he was wise, faithful, modest, scholarly, and completely dedicated to the crown.

Had he done nothing more, we would remember Bacon as a brilliant executive. But during all those years as an active lawyer and politician, he also wrote in bold, broad strokes about the process of reason. He accepted the Church and honored it in more than a perfunctory way, but he observed that religion might exert a limitation on ideas. He advocated experimentation and unstinting observation as the test of truth. As a practical matter, Bacon asked, how should we manage our affairs when so much of the information we are getting about the real world seems to disagree with official doctrine? Bacon thought the answer might lie in reason, but it was a process full of risk. He warned against what he called illusions of the mind. Beware of the idea that the universe is ordered; it may merely be a reflection of our own human desire to understand. Beware of personal bias; our observations and even our thoughts are easily colored by preconceptions and desire. Beware philosophy; words can be spun to form seductive abstractions that twist and then supplant reality. Beware false logic.[24]

It is interesting to speculate how Bacon must have reacted to Shakespeare's *Othello*, first played in 1604, shortly after he was knighted. In it the mighty general gets false but logical information convincing him that his wife has committed adultery with a trusted lieutenant, and he is led through cunning flattery and deception to murder her. Like Bacon (who was once thought to be the author of this play), Shakespeare presses the question of whether reason might not betray us, as Iago betrays Othello. How is a person to detect the skillful lie? Is there not another basis for truth—love, trust, morality—that is a better standard for action than reason, which is so easily twisted?

Following the rise of reason through this incredible period of intellectual enthusiasm is both difficult and misleading; the Enlightenment was about many things. But from time to time we see the arguments embodied in a pair of figures emerging as in a dance, taking up opposing positions and then whirling back into the crowd. Man could reason for himself, they said, but with every impudent new pamphlet on the subject, the philosophers were careful to touch their hat to the Crown and Church. Some argued that reason could be relied upon to help us test official truth, as long as it did not conflict with the teachings of God. Others were comfortable arguing against the Church but felt that reason should never be a justification for opposing the state. Some felt that reason was fine, but serious questions should be asked only by an educated aristocracy. No, said others, truth was everywhere around us and could be assayed by every man.

René Descartes, following in the path of Bacon, proposed to reduce all knowledge, except knowledge of God, to a process of rational analysis, and in common language he explained how logic and free will might work together to unlock all mysteries. Man could construct an ideology of his own, as long as he accepted the preeminence of God. "On no account will I publish anything that contains a word that might displease the Church."[25]

Thomas Hobbes, tutor to the English royal family and friend of Galileo, struggled with a comparably difficult question: How can man be rational and free, yet still be obedient to the laws of the state? While he was teaching mathematics to young Charles II, Hobbes wrote *Leviathan*, in which, after more argument than was necessary to the task, he announced that men are free to choose their government. But once the choice was made, they must obey it absolutely. Not surprisingly, Hobbes thought that in England, at least, the people had chosen the monarchy.

It was John Locke who took the final step, saying in 1690 that the rights of men were defined by "natural law" and not granted to them by government. Men had the right to think for themselves, and although they had a "contract" with society to obey the law and support the government, they could speak out, question authority, and even overthrow a tyrant if he became "lawless and arbitrary."

Trained as a physician, Locke traveled among liberal theologians and young philosophers for a decade in Paris and Holland but published none of his major works until his return to England at the age of fifty-seven. By then he was the leading liberal intellectual of his time. Man's knowledge, he wrote, comes from experience, organized by reason and reflection. From this "furniture" as he called it, men fashion ideas "intuitively," and those ideas, in turn, help him to gain a greater understanding of the world. He called this the "natural way of knowledge" and argued that reason is the judge. Members of a group might benefit greatly by discussing their conclusions in the open, even if some of these conclusions ran contrary to the ideas of those in authority.[26]

One is tempted to observe how closely history recapitulates adolescence. From Confucius, Plato, and others comes the parental assurance: Great ideas are the embodiment of truth, and we [the Church, the state, the academy] will provide them in good season. Sit up straight and pay attention. From Bacon, though, there is the whisper of youthful anarchy: Don't believe it. Gather the evidence yourself and trust to reason. And then from Locke: Look, it's not going to work if we just replace the official ideas with someone else's logical conclusion. Frankly, many of us see things a little differently. What we have to do is talk it out and decide as a group which ideas we want to accept as the basis for action. Inspiration, reason, consensus.

LES PHILOSOPHES

This was the issue facing the philosophers of the eighteenth century: Should the "truth" of new ideas be decided by an aristocracy of educated men or should it be decided by all the people thinking for themselves? Under what circumstances were common people permitted to question authority? In the years that followed, two voices were particularly clear. Opposed in thought and style, each personified the major philosophy of an age. And just as a dancer is permitted by the strength of his partner to test grander and more elaborate embellishments, each man was taunted by the other to search for more extreme forms of his own belief. They lived in mutual hatred, they died within weeks of each other, and they came in time to be buried like lovers in the same grave.

Voltaire was born in 1694 into Paris aristocracy; Jean-Jacques Rousseau was born poor in Geneva in 1712. Voltaire began a brilliant career as a playwright, an essayist, and a cynic. He attacked the Church with witty invention, arguing that men should strive for a better life through science and the arts, not settle for blessings after death. By 1740, at the age of forty-six, he lived like a millionaire in a liaison with Mme. Émilie du Châtelet, much younger but equally brilliant, ruling intellectual Europe, the finest flower of the Enlightenment. He had considered the possibility that every man should think for himself but dismissed it sarcastically: "When the people undertake to reason, all is lost."[27] People may be equally free, but they are not equally endowed, and to credit them equally with wisdom would be folly. While making great fun of the clergy, the patriots, and the philosophers around him, he nonetheless believed in education, in science, and in the obligation of the few to lead the many.

Rousseau was self-educated and earned his living as a music copyist and teacher. In 1745 he moved to Paris, took as his lover Thérèse Levasseur, a dull but devoted chambermaid, and was at one point hired by a friend to revise the score of a minor opera on which Voltaire had collaborated. The two corresponded but never met. A pretty man, Rousseau was a romancer as well as a romantic. But his poverty and lack of education blocked him again and again from ascending to the society he admired, and by the time he was thirty-seven, he was frustrated and afraid. Then, walking to visit a friend in prison, he read that the Academy of Dijon would conduct an essay contest on the topic "Has the restoration of the sciences and the arts contributed to corrupt or to purify morals?" He was struck by the question and, in a quarrelsome mood, he saw the dramatic potential of a negative answer: "man is by nature good, and only our institutions have made him bad."[28]

His essay won first prize and became the battle cry for romanticism. Rousseau proposed that society, sciences, and savoir faire had gone too far. Philosophers (by which he meant the elite) "sap the foundations of our faith, and destroy virtue. They smile contemptuously at such old words as patriotism and religion, and consecrate their talents . . . to the destruction and defamation of all that men hold most sacred. . . . Let men learn for once that nature would have preserved them from science as a mother snatches a dangerous weapon from the hands of her child!"[29]

Then their fortunes changed: Rousseau's rousing cry found immediate sympathy among the rabble of Paris. His essay was widely debated and he became famous. At the same time, Voltaire's enemies grew bolder, his plays less popular, and his protectors less tolerant. In 1748, in a melodrama of deceit and discovery, Mme. du Châtelet had an affair with a minor poet, became pregnant, and died in childbirth with Voltaire at her side. According to legend, he was emotionally destroyed and, returning to the house they had shared together for so many happy and productive years, the man—having risen to fame by ridiculing sentimentality—wandered all night through the darkened rooms, calling her name.

The brilliant aristocrat moved to Berlin, to Potsdam, and to Geneva, hounded in every city by lawsuits and criticism. His plays were banned. His books were refused by booksellers, and he retreated finally to Ferney on the Swiss border where he gathered his talents around him for a long and remarkable rebuttal. He was a skinny man who drank coffee constantly and fired off caustic letters in all directions. He said that a few men of wit and reason must do the thinking for the rest.

Rousseau disagreed, saying that what people really needed were good songs and a simple religion. He was in favor of slowing down the education of children until they reached the age of twelve, giving them a chance to develop their "natural" gifts. And as he railed against the philosophers he became bolder, more inflammatory, and harder to have around. In the course of this writing, he attacked Voltaire. In 1764 Rousseau received a pamphlet, *The Feelings of the Citizens*, penned anonymously by Voltaire, in which he found himself savagely ridiculed as a hypocrite and a madman. At least Voltaire had the facts on his side. Rousseau, who grew rapturous on the natural beauty of children, had actually abandoned five of his own to foundling homes, reasoning coolly that they would burden his career. The man who gave so eloquent a voice to natural passion, when caught stealing a ribbon, simply placed the blame on his girlfriend. And he was crazy. In his last years he grew deeply paranoid and antisocial, fleeing from town to town under assumed names, yet writing the extraordinary *Reveries* that epitomized romanticism.

Voltaire died on May 30, 1778, and was buried secretly lest the Catholic Church deny him a place in any cemetery. Rousseau died four weeks later. In 1791 the remains of Voltaire were removed in honor to the Pantheon in Paris, and three years after that, Rousseau's remains were buried nearby. In 1814, during the battles of the Bourbon restoration, revolutionaries dug up the bones of both men, threw them together into the same cloth sack, and flung it into a dump at the edge of the city where it disappeared.[30]

The exploding knowledge of the Enlightenment, obvious to every man, seemed to be dangerously challenging authority, and the history of such efforts was grim. But there remained one final attempt to reconcile this intellectual freedom with the traditions of religion and the organizing power of the state. There was one last chance to think freely about science and the real world without giving up entirely on the comforts of faith. It was undertaken by a fifty-seven-year-old professor of geography no one had ever heard of.

In 1781 Immanuel Kant was teaching natural science and metaphysics at the University of Konigsburg, now Kalingrad on the Baltic Coast of Russia, and he had published only a few papers on astronomy and anthropology. A little man who stood less than five feet tall, he was thought of as compulsively punctual and unassuming—certainly not a provocative thinker. He had never traveled more than twenty miles beyond the university and lived alone in rented rooms all his adult life. According to his contemporaries, he was a teacher of great affection and wit, although he managed to suppress both traits completely in his writings.

Kant had followed closely the debate over whether men could question the established truth and he was deeply troubled by what he read. According to Scottish skeptic David Hume, everything should be questioned. Man could not be certain that any of his perceptions were accurate, nor could he confirm the nature of anything outside his own mind. Science was, at best, the rationalization of guesses. But Kant's own experience told him otherwise. There was some kind of "natural" sense of order that permitted men to organize their experience—vaguely reminiscent of Plato's "ideas"—and while it couldn't be entirely explained, this "moral code within me" couldn't be so easily dismissed. In particular, he felt a knowledge of right and wrong, an impulse to faith, a love of freedom, and a sense of time and space that helped him remember and imagine. How could such instincts be reconciled with the evidence of science and the dictates of the Church?

Nothing in Kant's understanding of the mind could explain the source of these ideas. They were not taught in the schools, they were not obvious in nature, they were no longer whispered to men by muses. Yet he saw that people reached conclusions based on thoughts that were beyond their experience and contrary to their immediate well-being. Perhaps these were a palimpsest of God's own mind, the faintly visible remains of an older script, lying beneath our knowledge and experience and offering clues to a deeper order of things.

What if these organizing faculties are simply part of the way the mind works? What if they are not ideas in the sense that Plato meant them but the natural mechanisms of thought? Unity, plurality, and totality; existence and nonexistence; possibility and impossibility—these are not rational judgments; they are a framework used by the mind in managing the flow of information. "Cause and effect" is not a scientific conclusion reached after study but the way the mind has of associating two events at the moment of experience. The laws of nature are not in nature but in how the mind experiences nature. Reason might not be the lofty functioning of a coherent intelligence but just some kind of biological grammar. Man could certainly resolve for himself the conflict between information and ideas, but the way he went about it might be a lot less conscious and far less pure than anyone was willing to admit.

Kant peered into the roiling darkness of human behavior (about which, in fact, he knew little) and backed away, able to see where his reasoning led but unwilling to follow. It was one thing to say that God exists only in men's minds, but to suggest the possibility that right and wrong are only "ideas" was to challenge the fundamental social order. It was a notion contrary not only to prevailing philosophy and the opinion of the king but deeply opposed to Kant's own fastidious moral outlook. And in the end, he retreated.

With the same sort of *Deus ex cranium* solution that had saved Descartes, Kant concluded that morality offered a standard for truth that was superior to reason. We know what is true or not true by trusting our own hearts, not the preaching of the Church.

This brave and troublesome investigation had been tolerated for a decade. His persistent questioning of the accepted order had been permitted to continue because even his enemies had to admit that few people could read Kant, and even fewer could understand him. But Kant's view of the Church was uncharacteristically simple to grasp and harshly antagonistic. In 1794 an order from the king called for Kant to present an "exact account" of his impertinence and demanded that future work be more supportive of the Crown and Church on pain of "unpleasant consequences."

The old man capitulated and took upon himself a vow of

silence. He had said enough. In seeking to save science, Kant had raised it from the process of experiment and deduction to a subtler intellectual effort, as prone to inspiration as to error. In seeking to rescue God from the claws of the skeptics, he suggested that religion might be merely a useful invention, valuable to the extent that it helps us make sense out of otherwise contradictory experience. With noble intentions and traditional language he had, perhaps unintentionally, dragged the issues of truth, morality, and the right to reason into a harshly modern light.

When Jean-Paul Sartre turned to the question of truth, he concluded that it was whatever you wanted it to be. The group's truth was merely moral judgment. But trapped in their dark solipsism, the existentialists missed the point: we may dream alone, but we do not act alone. It is hard to be a productive part of most modern enterprises without sharing information with others, without depending to some extent on the truth of what they say, and trying in turn to speak truthfully to them. To do that we join truth systems that work, for as long as they work, even when it means adopting the language, the ideas, and, to some extent, the values of the group. It isn't the old truth—ideology—that matters. It is the power of the group to provide a new truth—accurate information—as the basis for action in a complex and uncertain world. The classic truths are useless. The real truth is found in experience and in the life we share with others.

In retrospect it is odd that philosophers spent so little time thinking about families, colleagues, and communities. But then we get a clue from looking at their lives. Plato never married. Thomas Aquinas and Giordano Bruno were both monks. Locke, Hobbes, and Hume never married. Descartes and Voltaire each had mistresses but never married. Rousseau married his mistress at the end of her life. Kant, Schopenhauer, Nietzsche, Spinoza, and Kierkegaard never married. Heidegger never married. Sartre had a mistress but never married. Bertrand Russell, ever the contrarian, married four times *and* had several mistresses. Without speculating on whether the profession of philosophy leads to the single life or vice versa, it is notable that much of Western philosophy has been written by men without families; in some cases by men who were aggressively antisocial. They weren't the kind to join groups or to place much value on the benefits of membership.

And yet the history of man's evolution is marked by nothing so much as an expanding awareness of and dependence on his tribe, his work partners, his village, and others of his faith. The shift from the hunter/gatherer era to the Agricultural Age was not just about learning to manage the land from one season to the next. It was also about bringing groups together in a cooperative project. Most agriculture in early America was done on communal farms. The Industrial Age was not just about managing energy and labor in new systems. It was about complex organizations and specialization of labor, about buyers and sellers forming markets, and economic enterprises engaged in broad commerce based on trust. And the Information Age is not just about ideas and information. It is also about creating groups empowered with extraordinary new truth-sharing capabilities. There is an obligation that attends this opportunity. The medical team that cared for Betsy Lehman and the pharmacists who prepared the medication for Tiffany Phillips should have questioned what they were being told, whether their concerns were based on reason or consensus or just a plain hunch. Authority is rarely the best judge of what is true, and it is lazy to think so.

A group united by a common set of ideas and information permits its members to know together what they could never know alone. Instead of concentrating decisions in the hands of a few general deciders who struggle to keep up with the facts, successful organizations often construct a truth system that distributes the analysis in advance. They build a process that gathers information quickly, they work hard at reconciling new facts with old knowledge, they permit a diversity of views, and they learn the risks of group information processing as well as its strengths.

Able to describe reality, provide an agenda, and establish a hierarchy of valid ideas, a group can come to understand a subject like medicine, politics, or science more broadly and in more detail than would be possible for any individual. But in the process the group can, and it must, test these ideas to make them stronger. This is the difference between thinking alike and thinking together. For groups, truth is not "revealed" as mystics claim, "proven" as philosophers argue, or "discovered" as scientists tend to say. Instead, it is an accurate description of reality assembled and tested by the group in a process both difficult and risky. As tragic as it was, the death of Betsy Lehman is merely a vivid example of a larger problem. Groups bat facts around as if truth didn't matter. Ridiculous theories are asserted by men and women in authority, and no one has the courage to give them the raspberry. Warnings are ignored, and those who keep pointing to contradictions and inconsistencies in the data are roughly silenced. We have not yet learned to take information seriously, and now we face trouble on a much larger scale.

5

THE INFORMATION WAR

In 2001 the United States fought and lost the first information war. At a cost of nineteen lives and less than a million dollars, the enemy smuggled a handful of terrorists past a poorly coordinated military, past the jealous infighting of undisciplined intelligence services, past a government without leaders, and past an amiable but inattentive bureaucracy to succeed in the greatest attack ever made on American soil. This was not like any other wartime attack. Their soldiers could not be identified, their homeland could not be invaded, their weapons could not be captured, their communications lines could not be severed, and their finances could not be traced. They lived among us in rented houses; bought cars under their real names; were issued pilot's licenses, driver's licenses, and visas by our own government; and at the last minute they used our own commercial aircraft as weapons. When United States forces finally surrounded their citadel high in the snowy caves of Tora Bora, they slipped away across the border into a country we treated then, and now, as an ally. In a fight between what the enemy knew about us and what we knew about them, the enemy was audacious and resourceful, and America was confused.

Whenever an army loses a major battle, the general must walk the perimeter in the stink of blood and gunpowder and ask, what did we do wrong? Were our barricades too low? Were our fields of fire uncoordinated? Did we lack the ammunition, or the men, or the necessary resolve? How did we miss the warnings? How did they get over the wall? If every man fought bravely, what is it about our fortifications, our preparation, or our command structure that failed us? How do we keep this from happening again?

But in the aftermath of the terrorist attack on September 11, 2001, America's leaders seemed befuddled.[1]

PRESIDENT BUSH: "Never in anybody's thought process ... about how to protect America did we ever think the evil doers would fly not one but four commercial aircraft into precarious US targets ... never."[2]

VICE PRESIDENT CHENEY: While acknowledging that threat information had been received during the summer of 2001, "no specific threat involving really a domestic operation or involving what happened, obviously—the cities, airliners and so forth."[3]

SECRETARY OF STATE POWELL: "In the first 24 hours of analysis I have not seen any evidence that there was a specific signal that we missed. In this case we did not have intelligence of anything of this scope or magnitude."[4]

VICE CHAIRMAN OF THE JOINT CHIEFS, GENERAL MYERS: "You hate to admit it, but we hadn't thought about this."[5]

FBI DIRECTOR ROBERT MUELLER: "There were no warning signs that I am aware of that would indicate this type of operation in the country."[6]

NSA DIRECTOR MICHAEL HAYDEN: "NSA had no [indications] that al Qaeda was specifically targeting New York and Washington, or even that it was planning an attack on United States soil."[7]

NATIONAL SECURITY ADVISER CONDOLEEZZA RICE describing
the president's daily briefing for August 6, 2001, titled: "bin
Laden Determined to Strike in the US": "I don't think anybody could have predicted that these people would take an
airplane and slam it into the World Trade Center. . . . It was
an analytical report that talked about his method of operation, talked about what he had done historically . . . in 1997,
in 1998. It was not a warning."[8]

How can such claims be true?

Shortly after 7 a.m. on September 11, 2001, Mohamed Atta
boarded American Airlines Flight 11 from Boston to Los Angeles.
He was thirty-three years old, born and brought up in Egypt but
carrying a Saudi passport that had recently been replaced, thus
removing all evidence of his travel history.[9] Since he had already
lived in the United States for a year, much was known about his
activities. He sent e-mail messages to thirty-one flight schools
from his own Hotmail account, describing himself and his associates as "a small group of young men from different Arab countries
[who would] like to start training for a career of airline professional
pilots. In this field we haven't yet any knowledge but we are ready
to undergo an intensive training program. M. Atta."[10] He enrolled
in flight school at Huffman Aviation in Venice, Florida, received
his instrument certificate in November, and with flight deck
videos purchased at the local pilot shop and time rented on the
Boeing 727 simulator at the Opa Locka airport, Atta was granted
his US pilot's license on December 21, 2000.

In fact he had been under surveillance off and on for the last
decade. When he was living in Germany, the intelligence service
there identified Atta as one of a small group of active Islamic terrorists. He was tailed by the CIA as well, and when he entered the
United States in June 2000, responsibility for watching him shifted
to the FBI. A Department of Defense data mining project called
Able Danger had identified him as one of twenty members of al

Qaeda active within the United States. Twice. He had been cited in a suspicious activity banking report,[11] and there was even a warrant out for his arrest for not appearing in court in connection with a speeding violation.[12] This was a passenger about whom much was known, and all of it bad.

At 7:59 a.m., Flight 11 took off from Boston. At 8:13 the transponder was turned off. At 8:19 an attendant onboard called flight control and reported that the plane had been hijacked. Flight controllers tried to contact jet fighters who were supposed to be on alert for such contingencies, but the budget had been cut and the jets were elsewhere. At 8:37 NORAD, responsible for the air defense of North America, alerted two jets stationed on Cape Cod on the coast of Massachusetts, two hundred miles from New York. But within six minutes, Flight 11, flying at five hundred miles an hour, carrying ninety-two passengers and crew as well as sixty tons of jet fuel, crashed into the North Tower of New York's World Trade Center. The jet fighters sent to intercept the plane had been mistakenly directed out over the Atlantic.

THE STAG HUNT

It was always clear that international intelligence services would have to share information if there was any hope of stopping terrorists, and from the beginning that had been a challenge. Al Qaeda operated in small, often independent cells, able to move quickly around the world—Manila one week and Madrid the next— without the burden of a central organization or bureaucracy. But national intelligence services had languages and customs to observe, sources and methods to protect, and governments with a complex past of enmity and alliance. Within the United States, sharing was even more problematic. The FBI had separate criminal and national security divisions with a deliberate policy of not exchanging information with each other. Neither group shared data with the CIA, which routinely withheld information from everyone else, and the Department of Defense had its own intelligence service. NSA was responsible for communications surveillance but rarely disclosed its findings. There were other organizations as well, operating even deeper in the shadows.

Had they shared information more readily, they might have seen the target that needed to be protected. Security surveys repeatedly ranked the World Trade Center as "very high" on everyone's hit list. As early as 1984 there had been rumors of a plan by Iranian terrorists to bomb the World Trade Center. In 1993 a twenty-year-old Ethiopian man hijacked a Lufthansa plane with the intent to fly it to New York and crash it into "something."[13] The same year a Pentagon panel warned that a plane could be used as a missile to bomb American landmarks, but the State Department edited this out of the final report. "It was considered too radical, a little too scary for the times."[14] In February of that year, Ramzi Yousef, with close ties to bin Laden, set off a bomb in the lower level of the building, killing 6, injuring 1,042, and coming very close to bringing the tower down. During Yousef's trial, an undercover agent testified that the FBI had known about the attack beforehand and planned to substitute a harmless powder for the explosives. But at the last minute an FBI supervisor called off the switch and then failed to tell anyone else what he knew.[15]

For the attack on the World Trade Center, there was no shortage of models. In 1994 four Algerian terrorists affiliated with al Qaeda hijacked an Air France plane with the intent of flying it into the Eiffel Tower, but they were stopped by French Special Forces. *Time* magazine ran the story on its cover, and a copy of that issue was found later among the al Qaeda papers captured in the Philippines.[16] Tom Clancy's novel *Debt of Honor* ended with a Japanese commercial airliner being deliberately crashed into the US Capitol during a joint session of Congress, and the Bojinka plot in 1995, another al Qaeda scheme, included a plan to have a pilot crash a large plane into CIA headquarters.[17] In 1997 the Catastrophic Terrorism Study Group, a collaboration of experts from Harvard, MIT, Stanford, and the University of Virginia, warned that the impact of a terrorist attack might go beyond the loss of life and property. Such an attack, they predicted, might "undermine America's fundamental sense of security. . . . Constitutional liberties would be challenged as the United States sought to protect itself from further attacks by pressing against allowable limits in surveillance of citizens, detention of suspects, and use of deadly force."[18]

Nor was there much confusion over the likely perpetrator. In 1998 a foreign intelligence service warned the FBI that Arab terrorists planned to fly a bomb-laden plane from Libya and crash it into the World Trade Center. This was dismissed by the FBI and the FAA on the theory that Libyan aviation was incapable of such an attack.[19] When the CIA repeated the warning, saying the terrorists were al Qaeda, the FBI dismissed it again, claiming that the evidence of an al Qaeda presence in Libya was not clear.

In 1999 British intelligence gave the United States embassy a secret report warning that bin Laden planned an attack on the United States, using commercial aircraft as a "flying bomb."[20] At the same time the FBI learned that a terrorist organization planned to send students to the United States for flight training. The FBI's Counterterrorism Section instructed twenty-four field offices to be on the lookout for Islamic students engaged in aviation training. But the 9/11 Commission later concluded that "there is no indication that field offices conducted any investigation after receiving the communication."[21]

German intelligence, monitoring al Qaeda's communications, learned the name of one of the hijackers and passed it on to the CIA.[22] NSA, the United States' own superagency for monitoring communications, was by then recording everything going in or out of the al Qaeda hub in Yemen. But when it learned the names of the hijackers it chose not to pass that information on to either the CIA or the FBI.[23]

In a courtesy program established only with Saudi Arabia, the State Department allowed the Special Consul in Jedda to grant US visas without requiring the applicants to appear in person. In April 1999, four of the hijackers received these visas, each one a known al Qaeda operative and an experienced killer.[24] No report was made.

Osama bin Laden formed al Qaeda in 1988, determined to keep the holy war alive after the Soviets left Afghanistan. The seventeenth son of one of the world's wealthiest families, he was thirty-one at the time and a devout Sunni, committed to inflicting US civilian and military casualties on a scale so large that the country would be forced to back away from its support for Israel and withdraw all military forces from Islamic countries. He seemed an unlikely soldier. In college he had studied economics, business, and engineering, and three of his four wives were academics. Six feet four inches tall, slight, soft-spoken, and something of an amateur prophet, he lived an ascetic life and was prone to sermonizing. But drawing on his family's wealth, and possibly on funds from the CIA, he went to Peshawar in western Pakistan where, for more than a decade, he ran couriers from Pakistan into Afghanistan providing news, money, and coordination to the mujahideen who were fighting against the Soviet army. His criticism of the Saudi royal family became increasingly strident and disruptive until the government was forced, if only out of courtesy to its American friends, to revoke the young man's citizenship. The gesture may or may not have been sincere; bin Laden continued to visit his family and even participate in public conferences from time to time. How could international organizations contain or eliminate such a potential threat if even Saudi Arabia was occasionally doing him favors?

The problem of getting cooperation among people or even countries who have separate goals is an old one, and the political philosopher who thought most deeply about this was Rousseau. In 1754 he argued that people need to surrender certain individual freedoms in order to achieve the benefits of a strong community, telling the story of a stag hunt that has since become the model for discussing whether an individual (or a country) should do what is good for himself or join others to do what is good for all.[25] In this story, the men in the village set out to hunt down a stag that has been seen abroad in the forest, but since none of them can kill the great beast alone, they decide that each will stand guard in a corner of the forest and when the stag appears, chase him toward the others. As Rousseau points out, each man might be tempted to leave his post and chase a rabbit, thereby satisfying his own appetite. But if any of them leave their station, the stag will escape, and though it may never be known who betrayed the agreement, all will lose. In game theory, which tries to understand social, political, and economic behavior in quantifiable terms, the stag hunt allows us to talk about how a rational player would make such a choice, how his understanding and commitment to the others would evolve, and how the game might ultimately lead to an equilibrium of trust and a better outcome for all. Countries must cooperate to defeat terrorists, even though any one of them might be able to shift the threat elsewhere or make a separate peace.

It is the same with information. When players are pitted against each other, the value of information is usually reduced by sharing. If one player knows that a horse has a good chance of winning, for example, he places his bet and keeps his mouth shut, because if he tells everyone what he knows, they will all bet the same way and the odds will drop to nothing. The most common behavior in organizations is that people keep valuable information to themselves in order to maintain its exclusivity, increase their own opportunity, gain power over a situation, or use it later in a trade. Factions within a group, departments within a company, and countries within an alliance never tell all they know. They focus on their own opportunity and hold back from making commitments to a larger, more abstract goal. Going for the rabbit, to use Rousseau's model, is human nature. That is the point the philosopher was trying to make. But the lesson of game theory since the 1950s has invariably been that in war, as in games, such victories are temporary. If you betray the others, on the next round they will betray you. The only lasting peace comes from an equilibrium of shared interest and a commitment to help each other. Mutual assured destruction, balance of power, "co-opetition," agreement to disagree—there are many successful variations of such a covenant. And they are always difficult.

Like other nations battling terrorism, the Saudis had a choice between seizing a selfish peace or joining with others—perhaps at greater short-term cost—in a broader and more substantial attack on al Qaeda. In May 1996, at a secret meeting held at the Hotel Royale Mönçeau in Paris, they apparently made their decision.[26] According to French terrorism expert Jean Charles Brisard and BBC journalist Greg Palast, French intelligence monitored a meeting there between a representative of al Qaeda and a group of Saudi billionaires, including Prince Turki al-Faisal, head of Saudi intelligence; a representative of Saudi businessman Abdullah Taha Bakhsh, who had rescued George Bush's Harken oil company from bankruptcy in 1990; an unnamed representative from the Saudi Defense Ministry; one of bin Laden's brothers; and billionaire Adnan Khashoggi, reputed arms merchant and storied participant in the Iran-Contra deal. The Saudis suggested to bin Laden's representative that al Qaeda would be generously rewarded for promoting their Wahhabi fundamentalism somewhere else—in Chechnya, Kashmir, Bosnia. Anywhere bin Laden wished, as long as he would keep his activities in Saudi Arabia down to a petty annoyance. The deal was apparently done quickly.

The Clinton administration had a different view of how to handle bin Laden. In 1998, after six months in office, President Clinton signed a memorandum of notification authorizing the CIA to capture him. A team was assigned to learn the details of his travel, his schedule, and his daily routines. As the picture grew more complete, the team proposed more specific actions, but each one was turned down by CIA executives.[27] Two submarines were stationed in the Indian Ocean with cruise missiles aimed at bin Laden's quarters, but it took six hours to get CIA approval, program the missiles, and have them reach their target. Each time an attack was proposed, it was deferred by CIA director George Tenet because the information seemed unreliable.[28] Finally, in June 1999, Michael F. Scheuer, head of CIA's Counterterrorism Unit, resigned, frustrated by the difficulty of coordinating the various US intelligence agencies and exhausted trying to get approval to hit bin Laden.[29]

Clinton signed another order imposing severe sanctions on any country, organization, or person providing "material assistance" to al Qaeda, and the Saudi government promised to help. But no information was forthcoming, and in private they protested against the sharp focus the United States was putting on bin Laden's family. "How can we tell a mother not to call her son?"[30]

FBI agent Robert Wright, whose project, Vulgar Betrayal, had been tracing the sources of money for terrorist activities, was told by his FBI superiors to shut the effort down because it was getting embarrassing for the Saudis.[31] In October 1999, the United States trained a detachment of sixty Pakistani soldiers to track down and kill bin Laden, but General Musharraf had reached an "understanding" with the Taliban, and when he was elected president of Pakistan the commandos were suddenly "no longer available."[32] Now everyone was going for the rabbit.

In late 1999, the US Special Operations Command began a project called Able Danger to scour news wires, online chat rooms, Web sites, e-mail, financial records, and other available data to identify and cross-index all references to al Qaeda. Called "data mining" by the direct marketing industry where this technique originated, the process almost immediately identified a significant presence of al Qaeda agents in the United States. According to Lt. Col. Anthony Shaffer and four others who participated, the data identified Mohamed Atta and three of the other 9/11 hijackers by name.

When Shaffer delivered the names to Navy captain Scott Philpott, the project manager, Philpott's reaction was: "Oh, my god, this is what we need. This is exactly what we need to do."[33] Philpott directed Shaffer to request additional data about these individuals from the CIA, but the request was refused. "The bottom line is," said a CIA officer, "CIA will never give you the best information . . . because if you are successful in your effort to target al Qaeda you will steal our thunder."[34]

Even as the project began turning up valuable leads, resistance to its work began to grow. In March or April 2000, according James D. Smith, a civilian working on the project, armed federal agents arrived at the site and confiscated all the Able Danger data, stopping the project cold. "To this day we don't know who [they were]."[35] At about the same time, Major Eric Kleinsmith, chief of intelligence for the supervising Army unit, was ordered by Army Intelligence and Security Command general counsel Tony Gentry to destroy all data and documents, "or you'll go to jail."[36] Although no explanation was offered at the time, analysts have later suggested that Defense Department lawyers worried that Able Danger might be gathering data on US citizens, which would be illegal. Data mining is a powerful tool for spotting activities that are illegal or "of interest," as the government puts it. A program to gather private telephone records, credit card charges, e-mail messages, and other digital records had been proposed by the Defense Department in the past and denied by Congress, and the concern was voiced by some that the Able Danger project might unwittingly shine the light on such data gathering continuing in secret without authorization.

Since they had now been prohibited from focusing on anyone in the United States, the team recommended that the investigation be taken over by the FBI. But this time Major General Geoffrey Lambert was particularly adamant in telling Shaffer not to pursue Mohamed Atta any further, "to the point where he had to remind me that he was a general and I was not."[37]

In October Shaffer met with the deputy director of the Defense Intelligence Agency and briefed him on the Able Danger results, offering him all the supporting information. The DIA official declined to accept the computer disc[38] but secretly assigned one of his own agents to spy on the project so they could build their own.[39]

At about the same time, the Able Danger team developed a new alert, and when General Peter Schoomaker, commander of the US Special Operations Command, arrived for a VIP visit on October 10, they made a presentation. There were three hot spots in their data, they said, places where a major al Qaeda attack seemed to be indicated, particularly in Yemen. "Two days before the attack they were jumping up and down because they knew something was going to happen . . . at the port of Aden."[40] But the warning never reached the USS *Cole*. The ship's commander later said that he "could have refueled the ship at sea. He had two other harbors. If he had [received] any indication that there was a problem with Aden in Yemen he would not have gone there."[41] At 11:18 on the morning of October 12, a small boat manned by al Qaeda suicide bombers approached the port side of the destroyer and blew itself up, tearing a thirty-five-foot hole in the ship's hull. Seventeen sailors were killed and thirty-nine injured in the blast.

When the Able Danger project was finally shut down, the data mining effort was absorbed into the intelligence activities of the Special Operations Command. But it was never again given the resources required. A request for fresh data from the Defense Intelligence Agency was denied.[42] In May 2001 Captain Philpott contacted Shaffer, asking for a computer facility where he could run his analysis. But Shaffer says that when he passed along the request to his supervisor he was severely criticized and subsequently relieved of his position.[43] In the last few months before the attack on the World Trade Center, Able Danger—which had shown an extraordinary ability to predict al Qaeda attacks—was just a memory that most of the intelligence establishment was trying hard to expunge. A memory and a few old charts showing bin Laden and his leadership structure.

Two weeks after the 9/11 attacks, one of those charts surfaced again. Congressman Curt Weldon showed it to deputy national security adviser Stephen Hadley and left it for Hadley to show the president. The White House later claimed that no one remembered seeing the chart, and a search of White House records turned up nothing. Now even the chart was gone.[44]

When the 9/11 Commission began its work in 2003, it received testimony about Able Danger from Shaffer and others but later said that the information was dismissed for lack of documentary evidence.[45] When the commission report came out, the project was not even mentioned. Congressman Weldon issued a response, questioning the truthfulness of the commission's work and asking why the record of this extraordinary warning had been buried.

Former FBI director Louis Freeh wrote in the *Wall Street Journal*:

> The Commission's dismissive and apparently unsupported conclusion would have us believe that a key piece of evidence was summarily rejected in less than 10 days without serious investigation. The Commission, at the very least, should have interviewed the 80 members of Able Danger, as the Pentagon did, five of whom say they saw "the chart." But this would have required admitting that the late-breaking news was inconveniently raised. So it was grossly neglected and branded as insignificant. Such a half-baked conclusion, drawn in only 10 days without any real investigation, simply ignores what looks like substantial direct evidence to the contrary coming from our own trained military intelligence officers.[46]

A Department of Defense investigation had concluded that Able Danger did not identify Mohamed Atta or any other hijackers prior to the September 11 attacks and that any chart the project might have produced was intended only to demonstrate how to "organize large amounts of data."[47] The Senate Judiciary Committee subsequently said that their investigation agreed with the Defense Department report.

And that was the end of Able Danger.

BLINKING RED

The warnings continued, more frequent, more specific, and more urgent. In late December the CIA's Counterterrorism Unit reported that bin Laden wanted to inflict massive casualties on the United States and was seeking to attack as many as fifteen targets around the millennium. "We must assume that several of these targets will be in the U.S." CIA director George Tenet delivered the report directly to outgoing president Bill Clinton.[48] Reports arrived about al Qaeda agents living in the United States, enrolling in flight schools, spending lavishly, and organizing themselves into "sleeper cells" of four and five, and still the FBI assured the White House that al Qaeda lacked the ability to strike within the United States.[49] In April 2000 an al Qaeda recruit told the FBI about a plot to fly a plane into a United States building. He was polygraphed and interrogated for three weeks, but when the agents asked for more resources to follow up the leads, FBI headquarters said to "send him back to London and . . . forget about it."[50] In December, in its annual National Intelligence Estimate, the FBI concluded that the risk of a terrorist attack on US aviation was "relatively low . . . notwithstanding historical intelligence information to the contrary."[51]

When the new administration arrived, the interest in counterterrorism declined even further. The senior military officers at the Pentagon had a long and collegial relationship with General Musharraf, president of Pakistan, and with the Taliban as well, and they were reluctant to attempt any action against bin Laden. President Bush and Vice President Dick Cheney had close personal ties with the Saudis, and further investigations into the complex financing of al Qaeda were ordered stopped. President Clinton, too, had been cautious about going after the Saudis, but according to reporter Greg Palast, "the difference was between closing one eye and closing them both."[52]

It was clear, too, that the new administration had come into office with a very different concept of who the enemy was. At the first National Security Council meeting on January 31, 2001, national security adviser Condoleezza Rice began by saying that regime change in Iraq could be the key to reshaping the entire Middle East. CIA director George Tenet reported that Iraq might be producing chemical or biological weapons, although he added that there was no confirming intelligence.[53] The new marching orders were clear. According to secretary of treasury Paul O'Neill, the president wanted Saddam Hussein gone. No discussion. "Go find me a way to do this."[54] Deputy defense secretary Paul Wolfowitz described White House counterterrorism chief Richard Clarke's concept of an al Qaeda terrorist threat as a "fabrication" and said that Saddam Hussein had obviously been the perpetrator of the 1993 bombing of the World Trade Center. Against that prevailing view there was no room for the bin Laden warnings that had so occupied the Clinton administration. As Wolfowitz put it, "Who cares about a little terrorist in Afghanistan?"[55] Even on the day following the 9/11 attack, he still had trouble believing that al Qaeda had been solely responsible and he began to argue that Iraq must have been involved.[56]

At the same time, the internal organization for gathering and evaluating these warnings became more vertical. According to a presidential directive issued February 12, 2001, heads of executive departments, agencies, and other senior officials were in the future to be excluded from the regular meetings of the National Security Council, cutting membership down to the topmost eight or nine officials in government. In addition, the directive abolished the existing system of Interagency Working Groups through which national security policy was discussed and coordinated. Finally, Dr. Rice was made secretary of the eleven surviving committees, charged with determining their meeting schedule and agenda. In short, she became the gatekeeper of all national security information rising into the Executive Office of the president. There were certainly advantages in simplifying the decision structure and getting control over the sprawling and sometimes undisciplined community of intelligence professionals. But there was also a disadvantage. Now all the warnings had to pass the narrow filter of Dr. Rice and her assistant Stephen Hadley, and those who were making the crucial decisions had difficulty hearing informed and well-intended dissent:

> PAUL BREMER, THEN CHAIRMAN OF THE NATIONAL COMMISSION ON TERRORISM, FEBRUARY 6, 2001: "What [the Bush administration] will do is stagger along until there is a major incident and then suddenly say, 'Oh, my god, shouldn't we be organized to deal with this?'"[57]
>
> NAVY VICE ADMIRAL THOMAS WILSON, DIRECTOR OF THE DEFENSE INTELLIGENCE AGENCY, TESTIFYING BEFORE CONGRESS ON FEBRUARY 7: "Within the next two years there will be a major terrorist attack against US interests, either here or abroad, perhaps with a weapon designed to produce mass casualties."[58]
>
> GEORGE TENET, DIRECTOR OF THE CIA, TESTIFYING BEFORE CONGRESS ON FEBRUARY 7: "Since 1998, bin Laden has declared that all US citizens are legitimate targets. [He] is capable of planning multiple attacks with little or no warning."[59]
>
> RICHARD CLARKE WARNED DR. RICE ON MARCH 23, 2001: Foreign terrorists might use a truck bomb on Pennsylvania Avenue. He said there were terrorist cells within the United States.[60]

Condoleezza Rice, in a press conference on March 24, 2004, denied that these concerns were ever voiced: "I have heard that

Dick Clarke has apparently said that he thought the attack was coming in the United States. He never communicated that to anyone."[61]

March 7, 2001. Russia submitted a secret report to the UN, detailing bin Laden's al Qaeda network, including all bin Laden's bases, his government contacts, and his foreign advisers, along with enough information to locate and kill him. According to Alex Standish, editor of *Jane's Intelligence Review*, the continuing lack of response from the United States was less an intelligence failure than a "political decision not to act against bin Laden."[62]

April–May. President Bush, Vice President Cheney, and their national security aides received briefing papers titled: "Bin Laden Planning Multiple Operations." "Bin Laden Public Profile May Presage Attack." "Bin Laden Network's Plans Advancing."[63]

June. German Intelligence warned the United States that Middle Eastern militants were planning to hijack commercial aircraft and use them as weapons to attack American and Israeli symbols.[64]

May–July. Over a two-month period the NSA intercepted at least thirty-three messages referring to an imminent terrorist attack. "Unbelievable news coming in weeks." "A big event, there will be a very, very, very, very big uproar." "There will be attacks in the near future."[65]

Summer. Congressman Porter Goss, chairman of the House Intelligence Committee, remembered that the "chatter level [went] way off the charts, and stayed high until September 11." Others called the volume of threat-related messages "unprecedented, in terms of their own experience." "The most urgent in decades."[66]

Summer. Israeli intelligence warned that bin Laden was planning a large-scale terror attack on the United States.[67] Jordanian intelligence intercepted a message between al Qaeda agents saying that a major attack, code-named "the big wedding," was planned inside the United States in the near future and that aircraft would be used.[68]

July 5. Richard Clarke told a meeting of the Counterterrorism Security Group that "something spectacular is being planned by al Qaeda." He directed every counterterrorism office to cancel vacations, defer nonvital travel, put off scheduled exercises, and place domestic rapid-response teams on short alert. But attention drifted. There was very poor follow-up to the warning, and by August the emergency measures were no longer in effect.[69]

July 10. FBI agent Ken Williams sent a memo to headquarters reporting that bin Laden associates were taking flight training in Arizona. He said they had a suspiciously complete understanding of airport security measures and he recommended that the FBI and the State Department get the visa dates and information on all Middle Eastern men enrolled in flight training in the United States. The memo was not uploaded for distribution by the FBI until the end of the month, and then it was marked "routine" and generally ignored. Authorities later claimed that it was only a "hunch."[70]

July 10. George Tenet received a report from CIA's Counterterrorism Unit that al Qaeda planned an imminent, multiple-target, simultaneous attack, possibly within the United States. He was so alarmed that he called Dr. Rice on her car phone and asked for an urgent meeting.[71] Together with CIA Counterterrorism chief Cofer Black, he briefed the White House on the threat and asked for $500 million to target bin Laden and kill him. Rice agreed to schedule a review of the situation, but the review did not happen until five weeks later. Rice later denied that her meeting with Clarke and Black had ever taken place.[72]

July 13. The White House denied the CIA authorization to capture or assassinate bin Laden.[73] According to John O'Neill, FBI counterterrorism expert, "the main obstacle to investigating Islamic terrorism was US oil corporate interests and the role played by Saudi Arabia." He said that the White House was opposed to any action in Afghanistan because Unocal and other American oil companies were trying to close a deal with the Taliban. The plan was to revive a project, stymied under President Clinton, to build an eight-hundred-mile pipeline that would bring gas across Afghanistan from the Caspian Sea to India, where Enron, then on the brink of bankruptcy, had just built a $3 billion gas-fired power plant.[74]

In the next four weeks, the United States received warnings from the intelligence agencies of Egypt, Morocco, the United Kingdom, France, and Israel, all describing an imminent al Qaeda attack *within the United States, using aircraft.*

August 6. A CIA representative went to Crawford, Texas, to brief the vacationing president in the most urgent terms: "bin Laden determined to strike in the US." "You've covered your ass, now," Bush told the briefer, and made the decision to spend the rest of the day fishing. He later described the report as "historical in nature" and said he was "satisfied that some of the matters were being looked into." The 9/11 Commission reported that there was no evidence of "any discussion or further actions taken by Bush and his top advisors in response to the briefing."[75]

August 16. Zacarias Moussaoui was arrested by the FBI and charged with immigration violations. He had in his possession a laptop computer, two knives, 747 flight manuals, a flight simulator program, fighting gloves, shin guards, and a computer disk with information about crop dusting. Suspecting him of being a terrorist, Harry Samit, the local agent, asked headquarters for permission to open Moussaoui's laptop, but permission was refused, citing Moussaoui's right to privacy.[76] The agent persisted. He pleaded with FBI headquarters to pass the information on to the Secret Service. They wouldn't. He even tried to get Moussaoui sent to France where a more interested intelligence agency might open the laptop. The laptop was later found to contain the names and phone numbers of the al Qaeda chain of command, as well as the names of the 9/11 hijackers.

In the last days before the attack, specific warnings began to trickle in from prisoners in Jordan and Brazil, and even from a priest in Italy. According the *New York Daily News*, mosques warned their people to stay out of lower Manhattan on 9/11.[77] An analysis of option market trading just before the attack, published in the *Journal of Business*, showed that there was an unusual level of puts, or short selling.[78] On September 10, according to *Newsweek*, several senior generals at the Pentagon canceled their flights for the following day.[79]

FACTS, VALUES, CONCEPTS

In the mid-1940s Herbert Simon observed that truth assessment and decision making occur at the intersection of facts and values.[80] Our ability to assess new information, he said, is heavily influenced by desire. But after sixty years of cognitive science, and a dolorous history of misjudgments and information management errors, we need to amend this insight. It may be more accurate to say that there are three elements present at the moment of truth assessment: facts, values, and concepts—what might be, what ought to be, and what is.

Simon described facts as new descriptions of events as they are, but for the unpersuaded mind, they are still things that might or might not be true. Values, as Simon suggests, are those currents of desire that distort our view. They are wishful thinking, offered by the emotional brain, nudging us through doubt to a happier conclusion. And concepts, from the mind's point of view, are what is. They are the settled truth on which we lead our lives, and we cling stubbornly to them as one might lash one's self to a raft at sea.

When we rationalize new knowledge, these three forces contend against each other. For a scientist devoted to a particular concept of how the world works, dissonant new data is difficult to accept, and the work required to reconstruct his understanding in light of this knowledge is sometimes too hard and too painful to undertake. Our values, too, can distort our thinking. It is hard to accept information that is contrary to one's desire. Just try balancing your checkbook without a calculator on a bad month. In the

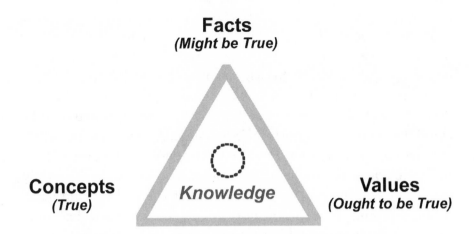

Facts
(Might be True)

Concepts
(True)

Knowledge

Values
(Ought to be True)

Rationalizing New Knowledge

middle of a truth assessment, it is often useful to ask yourself, how do you want this analysis to turn out? Which possible truth would be best for you? And then be on your guard against that conclusion as you go back to the data. Because with information analysis, what you want has a sneaky way of becoming what you get.

When Bruce Ismay was handed a warning of icebergs ahead, these three powerful forces were at work on his decision. Uncertain facts: The report might or might not be accurate or up-to-date. Values: He was very determined to set a new transatlantic speed record, and icebergs in the path would threaten that prize. Concepts: He believed that the lookout would give him "real" sightings in plenty of time to respond. In any event, *Titanic*'s hull was strong enough to survive any brush with an iceberg. These ideas were "truth" as far as he was concerned, and new information was an uncomfortable challenge that might or might not be accurate.

When Larry Mulloy was confronted by the Thiokol engineers, he was in similar difficulty. The "facts" about the O-rings were disputable and incomplete. The business side was urging him to put on his "manager's hat" and accept their values: all business entails a little risk, but we have to work as a team to achieve our goals. And the concepts he held about his environment were pressing hard on his assessment: engineers are annoying, undisciplined, and risk-averse prima donnas for whom any technical difficulty is a rare moment in the sun. The NASA decision regime was comfortably "scientific," and as long as he followed its well-established rules he could not be blamed later for the outcome. Accidents happen.

Neither of these men intended harm, nor did either see himself as reckless. It is no good to dismiss their decisions as perfidy, carelessness, or greed, and then claim that you and I would never do such a thing. That diminishes the problem. It makes bad truth assessment a mere moral lapse and denies the broader reality: we all make these mistakes, some on a larger scale than others. To the extent that we depend on each other to seek the truth, in spite of doubt, in spite of our desires, in spite of our preconceptions, we are all to blame and we are all at risk.

9/11: REALITY HITS HOME

From the beginning moments of the 9/11 attack, three kinds of communications channels appeared. A formal command and control hierarchy connected the pilot to the airport flight controller; the flight controller to the airline and the FAA; and in case military assistance was required, the FAA to NORAD and the Pentagon. All these organizations reported through the White House staff to the president. At the same time, open telephone and videoconferences were planned to coordinate the activities of the many different organizations involved. Additional "phone bridges," as they were called, also sprang to life and then just as spontaneously dissolved. The third channel was an unexpected ad hoc network of individuals calling on cell phones. Passengers on the hijacked planes called their husbands, wives and families, providing the only information available about what was really going on. Flight controllers and airline officials patched calls together and sometimes sat with a phone in each ear, relaying critical messages. And when communications with Air Force One failed during the crucial first hour, it was a borrowed cell phone that finally allowed the president to get a situation report.[81]

8:19 a.m., September 11, 2001. Twenty minutes after American Airlines Flight 11 left Boston, flight attendant Amy Ong called a colleague at a reservations office in North Carolina. Using a seat-back phone from the rear of the plane, she said that the pilot was not answering; someone in business class had been stabbed; and she could smell mace. She continued to keep the line open for twenty-five minutes as others passed her updates. "I think we're getting hijacked." The response on the ground was disbelief. No one expected a hijacking.

At about the same time another attendant, Amy Sweeney, called an American Airlines flight service manager. Using another phone, the manager called a supervisor at the Boston airport and repeated everything he heard from Sweeney, and the supervisor relayed it on to headquarters in Fort Worth, where the shift manager stopped the chain. "Do not pass this along. Let's keep it right here. Keep it among the five of us."[82] American Airlines executives did not hear of the hijacking for another nine minutes.

8:25. Alerted to the crisis, Boston flight control began to call up the chain of command, including the FAA Command Center in Virginia, where a teleconference was immediately set up to keep other flight control centers informed. But still they did not report the hijacking to NORAD. At 8:38, after some confusion over who was on duty, the FAA reached the National Military Command Center (NMCC) at the Pentagon, which was responsible for domestic military activities such as intercepting hijacked aircraft. But the NMCC did not take any action for another hour, finally setting up its own teleconference at 9:29.[83]

8:34. As instructed by standard operating procedure, Boston flight control called an air base in Atlantic City to scramble two fighter jets, but the procedures on the desk were out of date. The air base had ceased to provide that support in 1998, and flight control got no answer. By 8:37, though, Boston flight control had skipped protocol and reached Northeast Air Defense Systems, part of NORAD, but NEADS could not see the missing plane on radar. Nonetheless, acting without full authorization, NEADS sent the order to Cape Cod to scramble two jets in pursuit.

American Airlines opened its crisis center and informed the FBI of the hijacking, but even as they were talking, twenty-six minutes after the flight attendant's first call, Flight 11 crashed into the North Tower of the World Trade Center.

8:46. The United Airlines flight controller confirmed that a second Boston plane had been hijacked, Flight 175 bound for Los Angeles. Again it was a call from one of the flight attendants that provided the first direct evidence; her name is unknown. Reaching a mechanic on the ground, she whispered: "Oh, my god, the crew has been killed; a flight attendant has been stabbed. We've been hijacked."[84] Two minutes later Peter Hanson, a passenger, called his father with a similar report, adding that Middle Eastern men armed with knives had killed the flight attendants in an effort to break into to the cockpit. Another passenger, Brian Sweeney, tried to reach his wife, then called his mother: "We are going to try to do something about this." But within a few moments Flight 175 crashed into the South Tower, killing sixty-five passengers and crew.

9:00. Condoleezza Rice called President Bush, who was visiting a Florida elementary school to promote his education agenda. She told him that a twin-engine plane had accidentally struck the World Trade Center. Incredibly enough, as the president's national security adviser, she did not yet know that NORAD had called a full national alert, scrambled fighter jets, and was already working with the FAA and the Pentagon to put the country on a war footing. Misinformed by Rice, the president decided to go ahead with his photo op.

Vice President Cheney, having watched the news report on

television, also assumed it had been an accident and turned off the TV to continue with his staff meeting. Richard Clarke, who saw the same facts in an entirely different context, knew immediately that it was a terrorist attack. He directed the White House to set up a videoconference with the members of the Counterterrorism Security Group.

9:03. Through his Secret Service bodyguards, Cheney learned that a second plane had crashed into the World Trade Center and he called immediately for fighters to be scrambled from Andrews Air Force Base in Washington, fully armed with missiles. But there were no fighter jets ready at Andrews, and the vice president's order was not followed. At the same time, the Secret Service learned that two more planes were missing and presumed hijacked, but this information was not conveyed to Cheney.[85] The formal information system was breaking down.

In the crucial next hour, most of America's leaders were out of touch. President Bush continued to participate in the children's reading exercise, even after being told by his chief of staff that a second plane had crashed into the tower and "America is under attack." He later described his thoughts as he sat there: "I'm very aware of the cameras. I'm trying to absorb that knowledge. I have nobody to talk to." In the back of the room, his press secretary, Ari Fleischer, held up a sign: "Don't say anything yet."[86] When the reading exercise was over thirteen minutes later, the president was steered into a small room with his staff where he was able to talk briefly on the phone with Dr. Rice, Vice President Cheney, and New York's governor George Pataki. At 9:28 he read a short statement to the press and was then driven to Air Force One. Told by Cheney that the president's plane was a target of attack (there was no evidence for this then and is none now), the Secret Service ordered the plane into the air and then decided to head for Barksdale Air Base near Shreveport, Louisiana, two hundred miles from Bush's home in Crawford, Texas. A fighter jet escort was scrambled but never showed up, and because of a communications failure, Bush was unable to speak with the White House from the plane. He did not publicly address the situation again until 1:04 p.m., when his staff released a brief videotaped message to all Americans, recorded a half-hour before.

Secretary of State Colin Powell was in Peru and, for some strange reason, was unable to get through to the White House all day. Attorney General John Ashcroft was in Milwaukee. Secretary of Defense Donald Rumsfeld was in his office with a CIA briefer when the report of a second crash came through. While others went quickly to the Pentagon situation room a few feet away, Rumsfeld stayed at his desk for a while and then left the building for about an hour. He appeared again at 10:30. Since then, Rumsfeld has offered three conflicting explanations for his absence, but they all agree on two facts. He wasn't in his office or in the NMCC, and he couldn't be reached. It is still unclear where he was. General Henry Shelton, chairman of the Joint Chiefs of Staff, was in the air over the Atlantic. When General Ralph Eberhart, commander of NORAD, heard of the attacks, he decided to drive from Petersen Air Force Base in Colorado to the NORAD operations center thirteen miles away. The journey appears unaccountably to have taken forty-five minutes, during which he was out of contact.[87]

9:20. The FAA set up a teleconference, but NORAD was not on the line. According to the 9/11 Commission report, the joint American-Canadian command that is responsible for protecting the continent from an air attack learned about the situation accidentally at 9:34. A second teleconference was set up by the Pentagon, but at that time none of the information from Clarke's White House videoconference was reaching them, and the Pentagon's decisions were being conveyed to the FAA, CIA, FBI, State, Justice, or the White House only when one of the conference members left the room to join one of the other conferences.[88]

Dr. Rice went first to the Situation Room where Clarke was running the videoconference, then left after a few minutes to join Vice President Cheney in his bunker.[89]

As the situation developed, there appeared to be two epicenters of control: Counterterrorism chief Richard Clarke had set up a videoconference in the White House Situation Room and very shortly acquired an appropriate membership, a well-disciplined agenda, and an engagingly horizontal structure. Initially he deferred to Dr. Rice, but, according to Clarke's later account, she wisely declined. "You run it." And she stood at his side to authenticate her support. "Let's begin," Clarke then said to the group. "We will do this in crisis mode which means keep your microphones off unless you're speaking. If you want to speak, wave at the camera. If it's something you don't want everyone to hear, call me on the red phone." An important part of the recipe for Clarke's success seems to have been that he was of a lower rank than many of the participants, and no one felt the necessity to tailor their opinions. They could speak their minds. Clarke later remembered that when a similar conference had been convened immediately after the Oklahoma City bombing, President Clinton entered the room and joined in. "While it showed high level concern, and we were glad to have him there," wrote Clarke, "it would have slowed down our response if he had stayed."[90]

It is difficult to imagine a more different information management structure than the one that coexisted five hundred feet away in the Presidential Emergency Operations Center, a blast-proof, tubelike bunker buried beneath the East Wing of the White House. There, Vice President Cheney ran the show, supported by Dr. Rice, his aides David Addington and Lewis Libby, deputy chief of staff Josh Bolten, political adviser Mary Matalin, communications director Karen Hughes, Secret Service agents, and Cheney's wife, Lynne, who had arrived at the White House shortly after the crisis began. The information coming into the room was limited in volume and diversity. There was a one-way video feed from Clarke's conference in the other room, but Mrs. Cheney kept turning down the volume so she could listen to CNN. There was a secure telephone line between the two rooms, and Clarke suggested that it be left open, but the vice president kept hanging it up. No one in the room could reach the president.[91]

9:37. The third hijacked plane, American Airlines Flight 77, crashed into the Pentagon, killing all sixty-four passengers and crew, as well as one hundred and twenty-five people on the ground.

10:00. Cheney's military aide reported that a new plane, suspected to be hostile, was about eighty miles from the White House. Vice President Cheney gave the order to shoot it down, as his aide Lewis Libby later said, "in about the time it takes a batter to decide to swing."[92] A few minutes later the aide said that, based on the estimated air speed and position originally reported, the plane would now be about sixty miles away, and he continued to project the progress of this imaginary attacker: forty miles from the White House, now thirty miles from the White House. (There was no radar confirmation.) Again, Cheney ordered fighter aircraft to shoot it down. A few minutes later, a report arrived of another plane now about eight miles away, and again the vice president gave the order to "take it out." The second aircraft proved to be a medevac helicopter.[93] Nonetheless, the order to engage the enemy was communicated to NORAD, and at 10:31 the message was broadcast: "Vice President has cleared us to intercept tracks of interest and shoot them down if they do not respond." Still uninformed about the actual situation, Secretary Rumsfeld, arriving on the scene after an hour's absence, was told by Cheney that the shoot-down order had been given.

> SECRETARY OF DEFENSE: "So we've got a couple of aircraft up there that have those instructions?"
> VICE PRESIDENT: "That is correct. And it's my understanding they've already taken a couple of aircraft out."[94]

10:45. On orders from the Secret Service, more fighters were launched from Langley with instructions to shoot down other aircraft at the discretion of the pilot. Neither the president, the vice president, nor anyone at NORAD or the Pentagon knew that these additional fighters were in the air. Nor had the Langley pilots been briefed on the reason for their orders. They guessed they were looking for Russian aircraft, but a plane is a plane. NORAD later maintained that the fighters would have successfully intercepted and shot down the fourth hijacked aircraft, United 93, but the 9/11 Commission concluded, in the most generous possible terms, that "we are not so sure."[95]

As the events unfolded in the presidential bunker during the first hour following the attack, Vice President Cheney and his aides considered the future that had befallen them and determined that the president would require greater powers in this new and dangerous world. He needed the power to more broadly monitor people's communications—wiretapping without warrants. He needed the power to seize and interrogate suspected terrorists without the prissy constraints of the Geneva Convention or the creaky and unpredictable judicial system. He would need a swift authorization of force from Congress, broad enough to allow not only the cauterizing of Afghanistan but, less explicitly, the invasion of Iraq as well. In the imperial gloom of the bunker, with machine guns at the door, Vice President Cheney, David Addington, deputy White House counsel Timothy E. Flanigan, and John C. Yoo from the Justice Department began to wind the necessary legal ropes.[96]

Cheney also found time to set in motion the plan for "continuity of government," which prescribed that one hundred or more key officials from the major federal departments and executive agencies should be taken to a secure location in the event that government needed to be reconstituted after a devastating attack.[97] As it turned out, everyone selected for this secret Noah's Ark was a Republican loyal to Cheney, Rumsfeld, and Bush. No members of Congress or the Judiciary were included or informed, and the fact that the continuity of the government program had even been initiated was concealed from the public until it was reported in the *Washington Post* six months later.[98] The idea of a highly vertical structure for information management that so clearly reigned in the Presidential Emergency Operations Center that morning reached forward, proposing to become America's new form of government.

At some point shortly after the attack, in an extraordinary gesture of information management wisdom, Russian president Vladimir Putin called the White House and, unable to reach Mr. Bush, told Dr. Rice that the Russians were voluntarily standing down all military exercises around the world. He said he didn't want to add to the confusion.[99]

9:30. The twin towers of the World Trade Center were in flames. All bridges and tunnels leading in and out of New York were closed, and the city was on full alert, though jet fighters scrambled from Cape Cod had still not arrived. At 9:47, a man on the one-hundred-and-fifth floor of the South Tower, the second one hit, called 911 to report that the floors below him were collapsing, but this message was misinterpreted to mean that his own floor was giving way. In the flood of incoming calls, the message was not passed along.[100] Two minutes later, a New York police department helicopter reported to the Special Operations Division that large pieces were falling from the South Tower, but since the police and the fire department were using separate radio channels, this warning was not received by the fire department.[101] At 9:52, two firefighters, Orio Palmer and Ronald Bucca, had climbed to the seventy-eighth floor and they radioed that they had found "two isolated pockets of fire. We should be able to knock it down with two lines."[102]

Mayor Rudy Giuliani arrived at the scene and had a brief meeting with fire chief Pete Ganci and police commissioner Bernard Kerik. The city's fire and police departments had a decades-long tradition of fierce independence bordering on rivalry, but now, as never before, it would be important for these two proud organizations to work together. Nonetheless, Mayor Giuliani made the deadly decision to separate the two command posts. At Kerik's suggestion, he directed the police department to set up a temporary emergency command center first at 75 Barclay Street, two blocks away. Then he moved it a mile and half north to an empty firehouse on Houston and 6th Avenue and finally moved it again to an abandoned police academy another mile and a half uptown, where he would also control communications with government and the media. That put the police department in a position of great influence, but it separated the fire department from access to the best current information. Ray Kelley, who had preceded Kerik as police commissioner, later said: "The separate command post was a violation of the protocols. The radios would have been no problem if they had been at the same command post, if they'd been face-to-face. Giuliani had the power to direct that to happen."[103]

But he didn't, and the result was a rising chaos. As Mayor Giuliani and his twenty-five-member entourage led the media up the street through swirling smoke and gray debris blowing like Dante's whirlwind of souls, he was separating those responsible for safety from those responsible for rescue, and Police Commissioner Kerik was reduced to being little more than the mayor's bodyguard. A management consulting firm, hired later to evaluate the city's performance, criticized the police department for lacking a "strong operational leader commanding the response" and for the "absence of [a] clear command structure and direction," noting especially the "poor coordination between fire and police at the highest levels."[104]

9:59. John Peruggia, chief of the fire department's Emergency Medical Service (EMS), met with fire department captain Richard Rodanz and an engineer from the NYC Department of Buildings, who warned them that the South Tower was going to collapse. Peruggia grabbed a medic: "Things were hectic. We didn't have the tools that we normally have to communicate with our agency, you know, cellular phones were not working properly, radio was very difficult to get through. I work for the Chief of the Department, I don't have a fire ground radio, so I had no direct communications with my boss at that time, which is one of the reasons I needed to send EMT [Richard] Zarrillo with that message, which I felt was very significant, to the command post."[105]

But as the medic shouted his warning out to senior firefighters on the sidewalk, witnesses said later that they felt the ground shake beneath them for about thirty seconds, "like a train was coming." A giant fireball exploded at street level, probably from the building's fuel tanks, and at 9:59 the South Tower began to collapse.[106] Nearly all the occupants evacuated from the tower had crossed the street to safety, but 619 others and many emergency workers trapped above the seventy-seventh floor did not survive.

10:07. Police helicopters hovering over the North Tower radioed to police headquarters: "About 15 floors down from the top, it looks like it's glowing red. It's inevitable." And another helicopter pilot reported: "I don't think this has too much longer to go. I would evacuate all people within the area of the second building." What happened next was kept a secret for four years. The story Mayor Giuliani tells is that the warning was delivered. The firefighters still in the North Tower realized the terrible danger of the moment but chose to stay in the building to rescue civilians. But in August 2005, under court order, the city finally released twelve thousand pages of oral histories, and it became clear that because of poor communications management, the firefighters had never heard the warning. Trapped in stairwells or resting on one of the floors, they had no idea that the South Tower had already collapsed and heard nothing on their radios. According to the *New York Times*: "The ragged character of the [oral history] records does not yield a clear explanation for the isolation of the rescuers within the building, and whether it was because of radio failure, a loss of command and control, or flaws in the Fire Department's management structure. Some firefighters described receiving a radio message to evacuate; others used strong language to characterize the communications gear as useless."[107]

10:28. The North Tower collapsed. The *New York Times* later estimated that at least two hundred firefighters died, including many who could easily have escaped.[108]

In the hours that followed, firefighters, police, and medical first responders struggled bravely and at great cost to pull the living from the molten rubble. Mayor Giuliani instinctively provided compassionate support and encouragement, in person and through the media, becoming for many people the embodiment of New York's courage and resilience. Combat jets finally arrived and took up positions over the city. The horrific task of rescue and recovery began.

One last plane was known to have been hijacked. At 9:27, passenger Tom Burnett called his wife from a cell phone to tell her that his plane, United Airlines Flight 93, was in the control of terrorists. Over the next few minutes, thirty other passengers made similar calls: The hijackers were in the cockpit, speaking Arabic. One of them had a gun. They had already knifed a passenger. An announcement was made that the hijackers had a bomb. Two people had been killed. The passengers voted to attack the hijackers and they were already filling pitchers with hot water, their only weapon. Then there was a struggle in the cockpit, there was screaming in the background and the sound of wind. The caller whispered into his phone: "I know we're all going to die."[109]

As the plane descended over Lambertsville, Pennsylvania, 124 miles from Washington, the last moments were described by Tim Thornberg, who watched it from the ground: "It came in low over the trees and started wobbling. Then it just rolled over and was flying upside down for a few seconds . . . and then it kind of stalled and did a nose dive over the trees."[110] There were thirty-seven passengers and seven crew members aboard.

1:04 p.m. The White House released a video of the president's message to the people, recorded half an hour before. He assured Americans that the federal government had taken all appropriate security precautions and would assist local authorities to save the lives and help the victims. He asked all Americans "to join me in saying a 'thanks' for all the folks who have been fighting hard to rescue our fellow citizens." He attributed the attacks to a "faceless coward" and vowed that "the United States will hunt down and punish those responsible for these cowardly acts."[111] But the hunt went slowly, and over the next few months, the faceless cowards slipped away.

2:40. Secretary Rumsfeld was presented with a detailed analysis that concluded that Osama bin Laden was the mastermind behind the al Qaeda attacks, but Rumsfeld was interested in Iraq. His aide's notes say that the defense secretary wanted to get the "best info fast. Judge whether good enough [to] hit S[addam] H[ussein] at same time. Not only [bin Laden]."[112] Richard Clarke later reported that at a meeting the next day with President Bush and Secretary Powell, Rumsfeld repeated his view: "Rumsfeld was saying we needed to bomb Iraq . . . we all said, 'But no, no. Al Qaeda is in Afghanistan.' And Rumsfeld said 'There aren't any good targets in Afghanistan and there are lots of good targets in Iraq.'"[113]

The idea that Saddam Hussein was the source of horrors like this had been around for several years. In 1995 Dr. Laurie Mylroie published an article suggesting that Ramzi Yousef, the confessed leader of the group that bombed the World Trade Center in 1993, was in fact an Iraqi agent. Dr. Mylroie had the credentials: a PhD from Harvard, associate professor at the US Naval War College, and consultant on Middle Eastern affairs to Bill Clinton's 1992 campaign. And her theory at least begins with a set of facts on which everyone can agree.

In the months before the 1993 attack on the World Trade Center, one of the conspirators made frequent calls to his uncle in Baghdad. A short time later, Ramzi Yousef, born in Kuwait of Pakistani parents, arrived in the United States on an Iraqi passport. He was fingerprinted and detained for not having a visa but granted temporary asylum pending a hearing. Yousef then became the leader of the bombing plot and two months later applied to the Pakistan consulate for a replacement passport under the name

Abdul Basit, offering copies of previous passports. Basit was a real person who had also lived in Kuwait before moving to Pakistan, and Yousef was trying to assume the man's identity. This time he got a six-month visa that gave him greater mobility.

On the basis of these facts, Mylroie made two assertions. First, she alleged that in the early months of the conspiracy, Iraqi intelligence must have overheard one of the World Trade Center conspirators on a call home to his uncle, and they sent Yousef to take control of the bombing plot. There is no evidence for this. Second, she said that Iraq had created a false identity for Yousef while they were occupying Kuwait in 1990, three years earlier. The photo and certain other information items had been removed from the original Basit passport files in Kuwait, she claimed, and Yousef's fingerprints had been substituted for Basit's to create a legend for their agent. Therefore Yousef must have been dispatched by Saddam Hussein, and therefore the bombing of the World Trade Center in 1993 must have been an Iraqi plot.[114] Richard Perle, chairman of the Defense Policy Board Advisory Committee, called Dr. Mylroie's arguments "splendid and wholly convincing."

Her theory had a powerful following in Washington. In 2000, when she published an expanded version of this theory as a book, she made a special effort to acknowledge the help of Lewis Libby, John Bolton, David Wurmser, and especially Paul Wolfowitz, who "provided crucial support for a project that is inherently difficult."[115] The assertions in her book were examined and refuted by the CIA, FBI, and others, but they were just as ardently defended. As soon as he gained office at the Department of Defense, Wolfowitz flew over former CIA director James Woolsey to check the fingerprints. But unfortunately for Mylroie's thesis, the fingerprints really were Basit's. Still, Mylroie's description of reality fit a larger emotional bias against Saddam Hussein; it was consistent with the concepts held by many of the neocons and once adopted could not be easily dislodged.

The idea of Iraq as the enemy was nicely supported by another factor as well. As Wolfowitz put it, Iraq "swims on a sea of oil."[116] With global reserves being slowly drawn down, the United States needed to secure a long-term supply and perhaps deny that supply to its economic competitor, China. What better way to accomplish this than a military campaign to gain control of Iraq's long-term oil production?

The hunt for bin Laden went forward nonetheless but without enthusiasm. There were offers of help from foreign intelligence agencies as before. Sometime after September 12, according to *Time*, Mullah Mohammad Khaksar, former intelligence minister for the Taliban, offered to provide the United States information about the fugitive Mullah Omar, as well as the location of al Qaeda hideouts. But he was ignored.[117]

In October and November, as the United States continued to bomb Taliban targets throughout Afghanistan; the US Air Force tracked bin Laden's movements and on several occasions believed that they had his location identified. But, as before, they could not get approval from the CIA or the Department of Defense in time to make a strike. After ten weeks, they cornered him in Tora Bora, a fifteen-square-mile warren of mountain caves on the Afghan-Pakistan border, and as the Taliban and al Qaeda forces began to gather, the Pentagon made a deal with Pakistani president Pervez Musharraf. Pakistan's intelligence service, still riddled with pro-Taliban officers and bin Laden sympathizers, agreed to block the escape into Pakistan in return for a billion dollars in aid.[118] The CIA was nervous and recommended sending in US troops to surround the cave complex as well, but Bush, Cheney, and Rumsfeld believed that Musharraf's promise was sound. The trap began to close, the Pakistani troops seemed slow to form along the "back door" to Pakistan, and still no US troops were deployed. As the battle formed, Peter Bergen, a CNN reporter, claimed that there were more US journalists there than US soldiers.[119]

Around December 5, US Special Forces "painted" strategic targets with handheld lasers, but the fight was a lackluster and intermittent affair. Bombing targets were few, the Afghans fought without distinction, and the United States committed no additional troops. After ten days, bin Laden announced his retreat in a broadcast from somewhere within the snowy caves, thanking his "most loyal fighters" and promising to continue his battle on new fronts. According to independent reporter Ron Suskind, he formed up his last eight hundred soldiers and over the next day straggled south across the unguarded border and disappeared into Pakistan. The United States declared victory, but impartial observers called it the "Grand Charade." Twenty-one al Qaeda soldiers were captured, but as many as four thousand Taliban soldiers may have escaped, including most of the al Qaeda leadership. When challenged, General Tommy Franks, head of DoD's Central Command, said that he had no resources available to continue pursuit. All his forces were being shifted to Iraq.

WHAT WENT WRONG?

In the war against the al Qaeda terrorists in 2001, the United States made nearly all of the mistakes we have come to recognize as characteristic of an information disaster. First, America didn't listen very carefully to the warnings. At the FBI, those who were investigating the al Qaeda threat were vigorously blocked by others higher in the organization. In the White House and in the Department of Defense, Paul Wolfowitz was waging a concept war, aggressively pushing the theory that Iraq was the enemy, while opposing without consideration the growing evidence that al Qaeda might be able to strike from within the United States. Close relations between the White House and the Saudis, and between the Pentagon officers and General Musharraf, apparently discouraged any aggressive investigation into al Qaeda's finances or the activities of the Taliban.

Second, when the crisis began, communications systems

started to fail. The president, secretary of defense, secretary of state, chairman of the Joint Chiefs, and commander of NORAD were effectively out of touch for the first hour. Vice President Cheney had isolated himself in a bunker and was responding to false and imaginary warnings with shoot-down orders that were not obeyed. Videoconferences established by Richard Clarke and others effectively coordinated actions at a secondary level, but they were not connected to each other, and the FAA frequently failed to keep the Pentagon up to date.

Tragically, even systems as simple as radios failed. The coordination problems between the New York City police and fire departments were made worse, not better, by Mayor Giuliani's decision to separate the command centers. Hundreds of firefighters died because the warnings from the police never reached them high in the towers.

And third, consistent with the pattern of other information disasters, those most responsible for the failure—Deputy Director Wolfowitz, CIA Director Tenet, Secretary of Defense Rumsfeld, FBI Director Mueller, and Mayor Giuliani—received high praise from President Bush while their errors were covered up. The White House resisted a commission to examine the attack, stonewalled its requests for information, and then ignored its recommendations. The idea that Saddam Hussein was linked to the 9/11 attack continued to be promoted by the president and vice president, in spite of conclusions to the contrary reached by the CIA.[120] Even the enemy got away: the pursuit of bin Laden was effectively abandoned after a few months, as the administration shifted the focus to Iraq. And the possibility that a more attentive government might have anticipated the attack or even prevented it was blithely dismissed with the time-honored alibi: "we made the best decision possible given the information available at the time."

When the only reality is appearance, it is tempting to go around the battlefield and put lipstick on the dead. And that's what happened after 9/11. In matters large and small, those responsible for the failure campaigned tirelessly to distort and suppress any reports that could put them in an unflattering light:

In the summer of 2004, the CIA completed an internal review of its own operations leading up to the 9/11 attack, and it was apparently highly critical. The report identified twenty intelligence officials who could be candidates for possible disciplinary procedures, including Director Tenet. But delivery of the report to Congress was first delayed until after the election and then buried by Porter Goss, the new director of the CIA. He said he would not convene an accountability board to hold anyone responsible.[121] George Tenet was later awarded the Medal of Freedom.

A special report by the 9/11 Commission concluded that the Federal Aviation Administration was fully aware of the al Qaeda terrorist threat and that at least half of its daily briefings between April and September 2001 mentioned al Qaeda by name. Publication of this report was delayed until after the election and then released only in a heavily censored version.[122]

A report by the Justice Department inspector general called the FBI's inability to detect a hijacking plot a "significant failure" and said that the bureau missed at least five chances to catch two of the hijackers. It attributed the failure to "widespread and long-standing deficiencies" in the way the bureau handled terrorism and intelligence cases.[123] In response, FBI Director Mueller said that there has been no evidence of any threat: "In our investigation, we have not uncovered a single piece of paper—either here in the United States or in the treasure trove of information that has turned up in Afghanistan and elsewhere—that mentioned any aspect of the September 11 plot."[124]

Even White House chief of staff Andrew Card seized the opportunity to assert a more favorable description of the events in the Florida schoolroom. Card claimed in a newspaper op-ed piece that when the president was told that a second plane had crashed into the World Trade Center, it was "only a matter of seconds before President Bush excused himself very politely to the teacher and to the students, and left the Florida classroom."[125]

After experts pointed out that the Saudis had refused to cooperate with the 9/11 investigation, President Bush declined to ask Saudi intelligence for background information on the fifteen hijackers who were Saudi and refused to help US reporters get visas into the kingdom: "As far as the Saudi Arabians go, they've been nothing but cooperative. Am I pleased with the actions of Saudi Arabia? I am."[126]

The danger in minimizing errors, misjudgments, and conflicts of interest is that these risks then go uncorrected and they repeat themselves in other organizations. Nothing is learned. But more fundamentally, when leaders start to pretend that the errors never happened, the trust that glues the group together begins to dissolve, and subsequent communications are darkened by doubt and suspicion. When its report was published four years after the attack, the 9/11 Commission had obviously omitted a number of events that, as currently understood, reflect unfavorably on the military and on members of the administration.[127] It also ignored or oversimplified important issues raised by the growing chorus of skeptics:

The report makes no mention of FBI agent Robert Wright's blocked efforts to trace Saudi financing of bin Laden[128] nor of FBI headquarters' campaign to stop the opening of Moussaoui's laptop.[129] There was no response to engineering questions raised about the collapse of the twin towers, particularly the later collapse of Building 7 across the plaza.[130] Questions raised about the damage at the Pentagon were never addressed—the destruction seemed too small to have been caused by a Boeing 757.[131]

The commission sought to minimize the significance of the fact that, beginning on September 13, within hours of a meeting between President Bush and Saudi Ambassador Prince Bandar, as many as three hundred Saudis were flown out of the country, including twenty-six members of bin Laden's family, with only a perfunctory check of their identities. During the first day of these flights, all private aircraft in the United States were grounded. The Saudi exception, say the skeptics, could have been authorized only by President Bush, probably in response to a personal request from Bandar, his long-time friend.[132] While acknowledging that these flights occurred, the 9/11 Commission dodged the issue of who had given the authorization. "We found no evidence that anyone at the White House above the level of Richard Clarke participated in a decision on the departure of Saudi nationals. . . . The president and vice president told us they were not aware of the issue at all until it surfaced much later in the media."[133]

Patriotism is a powerful concept that lies at the heart of every healthy nation. Men and women willingly risk their lives for the country they love. And yet in a July 2006 poll, Scripps Howard Research found that 36 percent of American adults now consider it "very likely" or "somewhat likely" that US government officials either allowed the 9/11 attacks to be carried out or carried out the attacks themselves.[134] Five years after the tragedy, hundreds of studies later, a third of Americans believe that their own government conspired to blow up two of the most important buildings in the country and send a commercial aircraft crashing into its own military headquarters. In the same poll, 77 percent of those questioned said that they or others they know are now more angry with the government than they used to be, up from 25 percent before 9/11.

In a Harris poll conducted every year, the number of people who have a "great deal of confidence" in Congress, the White House, and the military dropped in 2006 to half what it had been five years before, while the level of confidence in medical, educational, and religious institutions rose slightly.[135] The trust in government is gone. A terrible blow has been struck at the foundations of democracy.

The price we are paying for the wink and wave of politics, for the stubborn failure of bureaucracies to handle dissonant information, and for the childish refusal of leaders to think critically about the real world is that the faith and confidence of United States citizens in the future of their country is now deeply shaken.

6

DEADLY DECISIONS

F alse knowledge is the problem. For reasons having to do with how individuals think and how groups communicate, inaccurate information has become a part of our shared knowledge, our virtual truth, and it is often the basis for our actions in a complex world. False knowledge is a growing cause of hospital deaths, the primary element in countless disasters, the principal reason we failed to stop the terrorist attack on 9/11, and the bugle that took the United States to war. But we can rise above these failures. On a personal level, we can learn to recognize and mitigate the biology of false knowledge. In those teams and communities and societies to which we belong, we can come to agree on a standard for determining the accuracy of information that will allow us all to be more effective. In time we might have greater respect for the truth. We might read the fine print, listen to warnings, report honestly to our colleagues without censorship or spin, and admit our information errors when they occur.

We can learn. The information disasters of recent years suggest a number of specific behaviors and information management tactics that may reduce the amount of false knowledge being introduced in an organization's truth system.

THE INFORMATION BUBBLE

In many of the situations considered here, a major reason for false information arriving at the decision-making point is that the decider was in an information bubble, listening to only one or two likeminded sources. Dissonant interpretations and even different descriptions were excluded from consideration, and the existing view of the world was not challenged and expanded but reinforced.

No example of this problem is more tragic in my own experience than the way a deeply flawed virtual truth about the threat of communism in Southeast Asia drew the United States deeper and deeper into the quagmire of Vietnam. I vividly remember my going-away party in New Haven the night before I left for Vietnam myself. A distinguished Yale professor of political science and one of the government's principal advisers on the war drew me aside after several drinks and told me with a grin that Vietnam was a courageous and romantic place with old French boulevards and beautiful women. He described the women in some detail. But during the year that I spent with the 25th Infantry Division along the Cambodian border, I saw instead a country torn to the sinews by war. The people were weary and old before their time. Their teeth were brown from chewing betel nut, and they lived along rice paddies that were pocked with bomb craters. I realized that most if not all of my friend's understanding must have come entirely from visiting Saigon, lunching at the *Circle Sportif* and riding around the city in guarded convoys. There the Vietnamese army was disciplined and loyal. There the people were eager for American support. There the streets were lined with trees and everyone was beautiful.

The American government had no direct understanding of

Vietnamese culture or of its government. It came to rely almost entirely on the reports of a few military commanders and State Department advisers who, like my friend, could neither speak nor read the language. The truth never made it to Washington. In *A World of Secrets*, his careful study of the nation's intelligence system, Walter Laqueur describes how even the faint warnings of failure in Vietnam were scrubbed from the official report:

> During [General] Harkins's tour, finished intelligence assessments for Washington produced by the CIA station and the US mission were coordinated with MACV before dispatch. In the process they were edited to reflect the optimism of the MACV commander lest any acknowledgment that the war was not being won, or that US military programs were not succeeding, might serve as an admission of failure. General Harkins's tenure began the fateful closing of the intelligence evaluation circle; its vested institutional self-interest and self-deception afflicted US intelligence for the remainder of the war.[1]

Dissonant facts need to travel quickly up an organization in the same way that even the slightest pain shoots through the nervous system, and for the same reason. Unpleasant as it is, these messages tell the decision-making center that the prevailing truth might not be accurate. Yet organizations and communities don't pay enough attention to such signals or to the people who send them. Salespeople who are in regular contact with the customer are often ignored by development engineers who have their own ideas about what the product ought to do, and engineers are in turn overruled—as they were at Morton Thiokol and Three Mile Island—by executives who are willing to take higher risks in order to expand the business.

As an executive considers whether to listen to another querulous and disrespectful opinion, he or she needs to recognize two possibilities: (1) the alternative description might be accurate and important, and (2) the normal channels have a bias for reinforcing the status quo. These questions and criticisms are often signals from the edge of danger.

It was clearly a mistake for then national security adviser Condoleezza Rice to reorganize the various counterterrorism working groups so they all reported to her. The result was that the concern about bin Laden's plans to attack inside the United States was effectively kept from the senior members of the administration. The fixed idea that Iraq was the enemy could not be dislodged or even effectively challenged as long as Paul Wolfowitz was in the Pentagon or Dr. Rice was in the White House. Even when George Tenet finally broke through with his July 10 warning based on CIA intelligence, it had so little impact that Rice could not even remember later that the meeting occurred.

Hurricane Katrina showed how isolated the White House had become. Just before dawn on August 29, 2005, the third-largest hurricane ever recorded in the United States swept in off the Gulf of Mexico to shatter the levees and flood the streets of New Orleans. More than a million people were driven from their homes, property damage was estimated at over $100 billion, and 1,836 people died. In the early hours of the devastation, one hundred thousand people were trapped in the rising waters with no transportation, no communication, and no emergency assistance. And yet the mayor of New Orleans and the governor of Louisiana were having enormous difficulty getting the attention of the White House, which was essential to deploying the federal resources they needed. Most assessments of the disaster now conclude that the president failed the city, and one explanation offered is that George Bush rarely listened to dissenting or disagreeable voices.

In evaluating the president's performance during the Katrina disaster, *Newsweek* criticized his habit of relying only on loyal aides and compared his information management style with those of other presidents:

Bush can be petulant about dissent; he equates disagreement with disloyalty. After five years in office, he is surrounded largely by people who agree with him. Bush can ask tough questions, but it's mostly a one-way street. Most presidents keep a devil's advocate around. Lyndon Johnson had George Ball on Vietnam. President Ronald Reagan and Bush's father, George H. W. Bush, grudgingly listened to the arguments of Budget Director Richard Darman, who told them what they didn't wish to hear: that they would have to raise taxes. When Hurricane Katrina struck, it appears there was no one to tell President Bush the plain truth: that the state and local governments had been overwhelmed, that the Federal Emergency Management Agency (FEMA) was not up to the job and that the military, the only institution with the resources to cope, couldn't act without a declaration from the president overriding all other authority.[2]

In *Team of Rivals: The Political Genius of Abraham Lincoln*, Doris Kearns Goodwin shows how President Lincoln followed a very different approach: "I have a good deal of news from New York," Lincoln told former congressman John Pettit, "but of course it is from friends, and is one-sided. . . . It would seem that assurances to this point could not be better than I have. And yet it may be delusive."[3]

Lincoln acted on his belief in multiple sources by bringing into his cabinet William H. Seward, Salmon P. Chase, and Edward Bates, all of whom had opposed him for the Republican nomination and were publicly scornful of his backwoods ways. But in spite of their occasional opposition to his ideas, they came to trust Lincoln and each other, and the difficult decisions these men made together carried the country through one of its darkest hours.

KATRINA: WARNERS AND WARNEES

Warnings are a special class of dissonant information and they are difficult to heed for three reasons. First, warnings like those from the

Babcock and Wilcox engineers often come from people deep in the organization who have few credentials and are frequently hard to understand. Second, they contain a prediction about the future based on facts, values, and concepts that may be different from those of the listener. It is important for the person giving the warning to remove as many of these obstacles as possible. If there are differences that are not essential to the warning, accept the listener's view on those issues and proceed from there. And third, there is a pathology of giving and receiving warnings to be overcome. Sherman Kent, CIA officer for twenty-five years and widely honored as the "father of intelligence analysis," chose in his retirement lecture to emphasize the difficult relationship between the analyst and his "customer." Kent noted that the "warner" always worries that the "warnee" will really listen, so he has a tendency to overstate the danger. The warnee, having experienced a pattern of persistent overstatements, now discounts the significance of the message, which in turn provokes the warner to even greater exaggeration. The two are caught in a loop. Kent has no solution, but an elementary school teacher might have suggested an old Socratic trick. Let the student connect the dots. Put the facts on the table and stand back. What conclusion do you draw? Sometimes a lesson learned is better than a lesson taught.

The history of warners is a sad tale of obsession, courage, frustration, and failure, as well as success. But here we find heroes:

Roger Boisjoly, the Thiokol engineer, gathered the data and warned NASA about potential failure of the O-rings, but he stopped too soon. With the evidence on his side, he could have brought his case to Stanley Reinartz, Shuttle Project manager or directly to Dr. William Lucas, head of the Marshall Space Flight Center, although it would clearly have cost him his job.

Joseph Kelley and Bert Dunn, the two Babcock and Wilcox engineers, wrote memos to their company for several years, trying to present their concerns in engineering language they thought would lend credibility to the case. The warnings were refuted, returned for being on the wrong form, and then simply ignored.

Richard Clarke was counterterrorism coordinator in the Clinton administration and during the first few months of the Bush administration. But as the danger drew nearer, his new superiors listened to him less. While Mohamed Atta and his conspirators made their final arrangements, Clarke was demoted to special adviser on cybersecurity. Criticized by his colleagues for what they saw as bureaucratic infighting and manipulation, he nonetheless kept concern for bin Laden alive in the White House against heavy opposition.[4] Even after the attack on 9/11, when he was asked by the president to document the link between Saddam Hussein and the attacks, he disproved the thesis and got his conclusions signed by all relevant agencies, including the FBI and the CIA. His paper was returned with the note "update and resubmit."[5] After working for the federal government for eighteen years, he quit in 2003.

In twenty-two years at the CIA, Michael Scheuer grew to become a fierce and obsessive advocate of stronger action against Osama bin Laden. As head of the CIA's bin Laden task force, he brought the necessary facts to his superiors and on at least ten occasions urged them to kill the man. More than anyone, he held a light on the target and reminded all who would listen that this was America's enemy. But frustrated by continued refusals to take action, he left the CIA in 2004. When the 9/11 Commission Report was published, he was referred to only once, as "Mike."

When Zacarias Moussaoui was arrested in Minneapolis, August 13, 2001, local agent Harry Samit campaigned for a search warrant to open the suspect's laptop and learn more about his terrorist connections. He was blocked at every step by Dave Frasca, chief of the FBI Radical Fundamentalist Unit (RFU). Over the next few weeks, Samit sent seventy messages to FBI headquarters, CIA, Secret Service, INS, FAA, and possibly the NSA, but these efforts, too, were stymied by Frasca.[6] When Samit sought approval from the court set up under the Foreign Intelligence Surveillance Act (FISA), FBI headquarters withheld supporting documentation and effectively scuttled the request.[7] When Samit found out that Moussaoui intended to go on "jihad," FBI headquarters claimed that "jihad" did not necessarily mean "holy war." When the Minneapolis office, with CIA support, requested a search warrant that would allow them to open the laptop, Mike Maltbie, a special agent with the RFU, blocked the request, withheld supporting evidence, and criticized the CIA office that had assisted Samit.[8] Maltbie later told Samit that when these warrants don't turn out well, the agents who requested them are usually demoted. He said he was blocking Samit to "preserve the existence of his advancement potential" within the FBI.[9] The laptop was not opened until after the 9/11 attack and then it identified several of the terrorists as well as the nature of their plan.

Coleen Rowley, one of the Minneapolis FBI agents, later tried to understand why these warnings had been so fiercely resisted by headquarters:

> I feel that certain facts . . . have, up to now, been omitted, downplayed, glossed over and/or mischaracterized in an effort to avoid or minimize personal and/or institutional embarrassment on the part of the FBI and/or perhaps even for improper political reasons. . . . Why would an FBI agent deliberately sabotage a case? The superiors acted so strangely that some agents in the Minneapolis office openly joked that these higher-ups had to be spies or moles . . . working for Osama bin Laden. . . . Our best real guess, however, is that, in most cases avoidance of all "unnecessary" actions/decisions by FBI managers . . . has, in recent years, been seen as the safest FBI career course. Numerous high-ranking FBI officials who have made decisions or have taken actions which, in hindsight, turned out to be mistaken or just turned out badly . . . have seen their careers plummet and end. This has in turn resulted in a climate of fear which has chilled aggressive FBI law enforcement action/ decisions.[10]

Rowley was right about one thing. Maltbie was promoted to supervisor in the Cleveland office, and Harry Samit, who had tried so hard to warn everyone about Moussaoui, was not.

Dr. Hans Blix, a distinguished Swedish diplomat and former head of the International Atomic Energy Agency, was summoned out of retirement to determine the extent of Iraq's WMD capability. But unhappily for his UN sponsors, he concluded in a 2003 report to the Security Council that there was no evidence to support claims that weapons were being actively developed. He accused the US and British governments of dramatizing the threat solely to justify the overthrow of Saddam Hussein. Dr. Mohamed El Baradei, an Egyptian diplomat who had succeeded Blix as director general of the IAEA, led the UN's inspection team in Iraq in the months prior to the US invasion. He, too, questioned the United States and British claims. He specifically refuted the key points of Secretary Powell's UN speech, saying that no weapons of mass destruction had been found. Allegations that Iraq was buying uranium from Niger were based on forged documents, and the aluminum tubes—claimed to be part of a uranium enrichment effort—could not be used for that purpose. The United States vigorously opposed El Baradei's reappointment as head of the IAEA in 2004, but he was finally approved in June 2005. In October, together with the IAEA, El Baradei was awarded the Nobel Peace Prize.

Sometimes warning the community about false knowledge in the system is more accidental than courageous. Four years after the little article that burst the Enron bubble, Bethany McLean described the circumstances that led her to write one of the most important articles ever published in the business press.

> When I think back to that time in early 2001, the idea that one of the largest companies in the country could be involved in fraud and be bankrupt—that wasn't conceivable. . . . I knew something was wrong, I knew something didn't add up. But the

idea that it would all collapse like this. . . . At that time, no one cared. It wasn't like I wrote a story and got calls from other journalists, saying "Good job." I got a few calls, but it was a very underground type of thing. . . . How do you know what's a big story? You just have to follow your instincts, report and see where the cards fall. . . . It wasn't until nine months later that I had any idea of the scope and significance of this story.

I don't think Enron is an isolated incident of people in a dark corner doing bad things. . . . With so many companies, their financial picture paints some mixture of reality and illusion. In Enron's case, it was more illusion than reality. In other companies, I hope it's more reality, but you have some illusion all of the time. . . . With talk about privatizing Social Security and people making decisions about the market for their financial future, it's important that people not be naive about the way information travels and how people lie to you. In the 1990s, I think people were sold on the idea that if you are an individual investor, you can compete and you are on a level playing field with institutional investors, and it absolutely is not true.[11]

Among the disasters of the last few years, the most successful single warning was probably a brief phone call on August 27, 2005, from Max Mayfield, director of the National Hurricane Center, to Mayor Ray Nagin of New Orleans. The circumstances were dire. By 7 p.m. that evening, it was clear that Hurricane Katrina would arrive with winds of one hundred and fifteen miles an hour, moving like a whirling scythe toward the mouth of the Mississippi. Computer projections at Louisiana State University (LSU) showed the city under water. Thousands of people trapped in the flooded city would die.

Warnings of a major hurricane had been a Louisiana ritual for a decade. The *Washington Post* ran a front-page story saying that if a hurricane hit New Orleans, the city would look like Bangladesh.[12] The *National Geographic* painted the result of a hypothetical hurricane and concluded that thousands would die in a "murky brew that was soon contaminated by sewage and industrial waste."[13] Even *Popular Science* said the city might be completely submerged if the levees failed.[14] But in 2003, LSU published a special five-year study showing that in the worst-case scenario, a third of the city's million-and-a-half people would not even leave their homes, and those who did would be trapped on highways jammed with cars. Busses and trains would stop running; emergency vehicles would be unable to enter the city.[15] A year later, a five-day exercise run by FEMA confirmed that if New Orleans was struck by a major hurricane, evacuation would be the biggest problem. One hundred thousand people did not even own cars. There would be casualties "not seen in the United States in the last century."[16] The only hope for avoiding such a disaster was to prepare the population to leave their homes and to begin the evacuation early.

In June the city began to distribute a million copies of an evacuation map. A video was made, "Preparing for the Big One," and seventy thousand copies of the DVD were distributed free. There were emergency drills, and from studying the results of those exercises it was estimated that at least seventy-two hours would be required to safely evacuate all the people.

On August 25, Katrina was declared a hurricane, and even before it struck Florida, New Orleans was forecast to be in its path. By the twenty-sixth, the governor of Louisiana had declared a state of emergency, but evacuation was still recommended, not mandatory; the city followed suit. Mayor Nagin was concerned that if New Orleans ordered the people out, the city might be sued by businesses for any looting or destruction from the resulting lawlessness. The seventy-two-hour mark came and went. By the afternoon of the twenty-seventh, with the eye of the hurricane three hundred miles away, getting the people out of the city had become more difficult than ever. The mayor and the governor were each working on plans, but people continued to cling to the idea that their homes might survive. And finally, sometime after 7 p.m. that evening, Max Mayfield, who had spent his professional life trying to get government officials to take these storms more seriously, called Governor Kathleen Blanco and pleaded with her to make the evacuation mandatory. He said later, "I wanted to be able to sleep that night."[17] She told him to call the mayor, the only one who could order the city cleared. And sometime after 8 p.m., less than forty-eight hours before the storm struck the city, Mayfield placed the call. Nagin later remembered the conversation: "At that point in time, [Mayfield] said definitively: 'Mr. Mayor, the storm is headed right for you. I've never seen a hurricane like this in my 33-year career. And you need to order mandatory evacuation. Get as many people out as possible' . . . Max Mayfield scared the crap out of me."[18]

Although it took Nagin another twelve hours to issue the mandatory evacuation, it was Mayfield's call that had forced him to the decision, and between them they undoubtedly saved thousands of lives. Mayfield retired the following year at the age of fifty-seven, saying "I'm tired and I want to go home."

UNCERTAINTY ABSORPTION

The mind abhors confusion, and when information is passed from person to person within an organization, ambiguity is removed; interpretations shift to favor the person delivering the message, and information is added to make the story conform more comfortably to the organization's existing view of the world. Not deliberately in every case, but so predictably that there might as well be a rule: the more people who stand between the event and the person who must make the decision, the more thoroughly the information about the event is distorted.

Economist Herbert Simon has suggested that as people try to understand an event or a message, they reason from the conclusions presented, not necessarily from the facts. They prefer to hear a reasonable story, one that makes sense, and if at all possible, one that fits their own view of the world. The biology of false information gives us a clue as to how and why this might happen: information is easier to store, process, and retrieve when it is consistent with an existing concept. Exceptions to the concept are recorded as new synaptic connections; they have fewer links to existing experience and are less likely to be reinforced. Thereafter, if our understanding of how the mind works is correct, the person retrieves the most "available" description, the one used most frequently, the one that creates the least dissonance with the rest of the person's knowledge. We remember what we understood, but more than that, we hear more easily what we are prepared to hear. It is important to listen with extra care precisely to those messages that seem most discomforting.

Newsrooms know that they will rarely get more from a story than what the reporter understood, so it is important to send the most knowledgeable person to the scene, someone who is prepared to hear the unusual, someone who won't throw away the good stuff.[19]

As information is transmitted from one person to another, uncertainty is eliminated. Evidence contrary to the main thesis or unflattering to the messenger is suppressed. Elements of the story that would provoke awkward or difficult questions are omitted in the cause of "cleaning up." Exceptions to the group's prevailing concept are forgotten. Even the vocabulary we use conspires to remove what we cannot understand or express. In a system that permits only "yes" or "no" it is difficult to express ambiguity. On the *Vincennes*, when Petty Officer Anderson had to tag the unidentified plane on his computer screen, he had no way to say "can't tell yet," so he tagged it "hostile." Others, unaware of Anderson's real intent, shot the plane down. In the case of the shuttle *Challenger*, the project manager reported to his boss at the Marshall Space Flight Center at the end of a long day, skipping over the hours-long debate about the O-rings. He said only that there had been some concern about "the weather." He knew his boss, Dr. William Lucas, would reject any unquantifiable "concerns."

But people don't stop at eliminating ambiguity; they also add "clarification." In disasters where communications failure was a factor, the message trail included interpreters who added information to make a more reasonable tale; just little things here and there to make the story more vivid, to connect it to the group's existing truth, to incorporate the messenger's own insight or clarification.

During the Vietnam War, two Associated Press reporters described a classic communication failure of the sort that may later have contributed to the massacre of civilians in My Lai:

> A reporter was present at a hamlet burned down by the US Army's 1st Air Cavalry Division in 1967. Investigation showed that the order from the division headquarters to the brigade was: "On no occasion must hamlets be burned down."
>
> The brigade radioed the battalion: "Do not burn down any hamlets unless you are absolutely convinced that the Viet Cong are in them."
>
> The battalion radioed the infantry company at the scene: "If you think there are any Viet Cong in the hamlet, burn it down."
>
> The company commander ordered his troops: "Burn down that hamlet."[20]

The anecdote seems too neat to be precisely true, but as an illustration of the problem, it accurately captures what often happened in a war where the political and military leadership sent messages out through command channels only to find them broadly distorted and ignored.

In the midst of the terrorist attack on the World Trade Center, Vice President Cheney, believing incorrectly that other hijacked aircraft might be headed for the White House, gave the order to shoot down any plane within twenty miles of Washington. General Larry Arnold of NORAD sent a message to his subordinates, "VP has cleared us to intercept tracks of interest and shoot them down if they do not respond." This caused immediate concern among those who would have to implement the order. Pilots were unaware of the hijack crisis and would be expected to start looking for Russian planes. They wanted to know whether "do not respond" meant that the target would not divert or would not acknowledge the warning. And there were other questions. As a result, the NEADS commander, not identified in the 9/11 Commission report, changed the order from "take out hostile aircraft" to "take down ID type and tail."[21]

Each messenger in the communications chain struggles to present a logical, interesting, attractive, and sometimes self-serving description of reality, and this tendency is most pronounced when the information is most ambiguous or conflicting. The messenger, whose understanding is already limited, further trims the picture until it makes a sensible presentation, eliminating in the process the elements that may have been the heart of the story.

The media, in particular, play this role in the larger community. The format of the conventional newspaper or television story requires that some overall theory of what happened should be presented at the beginning of the piece, supported by evidence marshaled in logical sequence. Reporters are encouraged to boil down the events, remove the ambiguous or uncertain material, and present the most important aspect of the story in terms as simple as possible. And in a larger sense, like any messenger eager to fit the news to the prevailing view of the group, the media is particularly sensitive about reflecting in its coverage what it perceives to be the "current understanding" of the issue. Over the years, as I have listened to briefings by foreign correspondents in particular, it has seemed to me that by sticking to the strict format and requirements of the traditional news story, the media are too often leaving out the best parts. If truth is the goal, there ought to be a line under the story, followed by a personal note from the reporter on the scene: "Here's what I think is really going on."

Reporters follow each other around, they feed at the same sources, they read each other's stuff, and they are cautious about going around the bend with a particularly unusual interpretation.

When it came to reporting the government's assertion that Iraq had weapons of mass destruction, for example, the media were too eager to adopt the official interpretation. Michael Massing, a contributing editor of the *Columbia Journalism Review*, studied how the media treated this issue in 2002 and 2003:

> In the period before the war, US journalists were far too reliant on sources sympathetic to the administration. Those [reporters] with dissenting views—and there were more than a few—were shut out. Reflecting this, the coverage was highly deferential to the White House. This was especially apparent on the issue of Iraq's weapons of mass destruction—the heart of the president's case for war. Despite abundant evidence of the administration's brazen misuse of intelligence in this matter, the press repeatedly let officials get away with it. As journalists rush to chronicle the administration's failings on Iraq, they should pay some attention to their own.[22]

We should distrust stories that are too tidy. When a committee or a project team sees no disadvantages to a new idea, it usually means they haven't thought about it enough. As Voltaire said: "Doubt is not a pleasant condition, but certainty is absurd."[23]

Whether or not the media were lazy in their coverage prior to the invasion of Iraq, and in my opinion they were, the format of the news story itself makes it difficult for the reporter to convey ambiguity. It is not acceptable for the anchorman to put the papers down on his desk after reading a piece, lean forward into the camera, and say, "I gotta tell you. There's a lot about this story that just doesn't make sense to me." And yet, let the record show, that is exactly what Walter Cronkite did on February 27, 1968, when he finally put his papers down, leaned into the camera, and said he thought the war in Vietnam had reached a stalemate.

> To say that we are closer to victory today is to believe, in the face of the evidence, the optimists who have been wrong in the past.

To suggest we are on the edge of defeat is to yield to unreasonable pessimism. To say that we are mired in stalemate seems the only realistic, yet unsatisfactory, conclusion. On the off chance that military and political analysts are right, in the next few months we must test the enemy's intentions, in case this is indeed his last big gasp before negotiations. But it is increasingly clear to this reporter that the only rational way out then will be to negotiate, not as victors, but as an honorable people who lived up to their pledge to defend democracy, and did the best they could.[24]

Taking a similar approach, Anderson Cooper left the beaten path of journalism to blurt out the truth that everyone else was dancing around. After one hundred hours of nonstop reporting from the roiling maw of Katrina's devastation, he confronted false information directly. As Jonathan Van Meter described the event in *New York Magazine*:

It was on the fourth day of coverage, at the most dire and terrifying moment of the crisis, that Cooper came unhinged. He was interviewing Mary Landrieu, the senator from Louisiana, who had a big, sweet, southern smile spread across her perfectly made-up face. In a nonanswer to one of Cooper's questions, she thanked President Bush for his "strong statements of support and comfort." Finally, Cooper boiled over. "I gotta tell you," he said, "there are a lot of people here who are very upset, and very angry, and very frustrated. And when they hear politicians . . . thanking one another, it just, you know, it kind of cuts them the wrong way right now. Because literally there was a body on the streets of this town yesterday being eaten by rats, because this woman had been lying in the street for 48 hours. And there are not enough facilities to take her up. Do you get the anger that is out here?"

[Cooper] didn't calm us down; he made us feel even more unsettled. He became a proxy, both for the victims of Katrina and for his viewers, building a bridge between the two. He reacted the way any of us might have—raging against government officials when help didn't come fast enough, and weeping when it all got to be too much. But it wasn't just his raw emotion that set him apart; there are plenty of hotheads on television, and tearing up became more and more common as the tragedy continued to unfold. It was his honest humanity; he comes off as genuine because he is. He connected to those in the hurricane's path, and to the people watching at home. He removed the filter.[25]

Up the organization and through the community go reports that are, with each repetition, more plausible, more comforting, more easily explained by concepts currently held, and less likely to be true. Like the childhood game of "telephone," the information traveling across an organization or around the nation is altered according to the limitations of the messengers until it fits the ideas and experience that prevail in the group. Virtual truth is strengthened, dissonant information is excluded, and no one is to blame.

MRS. ARISTOTLE'S TEETH

There is an antidote. Organizations that use aerial and satellite photography to assess the military situation, search for rare minerals, measure the size and health of a crop, or forecast future water supplies sometimes find an image that is not recognizable. It has never been photographed before or it seems different for reasons that cannot be explained. Over the years, the phrase "ground truth" has come into use to describe a process of confirming the photo interpretation by actually hiking in to the site to check a sample of observations. Is the portion of the photograph that looks like a swamp really a swamp? What is the real spectral pattern of the vegetation at normal temperature and humidity? How deep is the snow pack when it has that particular color?

While this process of corroboration may seem obvious, many serious errors have been made by guessing that if it looks like a bed of roses (from thousands of miles in space), it must be one. In preparing for the assault on the Bay of Pigs in Cuba during 1961, for example, satellite photographs of the landing site were misinterpreted. On the basis of the photography, the marines were told to be prepared for a beach littered with seaweed, but what they found when they hit the ground was a dangerous coral reef.[26]

In 1978 I saw how ground truth can work. As part of its military assistance program, the US government sent a team of information experts to Iran to build systems that would allow the shah's military commanders to communicate more effectively with their troops. Led by General James Gavin, former head of research and development for the Department of Defense and chairman of Arthur D. Little, Inc., the consulting firm, we were to design new publishing facilities, new training institutes, and new broadcasting capabilities. Early in the course of one of the team's visits we were becalmed by a local holiday, and there seemed to be little any of us could do but sit around the pool at the Teheran Hilton and write memos to each other. But Jim Gavin went out the front door that morning and, after talking to several taxi drivers, chose one car, jumped into the front beside the driver, and rode off.

That night the case team gathered again for dinner with a gentleman who was apparently responsible for America's intelligence activities in Iran. We engaged in the usual witty repartee and political speculation—more wine, please—and at each turn of the topic our host reassured us of the shah's plan to build from the rich oil reserves of his country a modern democracy that would be a beacon of freedom and technology in the Middle East. We could only nod in vigorous agreement. But when it seemed that we had exhausted ourselves in exuberant optimism, Gavin started to talk about *his* day. He had spent most of it in that taxi, riding first through every quarter of the city, up into the Elburz Mountains and out to the rural villages that lay beyond the city limits. He saw families living in tents with their animals; he saw people who still wore the curled-toe Turkish slippers. He drank yogurt with other drivers, gave someone's cousin a ride out to the desert, and, through his new best friend Mahmoud, the driver, had several long and candid conversations with cousins and associates, in and out of the ambit of government. They painted an entirely different picture of the shah's situation. What he heard, Gavin said, was that the shah's government was a house of cards, an artificial environment elaborately spun for Western eyes and existing only at the sufferance of a primitive and angry people.

The foundations of the buildings were too shallow, the concrete was cracking everywhere, the roads were breaking up, and the telephone system didn't work beyond a few miles from the palace. The shah's family was hated, his programs were widely ridiculed, and his police were feared. There was no education, no adequate public health system, no industry, no agriculture, and no way to make a living except within the government and its supporting infrastructure. Beyond the city limits, Gavin said, you step back into the sixteenth century where the people are impoverished, illiterate, conservative, and fiercely loyal to the mullahs. He said a revolution was in preparation, well organized and poised just beneath the surface. The government would certainly fall within a year.

Our host disagreed, arguing that the shah was a brilliant leader with a clear strategy and solid support from the United States. Gavin had been misled. Honestly, these taxi drivers will tell you anything. There followed an interesting but guarded debate— always be polite to people from the intelligence community—and then discussion turned, as I recall it, to rugs.

Gavin's analysis was penetrating and persuasive, and I repeated it over many drinks and dinners that fall. My colleagues thought his conclusions were fascinating if unconventional; I thought his methods even more so. In the end, Gavin's insights— widely respected within the government at the time—were ignored by the new administration. But he had been right. The shah's government fell four months later, swept from power by the fundamentalist mullahs.

The risk of mishandling information is greatest when the information itself is most abstract. High in a complex organization, errors of interpretation are based on several levels of analysis, and often no one in the room has ever been to the scene. But savvy intelligence officers and information executives often sense when they are being drawn into a virtual world where terrible inaccuracies can exist. They instinctively stop the process and go look at the situation directly. Ground truth is often what is being sought by executives who manage by "walking around," by politicians who go "back to the voters," and by scholars who return to the source materials. It is a process of degeneralization designed to reestablish the ambiguities and shake the loose ends loose again. It is a remedy for false knowledge.

The problem here is that information is a substitute for direct observation, and like all substitutes, it has its shortcomings. The abstract generalizations that are easiest to work with replace the gritty details of experience that are more accurate. The very power and usefulness of information derives from its ability to simplify reality in a way that makes a decision easier. But this presents a problem: Information becomes more "truthful" as it expands to include the real details, growing more complex in the process. On the other hand, it becomes correspondingly less truthful as it moves away toward general descriptions that are more easily understood. This is the paradox that ground truth tries to resolve. A sample of each abstract description is tested to establish its relationship to reality, and we then assume that this is representative of the whole picture. We gain the usefulness of broad concepts and efficient descriptions while getting at least some sense of their accuracy.

The process is not difficult. Pick an important element of the message and go to the source. You should find ambiguity and confusion, details that were omitted, opposing views and conflicting evidence as well as a general consensus in support of what you were told. If you start hearing voices in concert to the contrary—particularly if their view is unflattering—then you are probably headed for a coral reef. Venture capital firms planning to invest millions in new products often follow the simple, ruthless test of talking first to a potential customer. All of a sudden you are in the real world, trying to find out whether the product boldly outlined in the business plan can actually deliver value. But the answers are not always politely given, and for the analyst, being treated with such lack of respect is sometimes too great a punishment to bear. As Bertrand Russell pointed out, Aristotle believed that women had fewer teeth than men, even though, having married twice, he might arguably have confirmed this hypothesis by direct observation.

Is Occam's razor a useful tool? In the fourteenth century, William of Occam, a Franciscan monk battling furiously with the pope, suggested that the truest explanation for any phenomenon is usually the simplest one. We should believe the description that requires the fewest assumptions, leaps of faith, and vaulting complexities. In the medieval Church where angels danced on pinheads and Thomas Aquinas could construct an elaborate fourteen-point proof for the existence of God, Occam meant his rule to be as much a political statement as a philosophical one. It is still a good everyday heuristic, although the poor Franciscan was excommunicated for it—among his other heresies. But sometimes the simple description is merely the easy one. Einstein was once quoted in *Reader's Digest* (of all places), saying, "make everything as simple as possible, but not simpler." That is a highly simplified version of what he really said: "In my opinion the theory here is the logically simplest relativistic field theory that is at all possible. But this does not mean that nature might not obey a more complex theory. More complex theories have frequently been proposed. . . . In my view, such more complicated systems and their combinations should be considered only if there exist physical-empirical reasons to do so."[27]

Einstein had a point. There are times when you want to know that the doctor, the engineer, or the general has read the fine print. The codes and commands the president of the United States requires in a national emergency are all in the "football," a seventy-five-page loose-leaf notebook carried by his military aide. President Carter, who had a degree in physics and was one of the first navy officers to be recruited for the nuclear submarine program, took one look at the notebook and asked for a simplification. It now exists, we are told, as an executive summary in the form of a "cartoon."[28] That may not be an improvement.

The world is not simple. Go to a rally and listen to the candidate; don't take the media's word for what he or she is saying. Internal consistency in a presentation is rarely a good test for accuracy. More often it merely indicates that there has been a great deal of tidying up. Build redundant sources and use them. From time to time, on an important issue, see how the information you are receiving from your normal sources fits the impression you get yourself when you do the research. For one thing, you will be surprised at how much more interesting reality is than what you are accustomed to hearing in a committee room or on the evening news.

SIX TESTS FOR TRUTH

During the summer that my colleagues and I were interviewing police detectives, stock analysts, gamblers, and other professional truth testers, I began to collect anecdotes about how to tell when the tip or the tout is false.

Detail. Almost any broad generalization can be said to bear some truth: "Enron is an excellent investment." There was a point when it was. "This map of the Cold Bay, Alaska, airport is accurate." In fact, most of the map was. But a useful test for truth is to examine the information that backs it up. True statements are supported by rich and redundant detail, while the inability to provide such detail correspondingly suggests inadequate observation or risky judgment. Successful executives (and detectives) presented with a plan for action or an explanation of events often "drill down," picking one aspect of the presentation and examining it in more detail and then examining one of those details further, and so on until the presenter starts to sputter. Three levels of detail is a good indicator, but all executives have their own standard.

Evidence. A second and similarly simple test is to look for real evidence: actual documents, primary data, O-ring test results, visual confirmation of the plane's identity. Are there any examples where the valves actually stuck open? Could you find one al Qaeda agent actually in the United States in the summer of 2001? The information doesn't have to prove the truth in all its scope, but the listener should be able to pick one or two aspects of the assertion and see direct corroborating evidence.

Consistency. The third indication of truth is the extent to which the statement is consistent, not only internally but also with statements made by independent observers. Listen carefully to the argument; search for contradictory assertions however small, and for disconnected, irrelevant, or illogical conclusions. If this part of the description is true, how can that part be true? In a larger sense, compare the description to the world as we know it. Have the laws of physics been honored here? Is the market behavior they anticipate consistent with behavior we have seen in the past?

Witnesses. When another comparably trained professional evaluates the same information, does he or she make the same report? If not, be careful. Does the messenger generally agree with others who were there or who had the same experience? Witnesses seem an obvious way to evaluate the accuracy of a statement in court, but in business, politics, and science, they are rarely used. A simple way to do the test is to ask whether anyone else was involved or had that experience. What did he or she say? In the news business, when a story comes in that seems slanted, incomplete, or inaccurate, it is sometimes checked by another reporter. Send someone else out and see how the second account compares with the first. This is not a challenge to honesty; we all have biases that prevent us from seeing a dimension to the event that may be obvious to others.

Reputation. More frequently organizations look to the fifth index of accuracy—the reputation of the person who created the description. When a statement is made by an individual widely regarded for his or her powers of observation, it is quickly accepted as true, even if the report is surprising and inconsistent with what is known. On the other hand, a staunchly researched statement bristling with evidence and corroborating reports is likely to be dismissed if the messenger is also known to believe that aliens are molesting the cows. You are often, as the detectives told us, "buying the guy."

Katharine Graham, chairman of the board of the Washington Post Company, had many extraordinary friends and advisers— Warren Buffett, Robert McNamara, and Lillian Hellman, among them—and she often took their advice more seriously than she took the research and recommendations of her own executives (mine included). "Anyone who would work for me," she told me once, "can't be very bright." I'm sure she meant that in a good way.

Over time, across a series of reports, we develop a sense of whether a colleague has a habit of exaggerating the advantages, suppressing the problems, or coming up with descriptions that no one else seems to remember, and that appraisal goes into the truth calculation.

In fact, one of the most pervasive and powerful ways to present false information is to falsely attribute it to a reputable source. In the conference rooms at NASA the night before the launch, Morton Thiokol falsely presented a business decision as if it were an engineering assessment. The same conclusion, presented as a business decision, might have been understandably dismissed. In selling the invasion of Iraq to the public, the primary lie advanced by the White House was not the existence of WMDs, or an Iraqi/al Qaeda alliance. These assertions were widely rumored and plausible. The lie was that these were conclusions based *on solid intelligence* when everyone involved in the propaganda campaign knew that to be untrue.

Motivation. Finally, the motivation of the messenger is an index to be examined in testing for truth. For politicians, in particular, where the information is vague and the implications are personal, the loyalty of the messenger is the litmus test they turn to. "If you support me and share my goals, you are as deeply committed to finding the truth as I would be under the circumstances. Surely you would not lead me astray."

When faced with a choice between two witnesses, one credible, motivated, and reputable and another who knows all the facts, lawyers often choose to present the credible witness, even though he may have fewer facts.[29] For juries, as for most people who are judging the truth of information, the motivation and character of the messenger is often a more important indicator of truth than the content of the message itself.

Three of these characteristics are eloquent testimony on behalf of truth. But for three others presence means nothing—it is their absence that tells the tale. A high level of corroborating evidence and detail in a statement, for example, tends to indicate that it is true, but the lack of evidence or detail means little. Conversely, a high level of consistency in the statement does not necessarily mean truth, but when consistency is absent, when the statement contradicts itself or flies in the face of what is generally known, the message is hard to believe.

Witnesses reporting the same conclusion from independent observations are a strong indicator of truth, but the absence of witnesses does not necessarily mean inaccuracy. A poor reputation and self-serving motivation on the part of the messenger both raise doubts about any statement he or she might make. And under such circumstances the information, however true, is difficult to use. But a good reputation and noble intent do not by themselves prove truth. Honest people can be mistaken.

When all six indicators are strong, it is easy to make an assessment. Lots of evidence and detail, no inconsistencies, corroborating witnesses, and no record of lying or malicious motivation all point persuasively to truth—regardless of how startling or disagreeable the statement may be. On the other hand, serious inconsistencies in a message from a disreputable or malicious source, presented in the absence of any evidence or supporting witnesses, strongly suggest that the description is not accurate.

Finally, though not a test of accuracy, a truth must also be persuasive, or else the listener will simply cling to current beliefs. As Alfred North Whitehead observed: "It is more important that a proposition be interesting than that it be true."[30] The proposed truth must be sufficiently different from what is currently believed so that the unpleasant work involved in incorporating it into the listener's conceptual framework is work worth doing. It is one thing to conclude that the statement is not false: "Right you are if you think you are." But it is a substantially different matter to find the information so compelling that we must change our view of the world and accept it as a new basis for action.

A rudimentary test like this will not, by itself, uncover a careful fraud or pierce the calculated lie. It is a work-a-day tool, better for the normal range of information problems than for hard intelligence tasks where the messages have been craftily constructed to deceive. But the test has another, more serious limitation. Truth testing like this, as helpful as it is, doesn't deal with the aspect of intuition, revelation, philosophy, or faith. Not all true statements are the solemn product of a rational procedure, nor are they all provable by analysis. We have to examine our ideas about truth itself if we are to understand how accurate messages succeed or fail in a culture where the standards for truth can vary so widely. As Sir Francis Bacon pointed out four hundred years ago, there are errors of perception, errors of communication, and influences that the group exerts on everyone involved. Truth is not only the condition of accuracy, it is a process.

THE TRUTH/ACTION PARADOX

The most common reason for false knowledge is that important information has been left out. The Dana-Farber doctor didn't read the whole protocol; most Enron analysts didn't actually study the accountant's report; Dr. Lucas was not briefed about the difficult O-ring debate. The person responsible for the decision gathered information until he had a likely story and then stopped.

In July 2006, four ceiling panels fell on cars traveling through the newly built Ted Williams Tunnel in Boston, crushing Milena Del Valle to death and seriously injuring her husband. The safety of the whole tunnel came into question. In the investigation that followed, it was discovered that the panels, each weighing about three tons, were held up by bolts glued into the top of the concrete structure. But according to *Design News*, the glue used was a weaker "fast drying" epoxy, not "standard" epoxy, as the engineering drawings specified.[31] Apparently no one read the detailed characteristics of the glue.

Herbert Simon has suggested that most decision makers fail to gather all the relevant information. They don't "maximize" the search—get all the information available. They don't "optimize" it—get as much information as time or resources will allow. Instead, he said, they "satisfice" it. They gather information until it is possible to make a decision that fits the facts, values, and concepts available, and then they stop. The information is good enough to justify going forward, and nobody wants to spend a lot of time digging through the details. Analysis paralysis: when you bring more information to the table, more ambiguity is created, more work needs to be done, and you finally wonder whether anything in life, sufficiently analyzed, is worth doing.

What's happening here is a battle between truth and action, and action usually wins. Too little information leads to the wrong decision, but too much information makes a decision impossible. This is true in the biology of the brain, and it is true in the way

The Truth/Action Paradox

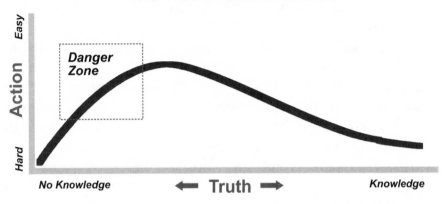

groups function. As information about the problem (truth) increases, the quality of the decision also increases, but beyond a certain point more information makes the decision more difficult. There are too many choices; there is too much uncertainty. In theory we reach a point where all the relevant information is there and a perfect decision can be made, but getting that moment right is very difficult. As a client told me once, "I can always make the right decision when I have all the facts, but I never know when I have all the facts."

In a study of wrongful convictions undertaken by the American Bar Association, it was found that mistaken eyewitnesses were a factor in 84 percent of the cases. And the most common form of mistaken eyewitness testimony is that the wrong person was picked out of a lineup. According to the ABA study, the witnesses often "made the best choice" instead of recognizing the person as the perpetrator. Urged by the police to decide, the witness selects the one person in the lineup or photo spread who looks *most* like the wrongdoer, rather than picking someone whom they are convinced is the *exact* match."[32] The ABA study speculates that since many of these errors occurred in death penalty cases, the error is likely to have occurred in an unknown number of other cases where an innocent person was subsequently convicted and executed.

In most cases, people make decisions as soon as the available information aligns itself. But that can happen because not all the facts are there. The truth is virtual: it seems to be consistent and detailed; it seems to conform to what everyone else is saying; but not all the possible suspects are in the lineup. No one has read the fine print. No one has actually tested the bolts. It is better to "satisfice-plus." Go beyond the point where the information seems to converge and keep listening until you start to get redundant confirmation from independent sources.

At some point in the future we will realize that our lives depend on doing this better. We will get past the "no one is to blame" stage and understand the importance of treating information as respectfully, and fearfully, as we treat nuclear energy, rocket science, stock markets, and medicine.

7

THE COMING EPIDEMIC

O n the farthest horizon of our consciousness, growing slowly in the fetid shadows of an Asian chicken farm, is an epidemic that will, according to some, sweep across the world in the next ten years to become the greatest human disaster in modern times.[1] In the darkest version of this warning, fifty million people may die, as many as thirteen million in the United States alone. Families will cower in their houses without food or water; schools and businesses will be closed. Hospitals will be useless because there will be no vaccines, no medical supplies, and only a skeleton staff of doctors and nurses. The National Guard will rumble through the streets in military convoys, relocating the sick, enforcing quarantines, and policing the vaccine distribution points. For weeks, electricity, telephone, and water will be spotty as the world economy falls to its knees. And it will be several years before life returns to normal in a society profoundly changed.

[Stop. Before we review the facts, consider your own values and concepts. Do you want to believe that a pandemic of avian flu will occur? Probably not. Do you think that such risks are often exaggerated by the media? Do you think that even if it does happen, it won't happen to you?]

It is difficult even to consider such a prospect. The gravity of the warning, combined with the ambiguity of its basic premise, challenges the mind where it is weakest, confronting our native optimism with facts that are difficult to prove. Yet here we have a chance to think about false knowledge prospectively. To what extent are we, once again, indulging in scaremongering on one hand or wishful thinking on the other? Is it possible to examine our virtual truth about a worldwide bird flu epidemic and sort out what is from what ought to be? Can we get it right this time? Here are the facts on which nearly everyone agrees:

AVIAN FLU: THE FACTS

A new strain of avian flu virus has been detected. Most wild birds, especially geese and ducks, have for thousands of years been infected with a mild virus that is occasionally transmitted to domestic poultry. The virus spreads rapidly in farms, particularly in Asia, and the infected birds nearly always die. There is no known cure.

Among poultry, the avian flu is hard to diagnose during incubation and contagious phases. The symptoms do not appear until a few days after the original infection, and even then they are easily confused with normal barnyard diseases, enabling the virus to sweep through a flock of birds before it is diagnosed. The farmer is understandably slow to believe that his flock has been infected, and for a few more precious hours or days, his birds continue to be contagious; some may even be shipped out. Farmers report the problem as a last resort, and governments that depend on poultry exports are slow to confirm the news. As soon as the virus is diagnosed in a bird, the entire flock must be destroyed.

The new H5N1 virus has infected dozens of humans in the last few years. As early as 1997, under circumstances that are not well identified, humans who had extended contact with diseased birds were infected with a new strain of avian flu, H5N1, that appears to take the same lethal course as its avian progenitor. Over an incubation period of two to eight days, it colonizes the lungs and other organs, causing pneumonia. The body responds dramatically to this invasion, producing a poorly understood reaction called the "cytokine storm," in which its own immune system floods the lungs with fluid, further weakening the patient. Young people age ten to seventeen are particularly vulnerable because their immune systems are vigorous, and the cytokine response is therefore correspondingly strong. And at the other end of the age spectrum, people with very low immune systems, respiratory problems, or other ailments are also at great risk. Once the infected person is diagnosed, he or she may be treated with antivirals and conventional pneumonia medication, but in 60 percent of the cases identified to date, the patient has died of respiratory failure within a few days. Because H5N1 mutates so easily, it is difficult to develop a specific vaccine that might prevent infection or an antiviral treatment to block its progression. There is no known cure for avian flu in humans.

The disease appears in clusters. Of the 380 cases of avian flu in humans reported by the World Health Organization through mid-2008, most appeared in forty to fifty family clusters, striking first at children from five to seventeen years old, then at the adults who cared for the children, and then at the extended families. Cases have appeared disproportionately in January and February of each year, with a slight rise again in October.

Infected humans may become contagious. The greatest concern about the avian flu is that this virus might mutate again into a form in which an infected person would be contagious to other humans. But there is disagreement over whether this might happen. The so-called species barrier normally prevents the diseases of one species from transferring to another species because of fundamental differences in their cell structures and RNA. But the rapidly mutating H5N1 virus may combine with the human flu virus to create a new and similar form, sharing many of the original avian characteristics. A rise in the number of infected birds makes bird-to-human infections increase, and as the human infections rise, the human-to-human jump grows more likely. This "jump" to a sustainable human flu virus may occur at any time in the next ten years. Or it may not occur at all.

If a human-to-human form of the virus appears, it will probably incubate for days before any flulike symptoms are apparent, and during that period the infected person could transmit the virus to others through a cough, a sneeze, or a touch. Cigarette smoke might also carry the virus. Early symptoms resemble those of a common cold or flu, including congestion, sore throat, dehydration, and fever. Diarrhea, vomiting, abdominal pain, and bleeding from the nose and gums have also been reported in some patients. But the characteristic symptoms are fatigue and muscle pain so extreme that victims are too exhausted to move from their beds; any gesture is painful. Coughing is so severe that patients bruise their throats and chest muscles. One observer says people "feel like they have been run over by a truck or beaten nearly to death."[2] As fluid fills the lungs, the patient develops difficulty breathing and then slips into a coma. Respiratory failure and death normally follow in three to five days.

No human-to-human cases of H5N1 have been confirmed, and some believe the virus can only be caught from infected flocks. But others point to at least three cases that suggest that the mutation may have already happened:

1. In Thailand, during September 2004, an eleven-year-old girl became infected from exposure to sick chickens and died of H5N1. Her thirty-two-year-old aunt and her aunt's son, who lived in the same house, became infected with the virus but recovered. Her mother who traveled from Bangkok to care for her became infected—she could not have been exposed to the chickens—and she died the next week.

2. In Vietnam, during February 2005, a twenty-one-year-old man became infected by eating meat from a sick chicken. His fourteen-year-old sister contracted the virus, having had no contact with poultry. A twenty-six-year-old male nurse who cared for the original patient became infected, as well as the man's eighty-year-old grandfather, his fourteen-year-old brother, and his sister, all without apparent contact with chickens. None died.

3. In Indonesia, during April and May 2006, a thirty-seven-year-old woman from the Karo district became ill and died. Her fifteen-year-old son died of H5N1 five days later. Her seventeen-year-old son died three days after that. Her twenty-eight-year-old sister, her sister's eighteen-month-old daughter, her ten-year-old nephew, and her thirty-two-year-old brother all became infected and died within two weeks. A twenty-five-year-old brother became ill but survived.

Although the reporting agencies and the World Health Organization have not confirmed these as human-to-human cases, the facts appear to support no other explanation. An individual who contracted the disease from sick birds then transmitted it to other humans. More recently, public health organizations have begun to focus on a "sustainable" human-to-human virus in which a person infected by the original patient would be able to infect others. If more than fifty people in a village, unrelated to each other, become infected within a week, that would be the signal that a real epidemic is about to begin. But by the time we learn of such an event, it may be too late.

On the other hand, H5N1 may never make the jump. In early 2008, Bernard Vallat, director general of the World Organization for Animal Health, called the risk of an avian flu pandemic "overestimated." He said that the H5N1 virus has not mutated into a human-to-human form as had been feared. "We have never seen such a stable strain," he said, describing the pandemic concern "just nonscientific supposition."[3]

[Stop again. For most readers at this point the stress of dealing with dissonant information is almost palpable. The facts are uncertain; the prospect is horrific. This is the point at which Bruce Ismay stuffed the iceberg warning into his pocket. The point at which the doctors closed Betsy Lehman's folder and decided that there was no real cause for worry. You can see how they felt. But don't run away. This is the dangerous maybe moment.]

If the virus jumps to humans in sustainable form, it will be hard to contain. Without a routine blood test for all travelers, it would be impossible to prevent undiagnosed persons from traveling out of the country by train or plane, infecting fellow passengers, and carrying the virus around the world within weeks.

An epidemic of avian flu would infect about a third of the world's population. The executive summary of the *National Strategy for Pandemic Influenza* uses 30 percent, based on a review of epidemics in the past, but at this point there is not enough actual experience to prove any projection. In the United States, that rate of infection would mean as many as ninety million people becoming sick.

There will not be enough hospital beds or supplies to care for the sick. If the number of sick in the United States rises above a few hundred thousand, there will not be enough diagnostic kits, traditional medical facilities, equipment, supplies, or trained medical staff to care for everyone. In the case of some flu viruses, the normal immune system can overcome the infection. But with the avian flu, doctors fear that weeks of treatment or hospitalization may be necessary. There are about one million staffed hospital beds in the fifty-seven hundred registered hospitals in the United States, including psychiatric and long-term facilities but not counting prison hospitals and college infirmaries. Over a period of six to eight weeks, there would be not only the people who are actually infected but also many more who fear they are infected but aren't.

In 1918 the Spanish Flu swept across the globe, killing between fifty and one hundred million, more than the Black Plague. Doctors and nurses fell ill as quickly as everyone else, so the available medical staff was cut by a third. And because there was no effective treatment, doctors were reduced to directing the sick to quarantine areas, severe treatment facilities, or the morgue. Adequate medical supplies and equipment were not available then and would not be available now. The only effective treatment—other than rest, liquids, and oxygen—would be antivirals such as Tamiflu. But to be effective, the antiviral has to be given shortly after the onset of the infection—difficult to do when the symptoms are often cryptic and slow to emerge. Many will request antivirals who seem to show symptoms but are not actually infected.

According to the Department of Health and Human Services Pandemic Influenza Plan, the rate of infection among children will be 40 percent and will decline with age. Among working adults, 20 percent will become ill during a community outbreak. Of those who become ill, 50 percent will seek medical care, even if effective antivirals are available.[4] If the epidemic is as severe as the one in 1918, the government says, ten million Americans will require hospitalization and two million will die. The existing hospital infrastructure in the United States is simply incapable of handling even a fraction of this load.

Some antivirals may be effective once the symptoms appear. Tamiflu and Relenza may slow or mitigate the growth of the flu virus in an infected person and may also reduce the likelihood of transmitting the virus to others. But as it mutates, the H5N1 virus will become resistant to any antiviral used against it, so the consensus now is that any antiviral not developed for the most current strain will probably have little effect. According to the US Centers for Disease Control and Prevention (CDC), Amantadine and Rimantadine, while effective in treating the normal flu, have not been effective against H5N1.

The US government has a stated goal of stockpiling twenty million courses of Tamiflu for healthcare professionals, politicians, and "infrastructure" personnel—key military, financial, and government executives. Responsibility for purchasing and distributing antivirals for the rest of the population has been assigned to the states. The federal government has even begun to recommend to businesses that they stockpile Tamiflu for their employees, shifting healthcare responsibility from the community to the employer.[5] At the end of 2007 it was estimated that there were only about five million courses of Tamiflu in the United States. With a 30 percent rate of infection, the country would require at least ninety million courses of antiviral medication, and no one currently believes that these can be produced in the next few years.

It will take at least six months to develop a vaccine. While antivirals may mitigate the effects of the virus, only a vaccine developed for the specific strain of H5N1 can actually block infection and bring the epidemic to a halt. In April 2007, the US Food and Drug Administration approved the first vaccine developed by Sanofi Pasteur, Inc., for the H5N1 flu as it was isolated in 2006. The vaccine, which requires two injections twenty-eight days apart, will not be available commercially. All supplies will be purchased by the US government as part of their rapid response program, to be dispensed by public health officials to health workers, government officials, and the military.

People will stay home rather than risk being exposed. In a national poll taken in early 2006, 75 percent said they would reduce or avoid travel in the event of an avian flu outbreak. Seventy-one percent said they would skip public events, and 68 percent said they would stay home and keep their children indoors while the epidemic lasted. People will be reluctant to gather in public places or shop in stores, even for food. As a result, experts agree, there would be a widespread shutdown of businesses, stores, and schools for a period of six to eight weeks. Vital services like electricity, water, telephone, Internet, and heating oil delivery would be interrupted in some locations.

During the SARS outbreak in Hong Kong in 2003, schools were closed for two months, 90 percent of the people began wearing surgical masks, and 70 percent avoided hospitals and medical clinics.[6] Based on this and other experiences, the Department of Health and Human Services estimates that eight out of nine infected persons will be treated at home.

A detailed study of the economic impact of a pandemic flu, prepared by the independent Trust for America's Health, concluded that the flu will lead to the second-worst depression in the United States, with the Gross Domestic Product dropping over 5.5 percent.[7] Arts, entertainment, hotels, and food service companies will lose 80 percent of their business for several months. Transportation and warehousing will lose 67 percent of its business.

Mechanical preventions are possible. The virus is transferred in the form of airborne droplets from sneezing, coughing, and even speech, and they can remain infectious on hard surfaces for as long as forty-eight hours. It is possible that they can be killed by ultraviolet light and normal disinfectant. N-95 medical masks, the kind sold in hardware stores, are a useful barrier to any airborne infections, but there are not enough of these masks in the United States to supply the needs of more than a few hundred thousand medical workers, and there is no current plan to increase the manufacturing level. The most effective prevention is to isolate anyone with symptoms or, in some cases, quarantine a house, a neighborhood, or a community.

The primary goal is to slow down the epidemic. Given the inexorable lethality of the H5N1 flu and the absence of any effective treatment, the stated goal of the United States government is to slow the advance of the virus long enough to create and administer an effective vaccine. This means an aggressive worldwide program that would try to contain the outbreak by rapid destruction of infected flocks and quarantine of communities where the outbreak has occurred. It means six months to get confirmation, gather a specimen of the human-to-human virus, and create and test a vaccine. To manufacture and distribute fifty to one hundred million doses will take even longer.

The federal government plans to play a limited role in prevention, care, and containment. *The National Strategy for Pandemic*

Influenza, released in May 2006, makes it clear that while the federal government will sponsor and support the effort to identify the virus and create an effective vaccine, it intends to rely on the private sector to manufacture the doses necessary, and on local governments to buy the supplies and manage the distribution. Even that now seems unlikely. The original report included a request for $8 billion for research for, among other programs, faster vaccine production methods ($2.8 billion), purchase of vaccine for essential government and infrastructure personnel ($1.2 billion) and the purchase of antiviral medications Tamiflu and Relenza ($1 billion). But only $3.46 billion of that proposed budget was finally approved by Congress, most of it earmarked for vaccine purchases from the private sector. In announcing the plan, Michael Levitt, secretary of health and human services, said that over the coming days he would be "asking governors, mayors and state and local officials to join me in a concern we all must share—preparing for a pandemic should one happen." The strategic plan left little doubt about who was going to be primarily responsible for distributing the vaccine, treating the infected, establishing quarantines, and maintaining order:

> State, local, tribal, and private sector entities have primary responsibility for the public safety and security of persons and non-Federal property within their jurisdictions, and are typically the first line of response and support in these functional areas. However, the unique challenges that might confront state, local, tribal, and private sector entities could require them to request additional assistance, either of a logistical or operational nature, from within their states, from other states pursuant to a mutual aid compact, or from the federal government. Civil disturbances and breakdowns in public order might occur in several different situations: as health care facilities are overwhelmed with those seeking care and treatment for themselves or family members; as persons vie for limited doses of vaccines and antiviral medications; as supply-chain disruptions cause shortages in basic neces-

sities; as individuals attempt to leave areas where outbreaks have occurred, or where containment measures are in place; and, potentially, in border communities if neighboring countries are impacted. 9-1-1 emergency call centers and public safety answering points may be overwhelmed with calls for assistance, including requests to transport influenza patients.

In addition to facing these challenges and dealing with the day-to-day situations they normally face, state, local, and tribal law enforcement agencies may be called upon to enforce movement restrictions or quarantines, thereby diverting resources from traditional law enforcement duties. To add to these challenges, law enforcement and public safety agencies can also expect to have their uniform and support ranks reduced significantly as a result of the pandemic, especially if they are not vaccinated.[8]

According to the HHS plan, the federal government proposes to provide advice and support when a full-fledged pandemic appears. When sustained human-to-human infections begin in the United States, the federal government will distribute the vaccine and antiviral stockpile to government employees, the military, and infrastructure personnel. It will advise states and localities to activate their epidemic response plans. And it will deploy medical personnel, equipment, and supplies to augment local capacity in affected areas. The plan does not identify where these medical personnel and supplies will come from, who will direct their activities, or how "affected areas" will be chosen.

The toll from H5N1 will be high. In the executive summary of the *National Strategy*, potential deaths from an avian flu epidemic are estimated to be about two hundred thousand. This is contradicted in the body of the report itself and is substantially lower than any estimates being offered by others. According to the report, 30 percent of the world's population was infected with the flu in 1918, and between .2 percent and 2 percent of those infected died as a result. If that experience is repeated with H5N1, about ninety million people in the United States will become infected and between two hundred thousand and two million deaths will result. With only a few outbreaks reported from third world countries over three years, there is no way to know at this time what the real rate of infection or death will be.

The World Health Organization records have documented 380 cases of H5N1 (239 deaths) occurring in reporting countries through mid-2008 and cited certain patterns. In 2003, 4 cases (4 deaths) were reported in China and Vietnam. The next year, 46 cases (32 deaths) were reported in Thailand and Vietnam. In 2005, 97 cases (42 deaths) were reported in Cambodia, China, Indonesia, Thailand, and Vietnam. In 2006, 111 cases (76 deaths) were reported, including new cases in Azerbaijan, Djibouti, Egypt, Iraq, and Turkey. In 2007, 88 cases were reported (59 deaths), down from the previous year, and as of mid-2008 new cases were occurring at about the same rate, 34 by mid-year with 26 deaths.[9]

BELIEVING WHO?

That may be the optimistic version. Chicken farmers are reluctant to have their flocks killed, and countries are reticent about officially admitting the danger their exports pose. As a result, the World Health Organization counts only those victims admitted to a cooperating hospital and has no way of determining how many nonlethal infections may have actually occurred. Dr. David Nabarro, United Nations influenza coordinator, acknowledges the difficulty of getting reliable data from governments around the world:

> I can never be sure when I'm talking to representatives of government or of other organizations, whether they're telling me everything that's happening in their countries. Perhaps even they can't be sure because in some of the countries that I visited, there is quite a strong decentralization of health and agricultural services, and information doesn't always flow to the centre in a

timely fashion, not least because sometimes there are disincentives for information to move.[10]

Knowing this, independent agencies on alert to the growing threat keep their own measure of the flu's progress and they say that in 2004 there were one hundred cases and fifty deaths, more than twice what WHO reported. A Japanese bird flu expert recently reported that China had actually experienced nearly a thousand cases of avian flu in 2005, with three hundred deaths, not the sixteen deaths they reported to WHO.[11] Turkey has said that it is reviewing its original WHO reports but has not yet provided any revised statistics. Singapore, which has one of the highest rates of infection, has decided not to report any data at all from now on. The good news is that when these additional cases are acknowledged, the rate of deaths as a percentage of all persons infected drops to about 20 percent. The bad news is that there may have been four or five times as many infections as WHO reported. The world's early warning system is badly out of synch with reality.

The public health community uses a system for describing epidemics in six phases, the last of which is sustained human-to-human infection. But it is the World Health Organization that decides when Phase 6 has begun and, as part of the United Nations, it is subject to certain political pressures. If it is systematically underreporting the experience of member countries, then the epidemic warning system, like the lookout on the *Titanic*, is lagging behind reality. The announcement of Phase 6 will be too late. At the rate of contagion expected of H5N1, sustained human-to-human infection—the beginning of the epidemic—will be well under way weeks or maybe months before the World Health Organization acknowledges it. Conversely, because people have already learned not to trust the WHO numbers, they will begin to follow the more informal counts, rumors, and speculation that abound on the many Web sites now devoted to this topic. For better or worse, news of a serious outbreak of the avian flu will be telegraphed around the world in hours, without confirmation or context. Real knowledge (and false knowledge) will precede official knowledge, and confusion will be added to panic.

How serious will the impact be? The rate of infection will be substantially higher in less-developed countries, particularly those who already suffer the ravages of various infectious diseases, and most particularly in those dense and impoverished cities of the developing world where the virus will spread in hours, not weeks. In 1918 nearly half the world's deaths occurred in India. Within the developed countries of the world, the poor, crowded, and under-privileged communities of even our greatest cities will be consumed. Living close together and lacking good medical care, the people may be unable to understand the public health warnings or follow the instructions. They will be the first to suffer and, if Katrina is any example, the last to get help. In Africa only six countries have the 2.5 health workers per thousand people considered necessary by WHO; compare this number to the United States, which has twenty-five per thousand. The continent is already wracked with widespread epidemics. It is deeply suspicious of Western medicine[12] and is likely to be devastated. In America, some poor and densely populated neighborhoods would wither into memory.

The "official" forecast of deaths as a percentage of those infected appears to be based on *normal* flu experience and it deliberately understates the gravity of the situation. In his *Bird Flu Manual*, Dr. Grattan Woodson estimates that during the epidemic of 1918, 30 to 50 percent of the world's population was infected and 12.5 percent of those infected died.[13] There is some ambiguity about the real infection rate and death toll of that epidemic, but if Woodson's estimates are used, and if the profile of the new H5N1 flu is similar to the 1918 Spanish flu, more than one hundred million people could become infected in the United States. As many as thirteen million could die, not the "two hundred thousand to two million" deaths anticipated in the government's plan.

The problem is not that the estimate is wrong; no one knows

what the new avian flu will be like. The problem is that in this case the US government has represented that its figures are drawn from history, but then it conspires to use the lowest conceivable estimate, encouraging citizens to take the risk less seriously. The *Titanic* is unsinkable again, the O-rings will seat properly, the levees will hold this time, we have nothing to fear from a "little terrorist in Afghanistan." The problem is that the information on which we are being told to plan our lives is foolishly optimistic and in some cases deliberately false.

The problem is that we will not be prepared. If a few million people need hospital care, the states that will be responsible for dealing with the epidemic might be forgiven for thinking that they can manage the situation. But if the number of people infected by the flu is ten times that, then a very different response must be considered. And in this context New York City's *Pandemic Influenza and Preparedness Plan*,[14] for example, is simplistic to the point of being silly. The public health function in New York City is one of the very best in the world and yet it repeats without comment the federal assumption that 30 percent of the population will become infected, even though history, the density of the population, and the general level of public health in some New York communities would suggest a higher rate. It assumes that 2.1 percent of those infected will die, substantially lower than the 1918 experience. But even if those assumptions are accepted, the greater New York City area will have 5.6 million sick and 118,000 dead. Including the twenty-three counties of New York, Long Island, and northern New Jersey, the area has about sixty thousand hospital beds in the best of times, and during an epidemic the staffing would be reduced. Even if only 11 percent of the sick are hospitalized, as the plan assumes, there will still be ten severely sick patients for every available bed. Children will be dying in the halls.

The New York plan ignores this. Instead, like its federal counterpart, it focuses on command, control, and management procedures, on counting the sick, on running the diagnostic labs, on recommending school closings and quarantines, on the management of hospital resources, and on distribution of antivirals—if they are made available from the federal stockpile. The plan for the state of California promises even less.[15] During Phase 6, the state's Department of Public Health plans to run the diagnostic labs and continue to monitor the course of the epidemic.

This is false knowledge. It is artificial certainty supported by rosy assumptions and elaborate language, presented to the public with the usual ceremonial flourish. These federal, state, and city plans may be intended merely to keep the political waters calm and create the impression that the government is doing its job—not in itself a crime. But in the process they are feeding false and misleading information to everyone in the community, encouraging a lower level of preparedness. More people will die because of this.

CONSIDERING DISASTER

Whatever assumptions are made about the deadliness of the avian flu, treating so many infected people will be difficult. But there are successful healthcare strategies and social responses that cities can prepare for, if properly informed. In the history of epidemics the response has nearly always been the same: small communities form to take care of their own. During the 1918 epidemic, ad hoc hospitals and neighborhood clinics emerged that were staffed entirely by volunteers. In Boston, where these volunteer community centers were especially successful, the death rate from the flu was half the national average. Cities can prepare to implement and support these groups.

In responding to the avian flu, there are a number of ameliorating treatments that are simple and successful. Treating dehydration with a mix of water, salt, and sugar, for example, is a crucial part of caring for the infected. Simple ingredients and equipment for home care like humidifiers, painter's masks, latex gloves, and blood pressure monitors can make a difference. Methods for preventing or limiting the spread of infection are straightforward, and instructions for the care of the sick are sadly simple. This information can be easily distributed in many languages and through illustrations.[16]

In establishing and maintaining official quarantines and unofficial blockades, some procedures are safer and more reasonable than others. Clarifying the legal issues and public priorities in advance will aid in maintaining social order when the time comes. But few governments, local or national, are paying enough attention. Dr. Nabarro, the UN influenza coordinator, said that this failure to the appreciate flu's impact on the community is characteristic of public health agencies around the world. "Most countries have now focused on pandemic as a potential cause of catastrophe and have done some planning. But the quality of the plans is patchy and too few of them pay attention to economic and social consequences."[17]

Going back as far as the fourteenth century, cities have responded to epidemics by creating local health boards to enforce the sanitary codes, protect the drinking water, control the sale of safe food, and bury the dead. But as the full gravity of the disease reaches into every corner of society, as the wealthy escape to safer locations and the poor remain behind, these committees turn to protecting property and controlling the movements of the "anarchic and unpredictable underclass." In Italy during the fifteenth and sixteenth centuries, these health boards became political, appointed and administered by the nobility. In Europe they became morality police, blaming the plague on the lepers, the beggars, the Gypsies, and the Jews. In Muslim countries, they blamed the plague on nonbelievers. Persecution followed in every case. Health boards even challenged the Church, canceling religious gatherings and practices and laying the groundwork for the Reformation. With their grip on the most intimate functions of the community, the health boards grew to become the new locus of law and order. Power shifted down from nations to states, and from states to cities.[18] And then, in Italy, at least, the cities became states unto themselves.

Epidemics fracture the social order. Societies devolve along existing fault lines as communities defined by ethnicity, language, and geography struggle to protect their children and keep their members alive. In such a crisis, gated communities will close their gates. The highway out to the northern suburbs will be blockaded by the residents. Medical checkpoints will be set up at bus terminals and train stations. The bonds of citizenship will be weakened in favor of the family, the neighborhood, and the community, and as people take up the task of caring for each other in a crisis, history tells us that the national government will become less relevant.

News of the epidemic's progress is likely to be swift, unreliable, and disorganized. In the United States and in most countries of the world, the government speaks only through the media and has few independent channels for getting out its message. And even when the government speaks to the public directly, political intentions now color the facts so thoroughly that, in the United States, at least, important public health issues are subordinated to party dogma and partisan political opportunities. In testimony to Congress, former United States surgeon general Richard H. Carmona described how the values and agenda of the White House distorted, and often silenced, the public health messages he was trying to deliver:

> The vetting was done by political appointees who were specifically there to be able to spin . . . my words in such a way that would be preferable to a political or an ideologically preconceived notion that had nothing to do with science . . . [To write an] emergency preparedness report . . . I brought my colleagues in, as I always do to achieve consensus. . . . I then . . . went to domestic policy at the White House, spoke to [Health and

Human Services] officials and I was given lots of different reasons. Well, this might incite, you know, scare the people.[19]

The Centers for Disease Control and Prevention has been a reasonably reliable source of public health information in recent years, but even they are not entirely to be believed. On the issue of sexually transmitted diseases, contraception, and abortion, the organization has a poor record of resisting political influence. On June 16, 2004, the Bush administration released a new regulation prohibiting any organization that receives federal funding for HIV/AIDS education from including any mention of condoms or "sexually suggestive" material in the information it provides the public. The CDC is the principal funder of HIV/AIDS education in the United States and its coverage on this issue has been frequently challenged. As a source of news about any H5N1 epidemic, the CDC reports only the World Health Organization data and then states the potential risk in language so bland that it borders on misinformation. In late 2007, it reported on the avian flu: "While most people . . . have been infected with H5N1 virus through direct contact with sick or dead poultry or wild birds, limited human-to-human transmission of H5N1 virus cannot be excluded in some clusters."[20]

Captain Smith of the *Titanic* might as well have said: "Based on regular reports about conditions in the North Atlantic, the crew and passengers should be advised that the possibility of encountering an iceberg this evening cannot be entirely excluded."

The conventional wisdom is that the Internet will deliver the real truth. With hundreds of sites now actively tracking the progress of the virus, it offers a vigorous diversity of views, along with primary data and detailed documentation. Government prevarications and platitudes are immediately challenged, new evidence is examined and debated, and knowledgeable researchers from every country in the world are pouring their time and skills into a community truth system that now transcends any library or panel of experts or scientific colloquium we could have imagined a few years ago. It has the jostling exuberance of a bright classroom when the teacher is out; brilliant insights fly back and forth like intellectual spitballs, competing with quirky rants and pompous obviosities in a rich and juvenile mayhem of ideas that refuse to clean up after themselves. The Internet is not for the faint of mind.

Such detailed knowledge matters, but not everyone seeks it with the same enthusiasm. If we care for each other, we need a simpler message system as well. We need to reach not just the bright and the curious but those who are afraid, in a hurry, or poorly informed. In impoverished communities and third world countries, the information needed to survive the avian flu can be distributed on a three-by-five-inch card. Elsewhere around the world, the best system for delivering alerts, education, and coordination is likely to be television. More than newspapers or radio, TV can compress the message and present it in simple, dramatic terms, telling the viewer how to protect against infection, how to identify the symptoms, and how to care for the sick. A familiar face and a local accent providing information about the community will encourage people to help each other effectively—the key to survival.

And the audience is ready. A survey done in May 2006 by researchers at the University of Minnesota showed that 42 percent of viewers want their television stations to give coverage of the flu the highest priority. Eighty-one percent said it was "important" (five on a scale of seven) for television news to focus on how the avian flu spreads and why scientists are finding it difficult to contain.[21] If it is integrated into national, state, and local epidemic planning, television might save more lives than science.

So why do we hear so little about it? Virtually every scientist and public health professional who has studied the situation concludes that a new Black Plague will blow across the globe in the next few years, striking hardest at our children and our parents, at the poor, and at the poorly informed. Millions will die. Communities and even continents will be devastated. And yet there seem to be no public information campaigns being designed, no disaster contingencies for local communities, no national or local television strategies. Why is the avian flu not being taken more seriously?

Maybe we hope the danger will go away. According to Nobel Prize–winner Daniel Kahneman and his collaborator Amos Tversky, people are more inclined to take a chance on success than live with the risk of failure. In a 1979 paper describing their "prospect theory," the two psychologists argued that people are prepared to stay with an investment that is doing poorly because they believe it will get better.[22] But they are quick to sell an investment that has done well because they want to grab the winnings while they can. Emotionally, people seem more comfortable with a bad situation that might get better than with a good situation that might get worse, even when the odds of winning and losing are exactly the same. It is our nature to wallow in hope.

But this might be a good time to rise above our nature, to learn that some risks need to be taken more seriously. Time to listen to warnings that make us uncomfortable. Time to discipline our information systems, make them more effective and more truthful.

8

WALTZING INTO WAR

L et's hope that by the time television is needed, it can still be believed. In the last few years there has been a sharp rise in the frequency, if not the boldness, with which the media have published or broadcast news that they knew, or should have known, was false. And the public's growing disbelief has been understandable. According to ongoing surveys by the Pew Research Center, the percentage of people who believe "all or most" of what they see on CNN has dropped from 42 percent in 1998 to 28 percent in 2006. NBC dropped from 30 percent to 23 percent, ABC News from 30 percent to 22 percent, and CBS from 29 percent to 22 percent. The number of those who believe all or most of what they read in their daily newspaper has dropped from 29 percent to 19 percent over the same period.[1]

FAKING THE NEWS

In 2004 Jack Kelley, one of *USA Today*'s star reporters, admitted that for twelve years he lied regularly and substantially in his work.

That night he spent with Egyptian terrorists in 1997, the Pakistani student who unfolded a picture of the Sears Tower and said, "This one is mine," the frightening visit to a terrorist crossing point on the Afghan-Pakistan border, the interview with the daughter of an Iraqi general, the high-speed hunt for Osama bin Laden—all made up. In Yugoslavia he interviewed a refugee who said that dogs were eating the body of his dead son. On a three-day assignment with the Kosovo Liberation Army in the mountains of Yugoslavia, he wrote about watching his companions shot down by Serbian gunfire and said he dragged one dying soldier over the mountains to Macedonia. These were lies. He stole quotes from other stories and shamelessly embellished the circumstances: "You don't need to talk to me. Just look at the reality. It speaks for itself," said Annalena Tonelli while running from machine-gun fire with a crying child under each arm.[2]

In 2002 Jayson Blair, a reporter for the *New York Times*, was fired for making up quotes and details, falsely claiming to have interviewed subjects, and plagiarizing materials from other reporters' work. The *Times* undertook a detailed investigation of the faked stories and published the results on page one. Editor Howell Raines and managing editor Gerald M. Boyd both resigned, in part because of the crisis the young reporter's lies precipitated.

In September 2004, months before the national election, Dan Rather, widely respected anchor of the *CBS Evening News*, reported on *60 Minutes* that documents discovered in the files of President George W. Bush's former commanding officer, Lt. Col. Jerry B. Killian, seemed to confirm a long-standing rumor that Bush, as a lieutenant in the US Air Force, had been found unfit for flight status because he failed to report for a physical examination. The authenticity of the documents was rigorously questioned by major newspapers and Internet blogs, but Rather and CBS stood by their story until former Texas Army National Guard officer Bill Burkett, the source of the documents, admitted that he had lied about how he got them and the whole thing started to fall apart. Rather interviewed Killian's secretary, who vouched for the truth of the content of the documents, but she couldn't confirm their authenticity. After two weeks of controversy, CBS retracted the whole piece, and Rather said he would not have aired it had he known more about the dubious documents. The story producer was fired, three others were asked to resign, and Rather left the anchor desk in 2006. Nonetheless, the producer and other experts continue to maintain that authenticity has not been disproved. Although there appears to have been no intent to mislead anyone, except by Burkett, the story became fodder for the election wars. Advocates for Mr. Bush claimed the documents proved that CBS, and by extension the mainstream media, was using its power to unfairly influence the election. Defenders of Mr. Rather argued that the content of the story was true and that the facts had been confirmed by the White House, even though the copies of the documents might be in question. In the end, the Killian documents had the effect of taking the topic of Bush's military service off the table and giving CBS an ugly bruise under its iconic eye.

On April 14, 2005, Lou Dobbs, news anchor and commentator on CNN, introduced a segment on leprosy—Hansen's disease—with the sonorous pronouncement that "the invasion of illegal aliens is threatening the health of many Americans." The correspondent, Christine Romans, took it from there and, citing Dr. Madeleine Cosman, a "medical lawyer," said that in the United States "there were about 900 cases of leprosy for 40 years. There have been 7,000 in the past three years."

"Incredible," Mr. Dobbs replied.[3]

Incredible indeed. Two years later, when Lesley Stahl interviewed Dobbs on *60 Minutes*, she asked about the evidence for this charge. "Well, I can tell you this," Dobbs said. "If we reported it, it's a fact."[4]

The next night, on his own program, Dobbs brought Romans back and had her repeat her assertion, adding that, if anything, it was probably an underestimate. In fact the original source for Ms. Romans's number was a poorly researched article called "Illegal Aliens and American Medicine," by a person with a doctorate in English, not biology or medicine. The publisher was the *Journal of American Association of Physicians and Surgeons*, a small conservative group not known as a reliable source on this topic. In her article, Cosman wrote: "Leprosy now is endemic to northeastern states because illegal aliens and other immigrants brought leprosy from India, Brazil, the Caribbean, and Mexico."[5]

According to the Department of Health and Human Services, the real number of leprosy cases reported in the United States in the last three years is 439. Seven thousand is the number of cases reported in the last *thirty years*. Cosman had apparently misinterpreted the public data to prove a political point. Romans, the reporter, had found the article supportive of the theory she was advancing and used it without confirming either the veracity of the data or the credibility of the source. And Dobbs refused to consider the possibility that he was wrong, then or since. In the interview, Stahl challenged him again. "How can you guarantee that [number] to me?" And Dobbs replied: "Because I'm the managing editor, and that's the way we do business. We don't make up numbers, Lesley. Do we?"[6]

Any major newspaper or national network news show would have fired its reporter for such a stunt, but cable television news apparently holds itself to a lower standard. During the devastation of Hurricane Katrina, some reporters were not satisfied with the drama and tragedy wrought by nature and felt compelled to make things up. On Fox News, correspondent Arthel Neville described the horror of what was going on:

> NEVILLE: One guy gets into a scuffle with a National Guardsman, takes the gun and kills the guardsman with the gun. Another guy, this is really sad, if there are any children watching take them out of a room. A man rapes and kills a 7-year-old girl.

About 10 guys, I don't know how many, but a group of guys turn around and beat this guy to death. This is just horrible. I cannot wrap my mind around how—the human—a human person can be reduced to such animalistic behavior. I don't understand it.[7]

The New Orleans police department said later that there were no substantiated reports of rapes—no victim reports and no eyewitnesses. There was a single homicide inside the Convention Center, but none inside the Superdome.

On December 6, 2001, Fox News correspondent Geraldo Rivera was in Afghanistan, reporting on the tragic deaths of several US servicemen as a result of another misguided US bombing raid. With an onscreen graphic showing his location as "Tora Bora," Rivera told his story:

We walked over what I consider hallowed ground today. We walked over the spot where the friendly fire took so many of our, our men and the mujahedeen yesterday. It was just, the whole place just fried really, and bits of uniforms and tattered clothing everywhere. I said the Lord's Prayer and really choked up. I can almost choke up relating the story to you right now; it was so melancholy, so sad.[8]

Except that David Folkenflik, then a reporter for the *Baltimore Sun*, pointed out the next week in his own story on the incident that the bombing raid had actually occurred in Kandahar, three hundred miles away. Rivera could not possibly have done or seen the things he claimed. But when challenged, he dismissed the discrepancy, explaining that he might have confused the Kandahar incident with another that occurred at Tora Bora. Except that couldn't be true either. As a Pentagon spokesman pointed out, the battle in Tora Bora to which Rivera was referring actually happened three days after his report aired.[9]

As *Fox News* commentator Bill O'Reilly said on another occasion:

> In my thirty years of practicing journalism, I have never seen things this bad. Newspapers will print anything. The Internet's full of lies and misinformation. And many TV and radio people will literally put anything on the air. So what is happening in America is that all of us are getting false information and forming opinions based on fallacious material. That of course also hurts others, and is devastating to a country that depends on truth to make fair policy.[10]

Faking the news has always had powerful enablers. For decades the tobacco industry sponsored research purporting to show that secondhand smoke was not harmful, and this research was published by even the most serious scientific journals.[11] The drug industry has long paid researchers under the table to write falsely favorable articles and get them published in the popular as well as the professional press, even about the most serious diseases.[12] But in 2001 the US Department of Defense took this deceitful practice to a new level. According to investigative reporting by David Barstow of the *New York Times*, the Pentagon recruited as many as seventy-five retired generals and high-ranking officers, many with business connections to defense contractors, and coached them to appear on television news shows as "military analysts," offering opinions that supported the department's current message. Participants were given private tours of critical military installations including Iraq and Guantánamo prison. They were provided access to classified intelligence and briefed by Secretary Rumsfeld and Vice President Cheney, as well as by White House counsel and later Attorney General Alberto Gonzales and others at the Department of Justice and the State Department. All in secret. According to Robert S. Bevelacqua, a retired Green Beret and former *Fox News* analyst: "It was them saying 'we want to stick our hands up your back and move your mouth for you.'"[13] Often the information they were given was dramatically different from what turned out later to be the truth. "Night and day," said Kenneth Allard, former *NBC News* military analyst. "I felt we'd been hosed."

As the administration ramped up its argument for an invasion of Iraq, the program shifted into high gear. This cadre of "independent experts" began to appear on every channel, shilling for the latest administration story, confirming the wisdom of whatever the Pentagon wanted to do. Under the direction of Victoria Clarke, assistant secretary of Defense for Public Affairs, talking points were prepared and distributed, program participants were coached on how to handle the different news organizations, and soon the air was filled with the sound of uniform approval. According to Brent T. Krueger, an assistant to Ms. Clarke:

> You could see that they were messaging. . . . You could see they were taking verbatim what the secretary was saying or what the technical specialists were saying. And they were saying it over and over and over. . . . We were able to click on every single station and every one of our folks were up there delivering our message. You'd look at them and say, "This is working."[14]

It is not surprising that the program was attempted. What is surprising is how easily it succeeded. News organizations didn't ask how it was that these men were so well informed. Or maybe the editors just didn't want to know.

In his book, *Bad News*, Tom Fenton, veteran foreign correspondent for CBS News, describes how in 1990 his colleagues in Sarajevo caught on video the details of a murderous attack on a schoolroom in which the teacher and several children were killed. It seemed emblematic of the tragedy of that war, and when New York didn't air the story, the reporters called to find out why. "The piece was fine," said Eric Sorenson, then Executive Producer of the *Evening News*. "It really was, a pretty good piece—solid, moving. But you know I just find that whole war over there very depressing."[15]

In 2008 the United States government will spend about $144 billion on the war in Iraq and Afghanistan, more than on NASA

($17 billion), National Science Foundation ($6.4 billion), National Institutes of Health ($28 billion), aid to elementary and secondary schools ($45 billion), energy research ($10 billion), and research into weather control and climate change ($10 billion) combined. But in mid-2008, according to Lara Logan, chief foreign correspondent for CBS News, CBS did not have a single reporter on the ground in Iraq.[16]

CBS Evening News had devoted less than sixty minutes to the subject over six months. The other networks have done only slightly better. According to the Project for Excellence in Journalism, network coverage of the Iraq war dropped from 23 percent of the newshole in the first ten weeks of 2007 to 3 percent for the same period in 2008. Coverage by cable network news channels dropped from 24 percent to 1 percent.[17] Whether these shows style themselves as "world news," "evening news," or "news headlines," they can hardly be called truthful reports on the important events in our world.

In their widely cited 1988 book, *Manufacturing Consent*, Edward Herman and Noam Chomsky argue that the news media are untrustworthy but for a different reason. The authors assert that news organizations are subject to influence in five ways. First, because the companies are owned by large corporations, the choice of news by print or broadcast editors is often tailored to reflect the profit interests of their owners. Second, because they depend on advertising revenue, editors filter the news to favor their largest advertisers. Third, editors depend on the cooperation of government and private sector sources and are reluctant to publish news that is critical or embarrassing to those sources. Fourth, editors are sensitive to public criticism of their product—Herman and Chomsky call this "flak"—and they don't run pieces that they know will generate a strong negative response. Finally, they argue, the media have a tendency to be "anti-communist" or, more broadly, anti-ideology. Today they might be antiterrorism.[18] In my own experience as a news executive and consultant to media companies, these assertions are only partly true and they miss the larger issue.

Small and medium newspapers are more likely than large ones to bend the news in response to the profit concerns of their owners. The major market newspapers and television stations that set the national news agenda depend on being able to hire from the senior ranks of professional journalists and they would not be able to do so if someone from corporate regularly phoned down to the newsroom and leaned on the editor. Whatever profit motives the owners have are difficult to transfer to the people who actually put together the news.

I spent a year as executive editor of UPI, the worldwide news service, moving the organization, news format, and communications systems toward a new model that we thought would be more successful in the emerging Internet environment and, although I am not a journalist, I had responsibility for the wire service content as well. One day I got a call from a man representing the Saudi sheik who owned the company at that time. He felt that a report we had done about the Israeli-Palestinian situation poorly captured the Arab view, and he was concerned. I listened, I looked at the story, and he was right. I passed his comments along to the bureau chief, and we tried harder to hear both sides after that. In the years I worked as a media executive or consultant, that was the clearest example I saw, and it wasn't much. Nor have I heard the bend-the-news argument from many inside the media. Of course it happens from time to time, but media employees make news for a living, and in their free time they write books. We would have heard more about it.[19]

The notion that advertisers might influence news coverage is also difficult to support. Advertisers worry all the time about having a sympathetic context for their messages. But they are savvy enough to understand that the most important asset of any news medium is the readers' trust, and as soon as stories start getting altered to fit the commercial interests of the advertisers, those readers will take their eyeballs and their buying power elsewhere. Herman and Chomsky argue: "In addition to discrimination against unfriendly media institutions, advertisers also choose selectively among programs on the basis of their own principles. With rare exceptions these are culturally and politically conservative. Large corporate advertisers on television will rarely sponsor programs that engage in serious criticisms of corporate activities, such as the problem of environmental degradation, the workings of the military-industrial complex or corporate support of and benefits from Third World tyrannies."[20]

This may have been true years ago, but TV news programs are rarely "sponsored" by a single advertiser anymore. Newspapers and newsmagazines have never been sponsored that way. Today, advertising agencies representing companies like Procter and Gamble, AT&T, Ford, Johnson & Johnson, and McDonald's buy space and availabilities based on reach, frequency, demographics, and cost per thousand. Not politics.

Editors and reporters do depend entirely too much, though, on sources they have cosseted for years. It is worse than that; they are friends. But Herman and Chomsky claim that the millions of dollars spent by government and corporations on press releases and story packages have overwhelmed the media's objectivity. Wrong. The average newsroom of a major newspaper or broadcast news program gets several thousand wire stories, press releases, photos, and independent contributions every day, and while the facts often inform the reporting, the point of view they contain is usually bleached out. The decision on which seventy or eighty items to run each day is usually made by a group: diverse, cynical, middle-aged, and of differing political persuasions. They don't like the government at all. They don't like large corporations very much, and their feelings toward publishers can be politely described as conflicted and confused.

It is true in my experience that newspapers and news broadcast programs shy away from stories that might offend their audience, and for the most persuasive reason. To make money in the current advertising-supported media business you have to cost-effectively attract and deliver a unique and desirable audience segment, and in the post–mass media age that segment is ever more specifically defined. It isn't like the old days. *Life Magazine* was subscribed to by 10 percent of all American households in the 1950s, becoming the nation's family album and a shared image of our lives. In the 1970s, Norman Lear's television comedy *All in the Family* was viewed every week by an astonishing 20 percent of American households, while bravely offering a common vocabulary for discussing the country's most controversial and divisive issues. But by the end of 2007, *CBS News with Katie Couric* was watched by only 6 percent of the television audience, flanked by *The News Hour with Jim Lehrer* (2 percent), and *The O'Reilly Factor* (2 percent), each serving very different segments. There is no longer a single news or information outlet trying to satisfy more than small, opinionated fraction of the community. And their content shows it.

Talking about her tenure as a television correspondent for ABC News from 2003 to 2007, Jessica Yellin described the pattern of spinning the news to fit what executives perceived as the current popular opinion:

> The press corps was under enormous pressure from corporate executives, frankly, to make sure that [the Iraq] war was presented in a way that was consistent with the patriotic fever in the nation and the president's high approval ratings. . . . And my own experience at the White House was that the higher the president's approval ratings, the more pressure I had from news executives . . . to put on positive stories about the president.[21]

All news organizations, including newsletters and Internet blogs, adopt the concepts and values of the community that supports them. They accept the reader's beliefs, they use the reader's language, and they abide by the truth system in place, establishing the veracity of whatever they are saying by appealing to the standard of truth their intended community employs—authority, tradition, science, or divine revelation. Publishers and broadcasters tell their intended readers what they want to hear, not always what they need to know. In the echo chamber of modern media the owners are struggling to survive by following the "least objectionable programming" model to its absurd extreme.

This means that an examination of any given newspaper, magazine, news program, or blog will show distortions of fact, editorial bias, and loaded language. But it also means that some news organizations, trusted by their engaged and skeptical readers, will support investigative journalism heroes like the fearless Seymour Hersh at the *New Yorker*, Walter Pincus at the *Washington Post*, Michael Isikoff at *Newsweek*, and many others who regularly swim out into the fog of secrecy and deception and bring back stories in their teeth. In the past, publishers large and small, liberal and conservative, have risked their profits, subjected themselves to libel litigation, and put their personal and professional reputations on the line, challenging government and special interests because the audience they have chosen to serve expects it of them. And they continue to do so.

The larger issue is not the fulminations of an overfed and self-important press, or the bias of a publisher who has friends in the military-industrial complex. It is that the information is often just not true. Through conspiratorial indifference and a kind of batty codependency with its sources, the media have allowed stories onto their pages and into their broadcasts that have proven to be false. More interested in accuracy than truth, and more interested in entertainment than accuracy, the media often serve as towel boys to power, fluffing the hard questions and overlooking the unflattering facts. They have to be nice to get the interviews. The threat of libel will stop a story cold; expensive lawyers will leap like Dobermans to the alarm. But the average newsroom lacks the resources and the time to go looking for truth. And in recent years the press has been fooled too often by corporations, special-interest groups, and government campaigns that seek to alter public opinion through dissemination of false information.

This is propaganda, and it has been part of American public discourse since colonial politicians adopted the practice of referring to King George III and his cabinet as boors, fuddy-duddies, too-little-and-too-laters, and conspicuous nincompoops.[22] Today companies do it through public relations. Special-interest groups and political parties do it through lavishly funded campaigns of misinformation, advertising, and phony news stunts. Industries do it through false flag "research" and lobbying. But no one has done it better or to greater effect in recent years than the United States government.

> See, in my line of work you got to keep repeating things over and over and over again for the truth to sink in, to kind of catapult the propaganda (*President George W. Bush*).[23]

MANUFACTURING TRUTH

The process of propaganda is ancient and well-known. Through the centuries, certain elements have emerged more frequently than others as necessary for success.

The Big Lie. The purpose of propaganda is to establish by surreptitious means the widespread belief in a single, simple, vivid proposition that, like every great lie, has elements of truth. Good advertising messages start with what the audience currently believes and then provide as little new information as necessary to bring the believer to a new understanding. Propaganda, too, succeeds most often when it is the alteration of an existing concept already connected to other strongly held beliefs. It doesn't launch a new brand; it makes the changes and calls it "new and improved." The best propaganda doesn't argue; it distorts and extends an existing concept.

Sometimes the big lie is played out on a small scale. In the fall of 2007, R. J. Reynolds, which manufactures six of the ten leading brands of cigarettes in the United States, mounted a campaign to defeat an Oregon ballot initiative that would have raised the cigarette tax 85 cents a pack to pay healthcare costs for uninsured children. Calling itself "Oregonians against the Blank Check," the company did not fight the idea of better healthcare for children, nor did it directly oppose the idea of increasing the cigarette tax. Both were established concepts widely supported by the public. Instead, it extended the popular preconception that the new funds would be squandered by the government, and blew on the coals of an existing debate over whether to amend the state constitution. With a war chest of $12 million, the company flooded local television with ads that, according to the *Oregon Daily Emerald*, distorted the facts of the program, lied about where the money would go, and fanned the fears of more government incompetence and corruption.[24] Healthy Kids Oregon, a not-for-profit advocacy group dependent upon donations, could not afford to compete in the media war and their initiative was defeated.

Emotions. The proposition should evoke strong emotions, preferably fear, pride, prejudice, or patriotism. It should appeal not to reason, which might be swayed in argument, but to deeper and more primitive values that will evoke an emotional reaction. We give too much credit to the rational mind and forget that opinions follow beliefs, and beliefs are usually rooted invisibly in some underlying conviction that has been there since childhood. The best propaganda reaches deep.

Framing. One of the most powerful tricks of the propagandist is to present his message using language, images, sounds, and even smells that evoke a strong memory, fear, or belief. This has a way of pretagging the experience for the lazy listener, establishing a synaptic link that reason alone might not have made. At a simple level, things are just misnamed. A program to expand logging on public lands is called the "Healthy Forests Initiative." "Patriotism," "Support Our Troops," and even the image of the American flag came to be associated with pro-war sentiment at the beginning of the Iraq invasion, even though many patriots who supported our troops were opposed to the war. Bill Clinton spoke of an America that "worked hard and played by the rules," implying that his opponent represented people who did neither. At a sillier level, slot machines in Las Vegas often jingle to the theme song from the television comedy *The Simpsons*, hoping, perhaps, that the gambler will look at risk the way the feckless father, Homer, does.[25] And Blockbuster, the video rental chain, experimented with releasing different aromas in different sections of their store: the smell of gunpowder in the action aisle, bananas in the comedy section, and roses in the romance row.[26]

The most powerful use of this technique, however, has been the careful and comprehensive presentation of a political program within the frame of a cultural metaphor. George Lakoff, professor of linguistics, describes how the second Bush administration carefully positioned its political views in language that evoked a deep-seated American myth:

> In foreign policy, the Bush administration uses a strict father model, and it says that only force works. Only punishment works. Moreover, it says that the strict father—in this case, Bush—is the moral authority. The U.S. knows better than anybody else. And they're certainly not going to ask other people who are presumably less moral than we are what we should do and how we should behave. That's why we go it alone. We have to preserve our sovereignty.
>
> A strict father [is one] who supports and protects the family, who raises children to know right from wrong, who raises his children to be able to take care of themselves in the world. He does it in only one way—by strength and punishment. Only punishment works. Only shows of strength work. That is part of the family model that's involved, and it's also part of the politics involved. When you have fear in the country, fear evokes a strict

father model. It's to the conservatives' advantage to keep people afraid, to keep having orange alerts, to keep having announcements that they have secret information that there might be a bombing somewhere in the country. As long as you keep people afraid, you reinforce the strict father model.[27]

Politicians, business executives and even siblings work hard to create a "narrative" about themselves, and particularly about their rivals.[28] "He's an elitist who doesn't understand what working families face every day." "Watch out for Charlie, he always has a trick up his sleeve." "She's a big fat liar." When the facts are sparse, ambiguous, or conflicting, information that fits the prevailing concept about your opponent's motivation and values tends to stick, and what doesn't is denied, ignored or forgotten.

Evidence. However it is presented, the premise of propaganda is supported by detailed information, witnesses, testimony, and science, all the trappings of truth. But this isn't a courtroom. Don't count on the logical process of testimony and cross-examination. What Geraldo Rivera knew how to do was take a few facts handed to him on a scrap of paper and invest in them the breath of life—the bits of uniforms and tattered clothing, the choking up as he spoke. That's why reporters use quotes. That's why fund-raisers present real case studies of their charity in action, and why politicians tell personal stories in their State of the Union addresses. Lofty, abstract descriptions do not tickle the thalamus.

Repetition. The proposition and the supporting evidence should be repeated as often as possible, and the biology of the brain tells us why. Synapses are strengthened through repeated use, and a strong concept, broadly extended through emotions, memories, visual images, and sound, will even inhibit competing concepts by repeated stimulation. "A lie told often enough becomes truth," said Vladimir Lenin over and over again,

Endorsement. To prevail, a false proposition should be attended by independent witnesses who will vouch for its truth. It is routine in advertising to have celebrities offer their endorsement of products, even in areas where they have little personal expertise. Movies are reviewed. Books are adorned with blurbs. A recent study of the factors that motivate online sales showed that 44 percent of shoppers cited independent customer reviews as one of the primary elements in their decision to purchase, even though the manufacturer and the retailer have made a great effort to provide more detailed and sometimes more accurate product descriptions.[29] Research over the years into how science and technology workers acquire information has always shown that the most important and most trusted source is a colleague. You not only get the information, you also get an independent appraisal of its value.

Certainty. Nothing is as painful to the mind as confusion. To prevail, a proposition must be stated in the simplest and most certain terms, using identical language every time. By the same rule, any competing proposition must be made to appear confusing and uncertain. It is often unnecessary to disprove the other concept; you merely have to make it hard to understand. To weaken the idea that global warming is caused by humans, for example, it is only necessary to persistently point out the complications, the ambiguities, and the conflicting testimony, while offering the simpler argument that global warming is just a theory and anyway there is nothing we can do about it. The truth is often complicated, while lies are simple by design. Sooner or later people will give up, or at least withhold commitment.

When Nobel laureate and climate scientist Steven W. Running agreed to talk to high school students in Choteau, Montana, residents of that largely conservative town complained, saying that the presentation should be cancelled unless both sides of the global warming issue were presented. Superintendent Kevin St. John agreed. Later, when Kirk Moore, one of the leaders of the group, was asked why he thought concerns about the climate were misplaced, and why the speech had to be cancelled, he said he had no comment.[30]

Punishment. And those who disagree shall be punished. The history of propaganda is a lurid tale of torture and repression, and modern propaganda differs only in degree. Roger Boisjoly was ostracized by his colleagues after challenging the NASA culture. In the months leading up to 9/11, people were harshly criticized for pushing the Able Danger project. When the accounting firm of Arthur Andersen began to publicly question Enron's books, the firm was fired. In advancing a false proposition, it is crucial that dissenters be silenced and threats of discipline and demotion should be wielded with an iron hand. What you don't want is a debate.

Momentum. Propaganda frightens and defeats people through the constant repetition of simple, evocative, and emotional messages. As people come to realize that the proposition is going to be accepted by everyone else, they cease to resist. In that way information wars are peculiar; when you win, the people don't come out with their hands up. They just pull down the shades and busy themselves at something else. The vote is taken, the propaganda prevails, and no one asks later how it was that truth could be so easily defeated.

In a speech to the officer corps on August 22, 1939, days before the German invasion of Poland, Hitler said that truth doesn't matter: "I shall give the propagandist a cause for starting the war. Never mind whether it is plausible; the victor is never asked whether he told the truth or not."[31]

There is no example in the last fifty years as broad in scope or as tragic in its outcome as the propaganda effort undertaken by a few men and women in the second Bush administration to justify the invasion of Iraq. In the summer of 2004, the Senate Intelligence Committee released a 511-page report on the intelligence community's pre-war assessments on Iraq, and it concluded:

> Most of the major key judgments in the Intelligence Community's October 2002 National Intelligence Estimate (NIE), Iraq's

Continuing Programs for Weapons of Mass Destruction, either overstated, or were not supported by, the underlying intelligence reporting. A series of failures, particularly in analytic trade craft, led to the mischaracterization of the intelligence.[32]

Iraq had no weapons of mass destruction. There was no affiliation or alliance between Iraq and al Qaeda,[33] and Iraq had nothing to do with the 9/11 attack on the World Trade Center. Although Saddam Hussein was a despot, there was no evidence to suggest that he represented a near-term threat either to the United States or to his neighbors. Nor was Iraq an important part of any international terrorism conspiracy. In his memoir, *At the Center of the Storm*, former CIA director George Tenet got it wrong when he said, "We got it wrong."[34] He should have said, "We lied."

At the time of its report on prewar intelligence failures, the Democratic members of the Senate committee made clear their hope that a second phase of the study would examine how this false intelligence was used by senior policy makers within the administration. But the chairman, Kansas Republican senator Pat Roberts, managed to put off that part of the study for a year, and even then he said there were two areas where questions should be further delayed. False statements made to the public by senior administration officials did not need to be explored, he said.[35] Nor do we need to know more about the Pentagon's Office of Special Plans, run by Paul Wolfowitz and Douglas Feith, which had been the source of so many of the "intelligence errors." Roberts said he thought it would be a "monumental waste of time to plow this ground any further."[36]

But with the war in Iraq still raging and the outlook for the Middle East far from certain, we need to ask these questions. It is not about the past, as Senator Roberts said. It is about the future. How was the false case against Iraq so easily won? How is it that the media, Congress, and the people of the United States were unable to see through the phony information in time? And what does it mean for the future of democracy when a small group of ideologues can manufacture and disseminate false information so skillfully that they roll the country into war?

THERE IS LESS TO THIS THAN MEETS THE EYE

In the next ten to fifteen years, the world's consumption of oil will begin to outpace production; demand will exceed supply. At that point, the petroleum reserves of many countries will have been exhausted and most of the oil remaining in the world will be in the Middle East. According to a recent report from the US Government Accountability Office (GAO), Saudi Arabia had 23 percent of the world's oil reserves in 2006, Iran 11.6 percent, Iraq 10.1 percent, Kuwait 9.1 percent, and the United Arab Republic 8.6 percent. The United States, which consumes a quarter of the world's production each year, has less than 2 percent of the world's reserves.[37] But as Stephen Pelletiére points out in his study *Iraq and the International Oil System*, the problem is not just that America is increasingly dependent upon the Middle East for the oil necessary to sustain its economy. It is also hostage to price. In 1974, when Saudi Arabia and OPEC blocked sales of oil to the United States in response to Israel's defeat of Egypt and Syria in the Yom Kippur War, the result was to immediately double the price of crude oil at the refinery level, toppling the US economy into recession. By 1974 the price of oil had quadrupled to $12 a barrel in the United States, gasoline rose 50 percent in a few months, and stocks on the New York Exchange lost nearly $100 billion in value in six weeks. The embargo was later lifted, but the inflation it triggered lasted in the United States for the rest of the decade. The ten largest oil reserves in the world came under the direct control of their respective governments, and in this war without bullets, America was defenseless. As long as Saudi Arabia remained a close ally, the United States could reasonably hope that another oil shock would be avoided, but with China rising as an economic competitor, roaring for oil, and Muslim fundamentalists gaining influence in Egypt, Iran, and Saudi Arabia, it was prudent for the United States to consider its alternatives.

One of those was military action. By 1999 the Department of Defense had expanded its understanding of "national security" to include economic security as well as military strength, and a report, *Strategic Assessment 1999*, prepared for the Joint Chiefs of Staff, envisaged that if "oil problems" arise, "US forces might be used to ensure adequate supplies."[38] Iraq, in particular, was a sentimental target. The Clinton administration had a policy to remove Saddam Hussein from power:

> Saddam Hussein must not be allowed to develop nuclear arms, poison gas, biological weapons, or the means to deliver them. He has used such weapons before against soldiers and civilians, including his own people. We have no doubt that if left unchecked he would do so again. . . . So long as Saddam remains in power he will remain a threat to his people, his region and the world. With our allies, we must pursue a strategy to contain him and to constrain his weapons of mass destruction program, while working toward the day Iraq has a government willing to live at peace with its people and with its neighbors. (*President Bill Clinton, 1998*)[39]

For the incoming president, George W. Bush, it was personal. Osama Siblani, publisher of the *Arab American News*, remembers that while he was campaigning for office, Bush said he would remove Saddam from power. "He told me he was going to take him out," remembered Siblani.[40] "He wanted to go to Iraq and search for weapons of mass destruction, and he considered the regime an imminent and gathering threat." Bush family friend Mickey Herskowitz remembers another occasion when Bush said essentially the same thing: "One of the keys to being seen as a great leader is to be seen as a commander-in-chief. My father had all this political capital built up when he drove the Iraqis out of

[Kuwait] and he wasted it. If I have a chance to invade Iraq, if I had that much capital, I'm not going to waste it. I'm going to get everything passed I want to get passed and I'm going to have a successful presidency."[41]

But the disruptive reality of 9/11 made the issue of Iraq not just economic, political, or personal. It demonstrated that if terrorists got their hands on biological, chemical, or nuclear weapons they could wreak unimaginable destruction. The policy of containment might have weakened Iraq, but the nightmare of a suitcase bomb, an anthrax attack, or a toxic cloud launched by an enemy with no country to protect was now more frightening than ever. The incoming administration worried that Iraq might make such weapons available to the growing ranks of terrorists. Thus, they reasoned, knocking Saddam Hussein from power was an act of self-defense. Not incidentally in this grand syzygy of interests, an invasion of Iraq would nicely address three other issues as well. Even if a post-Saddam government emerged as independent of US influence, the oil fields, having been administered by the Americans during the transition, would come out shackled to long-term price-controlled contracts with the major US oil companies. The brisk, muscular invasion of a troublesome Middle Eastern country might also provide a splendid demonstration of America's indomitable power while giving the US military a new long-term base of operations in the troubled region. And, finally, taking the country to war—if only briefly—would bring to the office of the president expanded powers and political influence that both President Bush and Vice President Cheney felt had been ceded in previous administrations.

The only problem was that for the last few years the US government had been saying that Iraq was no longer a threat.

We do not have any direct evidence that Iraq has used the period since [Operation] Desert Fox to reconstitute its WMD programs, although given its past behavior, this type of activity must be regarded as likely. ... We assess that since the suspension of [UN] inspections in December of 1998, Baghdad has had the capability to reinitiate both its [chemical and biological weapons] program . . . without an inspection monitoring program, however, it is more difficult to determine if Iraq has done so. (*CIA Director George Tenet, testifying to Congress on February 7, 2001*)

The Iraqi regime militarily remains fairly weak. It doesn't have the capacity it had 10 or 12 years ago. It has been contained. And even though we have no doubt in our mind that the Iraqi regime is pursuing programs to develop weapons of mass destruction— chemical, biological and nuclear—I think the best intelligence estimates suggest that they have not been terribly successful. (*Secretary of State Colin Powell, testifying to Congress on May 15, 2001*)

[While Saddam Hussein is] a threat to his neighbors, a threat to security in the region, in fact a threat to international security more broadly . . . let's remember that his country is divided, in effect. He does not control the northern part of his country. We are able to keep arms from him. His military forces have not been rebuilt. (*National Security Adviser Condoleezza Rice, on CNN, July 29, 2001*)

MR. RUSSERT: Do we have evidence that [Saddam Hussein is] harboring terrorists?

VP CHENEY: There is—in the past, there have been some activities related to terrorism by Saddam Hussein. But at this stage, you know, the focus is over here on al-Qaeda and the most recent events in New York. Saddam Hussein is bottled up at this point, but clearly, we continue to have a fairly tough policy where the Iraqis are concerned.

MR. RUSSERT: Do we have any evidence linking Saddam Hussein or Iraqis to this operation?

VP CHENEY: No. (*Vice President Dick Cheney on "Meet the Press," September 16, 2001*)

To lead the country into war, then, American public opinion had to be reshaped through press conferences, speeches, and stories placed in, or "leaked" to the media. But just as important, the intelligence community had to present or support incriminating evidence. The task was difficult, but the prize would be a congressional resolution giving the president the power to wage war.

Fortunately, the tools for shaping public opinion were already in place. The Rendon Group, a Washington public relations firm, had been hired by the CIA in 1989 to help oust Panama's President Noriega, and in 1991 the company got a second contract, according to James Bamford, "to create conditions for removal of Hussein from power." In his article "The Man Who Sold the War,"[42] Bamford describes how John Rendon—married to Lewis Libby's sister—organized the Iraqi National Congress (INC) as a focal point for Iraqi defectors and dissidents eager to overthrow Saddam. With a first contract of $16 million, Rendon acted as a public relations office for the campaign, following the press coverage and placing favorable stories in media around the world. "I am not a national security strategist," Rendon told cadets at the US Air Force Academy in 1996. "I am a politician, a person who uses communication to meet public policy or corporate policy objectives. In fact I am an information warrior and a perception manager."[43] Rendon and his team funneled money, moved people, planted stories, and created an aura of stability and purpose around the ragtag defectors. And for the INC he and his team chose a leader, Ahmed Chalabi.

Born in Iraq, son of the Shiite president of the Iraqi Senate, Chalabi moved to London at the age of thirteen when Saddam Hussein seized power. He was sophisticated, ambitious, smart, and dishonest. He had been convicted of defrauding his Jordanian bank of $230 million but left the country in the trunk of a friend's car before he could be taken into custody. Now he was looking at an even larger scam—becoming the next president of Iraq. Chalabi set up shop in a Washington row house and began, with

Rendon's help, to make friends with Dick Cheney, Paul Wolfowitz, Richard Perle, Newt Gingrich, and other conservative
Republicans. With his assistant Francis Brooke, he lobbied for and
won nearly $100 million from Congress to plant stories about Iraq
in the world's press and make plans to take over the government.
Chalabi said that Saddam was developing weapons of mass
destruction. Chalabi said that Saddam was a brutal and inhuman
dictator, willing to gas his own people. Chalabi said that Saddam
was a conniving and treacherous world leader who desired only to
destabilize and conquer his neighbors.

The INC set up lavish offices in London, hired Burson-
Marsteller to manage the conferences and publications, and began
to recruit defectors and insurgents in Iraq and Iran. They launched
a newspaper that didn't really publish anything and a satellite TV
channel that went off the air after a few weeks. Chalabi bought
executive memberships in health clubs and paid out half a million
dollars for "intelligence" that proved completely useless.[44] In 1994
Chalabi and the INC set up a forgery shop in Iraq, where,
according to CIA agent Robert Baer, "people were scanning Iraqi
intelligence documents into computers, and doing disinformation
. . . in order to bring down Saddam."[45] Chalabi hated the CIA and
blamed it for a number of failed schemes in which he had been
involved. And they hated him, too, saying—with the benefit of
evidence—that he was handing US secrets over to Iran.[46]

In her April 2004 *New Yorker* profile of Chalabi, Jane Mayer
described his Washington town house as "filthy." "Newspapers
were strewn alongside half-empty coffee mugs, and ants carried
cookie crumbs across a leather couch, giving the place the atmosphere of a frat house." Chalabi's assistant Francis Brooke, his wife,
and their two children occupied some of the rooms, rent-free, and
in the basement, according to Mayer, was a "succession of Iraqi
exiles camping out." But the group was so successful in placing
disinformation with the world press that the stories began to wash
back into the American media. Federal law prohibits the govern-

ment from distributing propaganda within the United States, but bouncing it off the British and the Europeans was both legal and easy. "It was amazing how well it worked," Brooke said later. "It was like magic."[47]

By feeding their information to congressmen and government officials as well as to the press, Chalabi and the Rendon Group made it appear that the intelligence came from many different sources corroborating each other. But most of what they produced was lies. When the Knight Ridder Washington bureau looked at 108 articles attributed to Chalabi by news media in the United States and around the world, it found that in many cases the real sources turned out to be just the half-dozen defectors living in Chalabi's basement. The stories were often contested by the intelligence agencies, and yet they were widely quoted by White House and Department of Defense officials in support of the plan to invade Iraq. Among the major stories planted by Chalabi:

- Saddam Hussein collaborated with al Qaeda for years and was involved in the attack on the World Trade Center.
- Iraq trained the 9/11 hijackers and prepared them for the attack.
- Iraq had mobile biological warfare facilities disguised as yogurt and milk trucks, and hid banned weapons in hospitals and palaces.
- Iraq had the technology to launch Scud missiles loaded with toxins, able to kill one hundred thousand people at a time, and it was aggressively developing nuclear weapons.[48]

All false.

A similar public relations operation was run by British Intelligence. Called "Operation Mass Appeal," the propaganda shop was set up in the late 1990s to place false stories in the media in order to gain public support for an invasion of Iraq.[49] Scott Ritter, who led the UN inspection team in Iraq, later admitted that he had been recruited by the British to provide the essential facts necessary for verisimilitude. (He was also being recruited by Chalabi, who promised to give him a piece of the oil business once his INC party was in power.) "The aim was to convince the public that Iraq was a far greater threat than it actually was," Ritter said. "Stories ran in the media about secret underground facilities in Iraq and ongoing programs [to produce weapons of mass destruction]. They were sourced to western intelligence and all of them were garbage."[50] According to Nicholas Rufford of the *Sunday Times*, Sir Derek Plumbly, then director of the Middle East department at the British Foreign Office, worked closely with the top secret team to spread this disinformation around the world, claiming that Iraq was secretly rebuilding its weapons arsenal. Prime Minister Tony Blair then referred to these stories in defending harsher sanctions against Iraq, and the United States referred to Blair's claims as corroborating evidence for its own campaign. Other high officials from the British government were involved, but the *Sunday Times*, which broke the story months before the bombing began, was prevented by the Official Secrets Act from revealing the names.[51]

Dealing with the intelligence community, though, required a different set of skills. In the earliest days of the new Bush administration, Deputy Secretary of Defense Paul Wolfowitz and Douglas Feith set up a top secret operation inside the Pentagon to gather, select, and disseminate intelligence favorable to the overthrow of Saddam Hussein. Feith had served as a Middle East specialist on the National Security Council in the Reagan administration, during which time he urged Israel to protect its borders by attacking Iraq. Opinions of his intelligence and skill were strong and varied. He was famously described by General Tommy Franks as "the dumbest fucking guy on the planet"[52] and by Secretary of Defense Donald Rumsfeld as "without question one of the most brilliant individuals in government."[53]

People working for Feith complained that he would spend hours tweaking their memos, carefully mulling minor points of grammar. A Joint Staff officer recalled angrily that at one point troops sat on a runway for hours, waiting to leave the United States on a mission, while Feith quibbled about commas in the deployment order. "Policy was a black hole," recalled one four-star general about Feith's operation. "It dropped the ball again and again." In the summer of 2001, Feith had been confronted on his management flaws by top aides at a large meeting. Lisa Bronson, a veteran specialist on weapons proliferation, stood and said, "This is the worst-run policy office I've ever seen." Another Feith aide agreed, saying later that the decision-making process in Feith's office was the most tangled he'd seen in twenty years of government work. Feith stood his ground, explaining to subordinates that "I don't treat you any differently than Rumsfeld treats me."[54]

Spurning the military intelligence professionals in place, Feith staffed the office with like-minded conservatives from the American Enterprise Institute who lacked intelligence experience but believed, as he and Wolfowitz did, that the CIA had been lax in gathering evidence of Saddam's evil intentions. They began to scour old reports and sketchy intelligence to support their view. They, too, were ardent sponsors of Ahmed Chalabi and they chauffeured him around the world as the president-in-waiting. They ridiculed existing intelligence organizations and piped their findings directly to Vice President Cheney and to his aide, Lewis Libby, who had been a student of Wolfowitz's at Yale. They called themselves the Office of Special Plans. Secretary of State Powell called them the "fucking crazies."[55]

As intelligence analysts, they were not impartial. In 1992, drafting a national strategic policy for Secretary of Defense Dick Cheney, Wolfowitz and Libby had urged a new posture in which the country would rely less on the United Nations and other international security agreements and instead create temporary US-led "coalitions" of nations that might not last beyond the limits of the immediate conflict. The paper advocated a substantial increase in the country's military presence around the world, "to discourage [advanced industrial nations, particularly Germany and Japan] from challenging our leadership or seeking to overturn the established political and economic order."[56] In subsequent papers they helped draft for the Project for a New American Century, Wolfowitz, Cheney, Rumsfeld, Libby, and Feith advocated the invasion of Iraq in order to establish new and incontestable American power in the Middle East and over the rest of the world:

> America has a vital role in maintaining peace and security in Europe, Asia, and the Middle East. If we shirk our responsibilities, we invite challenges to our fundamental interests. The history of the twentieth century should have taught us that it is important to shape circumstances before crises emerge, and to meet threats before they become dire. The history of the past century should have taught us to embrace the cause of American leadership.[57]

The movement had its big lie: Iraq was a clear and present danger. Manufactured news stories were reaching emotions still twitching from 9/11: anger, fear, and patriotism. They had two machines to produce the evidence: Chalabi's INC and Feith's Office of Special Plans. And now the administration required an endorsement. They needed a prestigious newspaper or television news network that would give their stories top play every day, a national news organization with an unflinching loyalty to the neocon's worldview and a jaunty disregard for truth. And for this they chose the *New York Times*. The newspaper itself had a strong history of opposing the policies of the second Bush administration and a stronger tradition of supporting internationalism and diplomacy, which made it even more miraculous that in its midst, and on its front pages with surprising regularity, was Judith Miller. With Laurie Mylroie, the Saddam conspiracy theorist, Miller had published a brief primer on

Saddam Hussein in 1990, just as the first Iraq war was breaking out.[58] Since then she had courted most of the politicians and power brokers of the emerging conservative leadership. According to her friends, she was ambitious, undisciplined, and ready to party.[59] According to her colleagues, she was a disaster waiting to happen. As early as 2000, *New York Times* editors were receiving, and ignoring, the reddest of journalistic flags. Craig Pyes asked that his byline be removed from a story on al Qaeda he had cowritten with Miller, and he sent a warning:

> I'm not willing to work further on this project with Judy Miller. . . .
> I do not trust her work, her judgment, or her conduct. She is an
> advocate, and her actions threaten the integrity of the enterprise,
> and of everyone who works with her. . . . She has turned in a draft
> of a story of a collective enterprise that is little more than dictation
> from government sources over several days, filled with unproven
> assertions and factual inaccuracies, [and] tried to stampede it into
> the paper.[60]

Miller was perfect for the job.

After years of ineffective argument and accusation against Iraq, the September 11 attack on the World Trade Center and the Pentagon was, for the United States government, an extraordinary opportunity. With the Rendon/Chalabi propaganda project being conducted surreptitiously by the White House and the war advocacy project churning away in the secret reaches of the Pentagon, the administration set about to shift the public's anger and fear onto Iraq.

Cheney, Rumsfeld, Wolfowitz, and Feith were beating the drums. Every ear was on alert for a premise, any premise, on which to hang the argument for war. The story to be established immediately was that al Qaeda had operated with Iraq's explicit support and collusion, and for this charge they needed evidence. That took two days. The Czech intelligence agency told a CIA liaison that

Mohamed Atta might have been seen talking to an Iraqi diplomat in a Prague restaurant in early April, and a week later the White House leaked the story to the Associated Press with all the uncertainty removed: "A US official, speaking on condition of anonymity, said the United States has received information from a foreign intelligence service that Mohamed Atta, a hijacker aboard one of the planes that slammed into the World Trade Center, met earlier this year in Europe with an Iraqi intelligence agent."[61]

Within two weeks, the Czech government appeared to climb down from this report, saying it could confirm only that Atta had connected through the Prague airport on his way from Germany to Newark. But by then the story was on the wing.

Over the next few weeks, a choir of memos, op-ed pieces, and public letters, all conducted by Wolfowitz and Feith, rose in song on the subject of a link between Saddam Hussein and the events of 9/11. Laurie Mylroie's old arguments were exhumed, and dire accusations were once again hurled. President Bush said he saw no distinction between bin Laden and Saddam Hussein. "The danger is, is that they work in concert. The danger is, is that al Qaeda becomes an extension of Saddam's madness and his hatred and his capacity to extend weapons of destruction around the world."[62] The following day, Secretary of Defense Rumsfeld announced that the United States had "bulletproof" confirmation of ties between the Iraqi government and al Qaeda members, including "solid evidence" of an al Qaeda presence in Iraq. Knight Ridder's Washington bureau refuted the claim after several days of research, saying there was no such evidence,[63] but the ardor slackened not at all. The eyes were glowing now, and the Atta story moved forward into the popular consciousness.

There was also a more subtle campaign. In press conferences, news program appearances, and official statements, the emphasis was shifted away from bin Laden. The attacks in Afghanistan went forward, but judging by the results—particularly at Tora Bora—it was a half-hearted effort. After all, if bin Laden was caught or killed, public demand for revenge would be sated. The war against the terrorists would have been won, and "the larger opportunity," as Wolfowitz called it, would be lost. No, the strategy for dealing with bin Laden was that he should fade away and the anger focused on him should be shifted to Saddam Hussein. The White House stopped mentioning bin Laden. On October 10, the US television networks were asked to stop showing bin Laden videos on the strange theory that they might contain coded messages to terrorists around the world. The networks agreed. And when it seemed for a moment that Pakistan might hand over bin Laden himself, the US government looked the other way. Leaders of Pakistan's two Islamic parties said that over the objections of President Musharraf, they had negotiated with Mullah Omar for bin Laden's extradition to Pakistan, where an international tribunal would either try him in place or turn him over to the Americans. But when the US ambassador heard this proposal, he indicated no interest, saying that "casting our objectives too narrowly" risked "a premature collapse of the international effort, if by some lucky chance Mr. bin Laden was captured."[64] By March 2002, six months after the attack on the World Trade Center, President Bush, when asked about the hunt for bin Laden, said "I don't know where he is. I truly am not concerned about him."[65]

The argument for invading Iraq was based on three principal assertions:

1. Iraq had been involved in the 9/11 attack and was supporting al Qaeda terrorists around the world.
2. Iraq had a stockpile of chemical and biological weapons, as well as the missiles necessary to deliver them.
3. Iraq was actively developing nuclear weapons and could be expected to have an operational bomb within three to five years.

By the time the White House propaganda campaign ended in October 2002, each of these assertions, while false, was widely believed by Congress and the American public. Much has now been written about the way the second Bush administration used lies and deception to lead the country into war. Other administrations have used similar tactics, as have other governments in recent history, including the United Kingdom. But the comprehensive nature of the Iraq propaganda campaign, the scale on which it was accomplished, and the near certainty that it will be emulated in the future require us to examine how at least one of those assertions came to be part of our virtual truth.

INVADING IRAQ: THE SMOKING GUN

In late 2000, Joe Turner, an engineer new to the export controls office of the CIA, learned from the Australian intelligence agency that a request for a proposal to produce thousands of aluminum tubes was being e-mailed to potential manufacturers by Al-Rasheed General, a division of the Iraqi Military Manufacturing Commission. One company in China appeared scheduled to deliver the tubes to a Jordanian company that was a known agent for Iraq. Turner, who had worked with gas centrifuges at the Oak Ridge National Laboratory twenty years before, thought the tubes might be intended for such a system.

Ranks of vertical tubes filled with uranium gas are spun in place so that the heavier molecules (U-235) go to the outside of the tube and the lighter ones are drawn up to other tubes and spun again. This cascade of thousands of tubes, spinning for months at a time, could produce the enriched uranium necessary to build a nuclear weapon. The new systems all use steel, but Turner knew that older systems had used aluminum, so the purchase looked suspicious. Over the next months, Turner followed the transaction and, in April 2001, he wrote his first memo, reporting the centrifuge possibility but noting that "using aluminum tubes in a centrifuge effort would be inefficient and a step backward from the specialty steel machines Iraq was poised to mass produce at the onset of the Gulf War."[66]

The Department of Energy, which had received a copy of the memo, responded the next day. Department experts pointed out several characteristics of the tubes, indicating that they could not have been intended for a gas centrifuge. The eighty-one-millimeter diameter of the tube was too small to be efficient, the walls of the tube were three times too thick, and the interior of the tubes had been treated with a coating that would react with the uranium. It was more likely that the tubes were casings for hand-launched antiarmor rockets. Moreover, the way the tubes were purchased—multiple quotes solicited publicly over the Internet, through purchasing agents, and by price haggling—seemed more like a conventional military procurement, not a secret scheme to build nuclear weapons.

In July, when the tubes arrived for delivery at the port of Aqaba, a carload of CIA agents and some Jordanian police went down to the docks. According to a news special produced by *Four Corners*, the long-time investigative journalism program of the Australian Broadcasting Corporation, the agents found two Iraqi men hanging around the crates, talking on their cell phones. The police persuaded the guards to look the other way, and the CIA put some of the tubes in their car.[67]

Still convinced the tubes were part of a nuclear weapons development plan, Turner took one of them to the International Atomic Energy Agency in Vienna and pressed his case to a pessimistic room of nuclear engineers. They pointed out that the dimensions of the tube were exactly those of tubes previously purchased by Iraq for eighty-one-millimeter rockets, but that didn't seem to change Turner's view. David Albright, a physicist, former weapons inspector, and expert on the proliferation of nuclear weapons, said Turner and his argument were not well received. "The view in Vienna in the summer of 2001 was 'Maybe this guy has a clever idea, but he really is just grabbing at almost straws to prove his case, and when he's debunked in one model, he then shifts it and tries to make his information fit another centrifuge model.' And yet whenever you confronted him with the facts or the weaknesses in argument, he always came back with the same answer—'It's only for centrifuges.'"[68]

While Turner was in Vienna, another dissenting voice emerged. Professor Houston Wood of the University of Virginia, one of the leading experts on gas centrifuges (and the only man in the world who had one of his own) said the tubes were wrong. Wrong dimensions, much too heavy, the uranium gas would be leaking out all the time. It was puzzling, he noted, that the tubes had been machined to a very high tolerance and that the aluminum was of a higher strength than rocket casings would require.[69] But he was convinced of his view and joined a panel of other experts from the Oak Ridge labs to file a dissenting opinion.

Then there was a mysterious and unexplained change of mood. Turner's discredited theory didn't die. During the month of August 2001, the idea that Iraq might be developing nuclear weapons caught someone's ear, even if the evidence seemed weak. It surfaced again in an August 7 Defense Intelligence Agency report titled "Iraq's Reemerging Nuclear Weapons Program."[70] By late August, Turner's suspicion was being promoted within the CIA as a legitimate theory.

Larry Johnson, a CIA intelligence officer who later served in the State Department's Office of Counterterrorism, said on an *Executive Intelligence Review* panel in 2007 that a theory like Turner's doesn't get promoted easily, and certainly not without some support and coaching from the top.

The [CIA] process of writing, whether it's for the Presidential Daily Brief, or the National Intelligence Daily, is, you start off in the morning, sort of like a newspaper reporter dealing with breaking news. We offer up a story-line; the section chief carries it forward to a morning meeting. At the morning meeting, the division chief says, "Yeah, I think we'll go with that." Then the division chief has to go upstairs and present it to an office chief. So it's very much a bureaucratic function, and it's amazing that anything gets done, but somehow in that process, you're able to turn these pieces out.

So, anything that gets written like [Turner's memo], it's not just because somebody is sitting there on their own saying, "Boy, I've got a great idea for a story!" It is overseen, it is supervised; and in fact, my understanding is, over the last seven years, they have actually added layers of management review to the process. So the fact that someone like this analyst Joe Turner, was able to run amok, it was not Joe Turner on his own: He was running amok with the witting cooperation of senior CIA officials, with Jamie Miscik, the DDI, with the people of Alan Foley who was in his chain of command. These people participated in that, willingly. These are not ignorant, stupid people.[71]

The CIA subsequently ran tests on the tubes but declined to consult with the experts at the Department of Energy. Two engineers were instructed to spin one tube up to sixty thousand revolutions per minute—real centrifuges operate at ninety thousand—and they concluded that the tubes were well suited for the task. What they didn't report was that in the majority of the spin tests the tubes failed. Another test showed that the tubes just didn't have the strength necessary for long-term operation in a centrifuge. All this information was kept secret from the DOE experts, as well as from everyone else.[72]

Turner presented his theory to the State Department Bureau of Intelligence and Research (INR). They said that "he seemed far more a man on a mission than an objective analyst. He had something to sell."[73] In November 2001, the CIA reported that the consensus view was that the tubes were for a gas centrifuge, although the report acknowledged that there were "divergent views."[74]

Vice President Cheney, who had started visiting the CIA regularly that summer, pushed the organization to "clarify" its analysis, and by December the remaining ambiguity had been removed. The CIA issued a Senior Executive Memorandum concluding that the tubes were intended for a gas centrifuge. The memo was titled "The Iraq Threat." In March 2002, just as Cheney was arriving in the Middle East to urge the US view on its allies in the region, the CIA shifted the message even further. The aluminum tubes were now evidence that Iraq was "trying to reconstitute its gas centrifuge program."[75]

When the Senate Committee later reviewed the development of prewar intelligence, it was critical of the CIA:

> In some cases CIA analysts were not open to fully considering information and opinions from other intelligence analysts or creating a level playing field in which outside analysts fully participated in meetings or analytic efforts. This problem was particularly evident in the case of the CIA's analysis of Iraq's procurement of aluminum tubes during which the Committee believes the agency lost objectivity and in several cases took action that improperly excluded useful expertise from the intelligence debate. For example, the CIA performed testing of the tubes without inviting experts from the Department of Energy (DOE) to participate. A CIA analyst told Committee staff that the DOE was not invited "because we funded it. It was our testing. We were trying to prove some things that we wanted to prove with the testing. It wasn't a joint effort."[76]

But from Cheney's point of view, the evidence had been wrenched around to where he wanted it. With the active assistance of George Tenet, he had jawboned the analysts into certainty and he could take it from there. The next week, on CNN, Wolf Blitzer asked Cheney if the United States was still trying to get weapons inspectors back into Iraq. Cheney, rarely an advocate for diplomacy, dismissed the idea:

> The issue is not inspectors. The issue is that [Saddam] has chemical weapons and he's used them. The issue is that he's developing and has biological weapons. The issue is that he's

pursuing nuclear weapons. It's the weapons of mass destruction and what he's already done with them. There's a devastating story in this week's *New Yorker* magazine[77] on his use of chemical weapons against the Kurds of northern Iraq back in 1988; may have hit as many 200 separate towns and villages. Killed upwards of 100,000 people, according to the article, if it's to be believed. This is a man of great evil, as the president said. And he is actively pursuing nuclear weapons at this time, and we think that's cause for concern for us and for everybody in the region.[78]

Most of this answer is false. The chemical weapons charge was based on claims by Adnan Ihsan Saeed al-Haideri, a defector recruited and trained by Chalabi's INC, under direction from the Rendon Group and the White House. He had failed a comprehensive lie detector test by the CIA, and his story was concluded to be false in every respect. Nonetheless, Chalabi tipped off Judith Miller, and the *New York Times* ran it on the front page.[79] The charges of biological weapons were based on testimony by Mohammad Harith, also a defector supplied by INC and considered by State Department Intelligence to be a liar. He appeared that month on CBS's *60 Minutes* with his identity dramatically shielded. Weeks later the Defense Intelligence Agency analysts issued a "fabricator notice," warning the intelligence community to disregard any intelligence that he had provided.[80] The charge that Saddam was trying to purchase five hundred tons of yellowcake uranium from Niger was transparently false—no one could have moved that much ore in secret—and it was almost immediately shown that the documents had been forged, probably by Americans close to the White House. The charge that Saddam had gassed his own people had been made for years and had been effectively disproved by Stephen Pelletiére, former CIA analyst and professor at the Army War College. Pelletiére's research showed that the five thousand innocent Kurds who died in Halabja were killed in a chemical war crossfire between Iraq *and* Iran. The gas Saddam Hussein used (technology and materials provided by United States, West Germany, United Kingdom, and China) was probably not intended to kill his own people.[81] In all these cases, like the argument over the aluminum tubes, the intelligence community had provided substantial doubt, conflicting evidence, and sometimes direct refutation. But in all these cases, Vice President Cheney, more than anyone else in the administration, chose to suppress this dissent and ambiguity, presenting his case to the American people as certainty.

During the summer of 2002, the White House made its plans for a final push. The goal was to get Congress to approve a war powers bill that would give President Bush the latitude to act more forcefully against Iraq, including an invasion, if necessary. A five-week publicity campaign would begin with senior administration officials appearing on all the news programs. Then on September 11, as Chief of Staff Andrew Card explained it to Elizabeth Bumiller of the *New York Times*, the president would make a speech on Ellis Island—they thought having the Statue of Liberty in the background would lend a nice touch. Given the rising level of doubt and criticism, Bumiller asked why the White House would wait until September, and Card said, with perhaps more candor than the occasion required, "[F]rom a marketing point of view, you don't introduce new products in August." It was a bold plan that would deploy all the resources of the executive branch, using the media to stimulate public concern that would reflect back onto the members of Congress. "In the end," an unnamed White House official said, "[i]t will be difficult for someone to vote against it."[82]

On September 8, 2002, Judith Miller and Michael Gordon wrote an article for the front page of the *New York Times*, "Iraq Intensifies Quest for A-Bomb Parts," in which they cited unnamed administration officials.

More than a decade after Saddam Hussein agreed to give up weapons of mass destruction, Iraq has stepped up its quest for nuclear weapons and has embarked on a worldwide hunt for materials to make an atomic bomb, Bush administration officials said today.

In the last 14 months, Iraq has sought to buy thousands of specially designed aluminum tubes, which American officials believe were intended as components of centrifuges to enrich uranium. American officials said several efforts to arrange the shipment of the aluminum tubes were blocked or intercepted but declined to say, citing the sensitivity of the intelligence, where they came from or how they were stopped.

The diameter, thickness and other technical specifications of the aluminum tubes had persuaded American intelligence experts that they were meant for Iraq's nuclear program, officials said, and that the latest attempt to ship the material had taken place in recent months. Iraqi defectors who once worked for the nuclear weapons establishment have told American officials that acquiring nuclear arms is again a top Iraqi priority. American intelligence agencies are also monitoring construction at nuclear sites.[83]

On the contrary, the diameter, thickness, and other technical specifications of the tubes were exactly the reason experts felt the tubes were *not* intended for a centrifuge. Chalabi's live-in defectors were once again doing their work as expert witnesses, and the report that intelligence agencies were monitoring nuclear sites was a complete fabrication. There were no sites. Under the subhead "On the Brink of War," the article went on:

Hard-liners are alarmed that American intelligence underestimated the pace and scale of Iraq's nuclear program before Baghdad's defeat in the Gulf War. Conscious of this lapse in the past, they argue that Washington dare not wait until analysts have found hard evidence that Mr. Hussein has acquired a nuclear weapon. The first sign of a "smoking gun," they argue, may be a mushroom cloud.

That same day, Secretary of State Colin Powell appeared on *Fox News Sunday* to restate the administration's conviction that Saddam Hussein must be removed.

> With respect to nuclear weapons, we are quite confident that [Saddam] continues to try to pursue the technology that would allow him to develop a nuclear weapon. Whether he could do it in one, five, six or seven, eight years is something that people can debate about, but what nobody can debate about is the fact that he still has the incentive, he still intends to develop those kinds of weapons. And as we saw in reporting just this morning, he is still trying to acquire, for example, some of the specialized aluminum tubing one needs to develop centrifuges that would give you an enrichment capability. So there's no question that he has these weapons, but even more importantly, he is striving to do even more, to get even more.[84]

Then Vice President Cheney appeared on NBC's *Meet the Press*, also referring to the article in the *New York Times* as an endorsement of his concern:

> MR. RUSSERT: What, specifically, has he obtained that you believe would enhance his nuclear development program?
>
> VP CHENEY: . . . What we've seen recently that has raised our level of concern to the current state of unrest, if you will, if I can put it in those terms, is that he now is trying, through his illicit procurement network, to acquire the equipment he needs to be able to enrich uranium to make the bombs.
>
> MR. RUSSERT: Aluminum tubes.
>
> VP CHENEY: Specifically aluminum tubes. There's a story in the *New York Times* this morning—I don't want to talk about, obviously, specific intelligence sources, but it's now public that, in fact, he has been seeking to acquire, and we have been able to intercept and prevent him from acquiring through this particular channel, the kinds of tubes that are necessary to build a centrifuge. And the centrifuge is required to take low-grade

uranium and enhance it into highly enriched uranium, which is what you have to have in order to build a bomb. This is a technology he was working on back, say, before the Gulf War. And one of the reasons it's of concern, Tim, is, you know, we know about a particular shipment. We've intercepted that. We don't know what else—what other avenues he may be taking out there, what he may have already acquired. We do know he's had four years without any inspections at all in Iraq to develop that capability.

And we also, if you harken back to the past, as I mentioned earlier, before the Gulf War, back in 1990, we had reason to believe then that he had established a program to try to produce a nuclear weapon. I was told then, as Secretary of Defense, that he was several years away from being able to do that. What we found out after the Gulf War, once we got in there, and got the inspection regime going and so forth, was that he had been much farther along than we anticipated, and that he, in fact, might have been within six months to a year of actually building a nuclear weapon.

MR. RUSSERT: Do . . .

VP CHENEY: So the point to be made here is we have to assume there's more there than we know. What we know is just bits and pieces we gather through the intelligence system. But nobody ever mails you the entire plan—or that rarely happens. It certainly has not happened in this case. So we have to deal with these bits and pieces and try to put them together in a mosaic to understand what's going on. But we do know, with absolute certainty, that he is using his procurement system to acquire the equipment he needs in order to enrich uranium to build a nuclear weapon.

MR. RUSSERT: He does not have a nuclear weapon now?

VP CHENEY: I can't say that. I can say that I know for sure that he's trying to acquire the capability. . . . Some people say, "Well, if you're going to use this process, if you're going to go through the enrichment process, it could take five, six years maybe." But then the question is: "Well, when did he start?"

Did he start back when the inspection regime was still under way, prior to '98? Because he did have, for example, a robust biological weapons program then, even though there were inspectors present. Did he start in '98 when the inspectors left? Has he had four years already to work on this process? Or is he only beginning now? We don't know that. We can't tell what the start date is. We do know that he is, in fact, embarked upon this venture. We don't have any way to know, at this point, to specify the date by which he will actually have a weapon he can use.

MR. RUSSERT: There seems to be a real debate in the country as to his capability. This is how the *New York Times* reported comments by Senator Chuck Hagel, a Republican, who said, "The Central Intelligence Agency had 'absolutely no evidence' that Iraq possesses or will soon possess nuclear weapons." Is that accurate?

VP CHENEY: I disagree. I think the accurate thing to say is we don't know when he might actually complete that process. All of the experience we have points in the direction that, in the past, we've underestimated the extent of his program. We've underestimated the speed at which it was developing. It's important for people to understand, as well, too, the difficult nature of the target here, in an intelligence perspective. This is a guy who runs a totally controlled system. There is no—he doesn't have to go to Congress to get funds appropriated to build a system. It's a dictatorship. Secondly, it's a police state. He runs a very brutal regime. Third, he has been very good at denial and deception. He's good at hiding whatever he's doing from public view. And therefore, as an intelligence target, it's an especially difficult proposition for us.

We have a tendency—I don't know if it's part of the part of the American character—to say, "Well, we'll sit down and we'll evaluate the evidence. We'll draw a conclusion." But we always think in terms that we've got all the evidence. Here, we don't have all the evidence. We have 10 percent, 20 percent, 30 percent. We don't know how much. We know we have a part of the picture. And that part of the picture tells us that he is, in fact, actively and aggressively seeking to acquire nuclear weapons.

MR. RUSSERT: Why haven't our allies, who presumably would know the same information, come to the same conclusion?

VP CHENEY: I don't think they know the same information. I think the fact is that, in terms of the quality of our intelligence operation, I think we're better than anybody else, generally, in this area. I think many of our European allies, for example, who are reluctant to address this issue or who have been critical of the suggestion that somehow the United States wants to aggressively go address this issue—I think many of them do not have access to the information we have. Now, some of this clearly comes from very sensitive sources, and we have to be very careful to try to protect those sources. And I know I can cite specific examples. During my time in government, where we have, in fact, had agents, people reporting to us on sensitive matters caught and executed. Their lives are at stake, and our ability to get access, to continue to get access to these programs, depends upon our trying to preserve the classification of some of this information. Having said that, the president, though, still knows and understands very well that we need to provide as much information as we can, especially to the Congress

And he directed me last week, together with Director Tenet of the CIA, to begin that process. We sat down on Thursday afternoon with the big four congressional leaders in the House and Senate—Lott, Hastert, Daschle and Gephardt —and began to share the most sensitive information with them about these new developments that we think are so disturbing.

MR. RUSSERT: You can't just send the military to war. You have to bring a country to war and convince them it is the necessary and right thing to do . . .

VP CHENEY: Well, I think we've started that process already, Tim. The president's going to address the General Assembly of the United Nations this week. He will lay out his concerns at that point. We have begun to share, as much as we can, with committees of Congress. A lot of this, I hope, eventually will be in the public arena so that we'll be able to discuss it not only with our allies overseas, but also with the American people here at home. They have a right to know and understand what it is that's happened here.

It's also important not to focus just on the nuclear threat. I mean, that sort of grabs everybody's attention, and that's what we're used to dealing with. But come back to 9/11 again, and one of the real concerns about Saddam Hussein, as well, is his biological weapons capability; the fact that he may, at some point, try to use smallpox, anthrax, plague, some other kind of biological agent against other nations, possibly including even the United States. So this is not just a one-dimensional threat. This just isn't a guy who's now back trying once again to build nuclear weapons. It's the fact that we've also seen him in these other areas, in chemicals, but also especially in biological weapons, increase his capacity to produce and deliver these weapons upon his enemies.[85]

And finally Condoleezza Rice appeared on CNN—employing repetition and momentum—to say the same thing:

BLITZER: Based on what you know right now, how close is Saddam Hussein's government—how close is that government to developing a nuclear capability?

RICE: You will get different estimates about precisely how close he is. We do know that he is actively pursuing a nuclear weapon. We do know that there have been shipments going into Iran, for instance—into Iraq, for instance, of aluminum tubes that really are only suited to—high-quality aluminum tools that are only really suited for nuclear weapons programs, centrifuge programs. . . . The problem here is that there will always be some uncertainty about how quickly he can acquire nuclear weapons. But we don't want the smoking gun to be a mushroom cloud.[86]

In the face of false information and innuendo so skillfully presented, it is difficult to remember that nuclear scientists at the IAEA and a panel of gas centrifuge experts at Oak Ridge National Laboratory had concluded the opposite: the aluminum tubes were for rockets, not a centrifuge, and Senator Hagel was right. If Cheney had been compelled to speak the truth on *Meet the Press*, he would have explained that the administration's determination to invade Iraq was really based on this fortyish-year-old engineer who had just joined the CIA and thought the tubes looked like ones he had seen twenty years before when he worked as a technician on a gas centrifuge at Oak Ridge. Plus, of course, they had these guys living in Chalabi's basement over in Georgetown.

And, as Cheney certainly knew, the *New York Times* story had been spun up by the White House itself; the line about the smoking gun had been written by Michael Gerson, one of President Bush's speechwriters.[87] All the talk about an intelligence capability superior to any of its European allies, piecing together a mosaic of complex information too secret to be discussed, the importance of protecting the country's sensitive intelligence sources in this case, the determination of the White House to share what they could with the American people—all that was window dressing. And it would have been obvious as such to an experienced political reporter like Russert. But it made for great television. NBC should have awarded Vice President Cheney both ears and the tail and carried him out of the studio on their shoulders.

When David Albright saw the *New York Times* article, he was appalled. The expert on nuclear proliferation called Miller immediately and explained, as he had done before, that the tubes were not for a gas centrifuge. The government's own experts in the field strongly disagreed with the CIA position and said the *New York Times* was presenting only one side of the debate.

Partly in response, she decided to do another article, which appeared on September 13 [but] the article was [again] heavily slanted to the CIA's position, and the views of the other side were trivialized. An administration official was quoted as saying that "the best" technical experts and nuclear scientists at laboratories like Oak Ridge supported the CIA assessment. These inaccuracies made their way into the story despite several discussions that I had with Miller on the day before the story appeared—some well into the night. In the end, nobody was quoted questioning the CIA's position. (*David Albright, on Australia's "Four Corners"*)[88]

Inside the CIA and State Department, senior analysts were also concerned to see that the true nature of the aluminum tubes, which had been so thoroughly examined, was not being accurately disclosed by the White House. Greg Thielmann, the person at the Department of State responsible for analyzing the Iraq weapons threat, felt that the professionals had lost control of the analysis. He repeatedly warned Secretary of State Powell that the claims being made by the White House had no basis in fact. They were "faith-based intelligence" being spun by the media. But there wasn't anything he could do. "Our job was not to straighten out the press on these issues," he later said. "It was all classified and we were not authorized to do that. So our frustration from within the government was that the leadership of the country was not being totally honest with the people on an important issue."[89]

David Albright was more rueful. "Now this is a war, in a sense, over the truth. . . . We started hammering away at this, but we felt we could never catch up, that the administration had gotten such an advantage by going public with a distorted story that we couldn't correct it."[90]

MISSION ACCOMPLISHED

With the evidence mustered, the endorsements in place, and the momentum gathering, the White House began the last stage of its campaign to get a war resolution passed. In a series of private presentations for leaders of Congress, Vice President Cheney and his staff made the case for invasion using satellite images of "weapons sites," sketches of how the mobile biological labs were thought to look, and a photo of the aluminum tube. The audience was skeptical. House Majority leader Dick Armey called it "not very convincing. If I'd gotten the same briefing from President Clinton or Al Gore, I probably would have said 'Ah, bullshit.'" Cheney asked him to keep his concerns to himself, though, and give them a chance to make a better case.[91] A White House aide was invited to look over the evidence and he was surprised at how flimsy it was. One photo of an "Iraqi" drone had a Czech flag in the background; an assistant to Dr. Rice admitted it had been taken at a German air show, but the Iraqi weapons were "like this one." Other photos of weapons sites were from 1998. The aide later told Michael Isikoff of *Newsweek* that he had "this sinking feeling. Oh, my god, I hope this isn't all we have."[92] Tom Daschle, Senate Minority leader and a former air force intelligence officer trained to interpret satellite images, thought the blurry pictures on the table showed nothing. But he, too, kept his silence. They understood what was happening. At one point the president walked in on a group of congressional leaders being briefed and said: "Look, I want your vote. I'm not going to debate it with you." When one of the senators tried to ask a question, Bush snapped back, "Look, I'm not going to debate it with you."[93]

The reality was that with a Republican majority in the House and Senate, President Bush was going to get whatever resolution he wanted. In the complex judo of Washington, the White House was just asking for a bipartisan vote in order to shore up public support. In any event, the Democrats who faced an election in a few weeks were deeply reluctant to vote against a war resolution at a time when feelings of unquestioning patriotism were still running very high. As they say in Washington, there are times when you have to rise above principle.

According to an ABC News/*Washington Post* poll taken in the last week of September 2002, 61 percent of Americans favored international military action against Iraq, even if Saddam cooperated fully with UN inspectors. Forty-six percent would still be in favor of an invasion if the United States had to go it alone. When asked whom they trusted to manage the Iraq situation, voters chose Republicans over Democrats two to one. President Bush's overall job approval rating stood at 67 percent, down from a high of 91 percent after the 9/11 attack but still very good for any president. Only 51 percent approved of the way Congress was doing its job. And just in case a congressman might be thinking of voting his doubts, 38 percent said they would vote against such a legislator.[94] The campaign had succeeded in shifting the 9/11 anger onto Saddam Hussein and in gathering up the will to war.

Democrats joined the cause. Richard Holbrooke, UN ambassador in the Clinton administration, called Saddam the most dangerous man in the world. Kenneth Pollack, a former CIA analyst and a member of President Clinton's National Security Council, said that Iraq could have a nuclear bomb in a few years. Even Madeleine Albright, secretary of state in the Clinton administration, agreed with a policy of regime change, saying that Iraq was developing nuclear weapons and could no longer be contained.[95]

On October 1, 2002, the National Intelligence Council, an independent board of senior analysts drawn from several intelligence agencies, delivered a classified National Intelligence Estimate that generally supported a strategy of regime change in Iraq but included a number of concerns, doubts, and cautionary comments. It concluded that Saddam might have chemical and biological weapons, although the United States lacked "specific" information. But it said Saddam was unlikely to make those weapons available to terrorists except when the survival of Iraq itself was no longer likely.[96]

The council said that "most" of the nation's intelligence agencies believed that Saddam was reconstituting Iraq's nuclear weapons program and offered a chart that appeared to show the similarities between the aluminum tubes grabbed off the dock in

Aqaba and the 1950s "Zippe-type" centrifuge that Joe Turner claimed was the new Iraqi design. But the NIE neglected to show that the tubes were *exactly* like the eighty-one-millimeter rockets Iraq was already using. The estimate also claimed that the tubes could not be used for rockets, in spite of the fact that almost identical tubes were used as rocket casings in many countries, including the United States. Both the Department of Energy and the State Department dissented from the NIE's primary conclusion, and those dissents were prominently included in the Key Judgments section of the report.[97] Even the president's summary of the NIE noted that "INR [State Department Bureau of Intelligence and Research] and DOE [Department of Energy] believe that the tubes more likely are intended for conventional weapon uses."[98] CIA analyst Stuart Cohen, acting chairman of the National Intelligence Council, later told an Agence France-Presse reporter, "Any reader would have to read only as far as the second paragraph of the Key Judgments to know that we lacked specific information on many key aspects of the WMD program."[99] Peter Zimmerman, scientific adviser to the Senate Foreign Relations Committee, remembered his reaction later: "Boy, there's nothing in there. If anybody takes the time to actually read this, they can't believe there actually are major WMD programs."[100]

But the essence of propaganda is certainty, and in the last few days before the vote, the administration moved to expunge all evidence of doubt and then deny that dissent had ever occurred. They later claimed that President Bush, Vice President Cheney, and National Security Adviser Rice had never been aware of a disagreement.[101] Senators Bob Graham and Carl Levin wanted the NIE to be declassified and made public, particularly the dissenting views. Two days later, the CIA produced a twenty-five-page version of the NIE on glossy paper with maps, graphs, tables, photos, and no dissent at all. Paul Pillar, who wrote the document, later described it as "policy advocacy."[102] It certainly wasn't the truth.

At the last minute, there were signs that the administration's story might come unraveled. Testifying to the Senate Select Committee on Intelligence, Robert D. Walpole, national intelligence officer for strategic and nuclear programs, said there were troubling questions about the accuracy of the NIE claims, particularly in the area of nuclear weapons.[103] Senator Graham, furious at the sanitizing of the NIE, challenged CIA director George Tenet on whether the "White House is telling the truth, or even has an interest in knowing the truth."[104] CIA deputy director John McLaughlin admitted that the likelihood of Saddam actually launching an attack with weapons of mass destruction was probably "low."[105] But in his speech to the nation on October 7, 2002, President Bush repeated all the charges that had been developed over the past months and, in spite of doubts building up inside the CIA, he claimed that the aluminum tubes were a clear sign that Saddam was building a nuclear bomb. He hit all the themes—the chemical and biological weapons, the training facilities for al Qaeda, the testimony of defectors—and finished off with the link to 9/11:

> The attacks of September the 11th showed our country that vast oceans no longer protect us from danger. Before that tragic date, we had only hints of al Qaeda's plans and designs. Today in Iraq, we see a threat whose outlines are far more clearly defined, and whose consequences could be far more deadly. Saddam Hussein's actions have put us on notice, and there is no refuge from our responsibilities...
> May God Bless America. [Applause][106]

On October 10, 2002, the US House of Representatives took up Resolution 114, authorizing the president to use the Armed Forces of the United States, as he determines to be necessary and appropriate, in order to defend the national security of the United States against the continuing threat posed by Iraq.

REPRESENTATIVE PETE STARK OF CALIFORNIA: I rise in opposition to this resolution. I'm deeply troubled that lives may be lost without a meaningful attempt to bring Iraq into compliance with U.N. resolutions through careful and cautious diplomacy.

Make no mistake, we are voting on a resolution that grants total authority to a president who wants to invade a sovereign nation without any specific act of provocation. This would authorize the United States to act as the aggressor for the first time in our history and it sets a precedent for our nation or any nation to exercise brute force anywhere in the world without regard to international law or international consensus.

What is most unconscionable is that there is not a shred of evidence to justify the certain loss of life. Do the generalized threats and half-truths of this administration give any one of us in Congress the confidence to tell a mother or father or family that the loss of their child or loved one was in the name of a just cause? Is the president's need for revenge for the threat once posed to his father enough to justify the death of any American? I submit the answer to these questions is no.

REPRESENTATIVE MIKE CASTLE OF DELAWARE: We know that Iraq has continued building weapons of mass destruction, energized its missile program and is investing in biological weapons. Saddam Hussein is determined to get weapons-grade material to develop nuclear weapons. Its biological weapons program is larger and more advanced tha[n] before the Gulf War. Iraq also is attempting to build unmanned vehicles, U.A.V.'s, to possibly deliver biological warfare agents. All of this has been done in flagrant violation of the U.N. Security Council resolutions.

Some may react to this evidence saying that in the past other countries have had similar arsenals and the United States did not get involved. But as President Bush has told us and as Secretary Rumsfeld reiterated yesterday in a meeting, Saddam Hussein's Iraq is different. This is a ruthless dictator whose record is despicable. He has waged war against his neighbors and on his own people. He has brutalized and tortured his own citizens, harbored terrorist networks, engaged in terrorist acts, violated international commitments, lied, cheated and defied the will of the international community. I have examined this information in some of the more specific classified reports. The bottom line is we don't want to be caught off guard. We must take all precautions to prevent a catastrophic event similar to September 11.[107]

The House made its decision, passing the resolution 296 to 133. The next day the Senate approved a similar measure, 77 to 23.[108]

9

TRUTH SYSTEMS

In his magisterial book, *Public Opinion*, published in 1922, Walter Lippmann said America can't handle democracy.[1] The father of modern political commentary had served as a propaganda writer during World War I and, at thirty-two, in the fullness of his youthful disillusionment, he realized that public opinion was easily manipulated. The country was too large for representative democracy, he thought. People had no way to corroborate the information they were given about national issues, and their understanding was often colored by emotion, prejudice, and habit. He said the press was an unfaithful messenger, less interested in truth than in covering events, episodes, and interruptions "like the beam of a searchlight that moves restlessly about." This created what he called a "pseudo-environment" of information that was unreliable and subject to distortion by a "specialized class."

The question Lippmann raised then and in his later writings was whether the size, type, and behavior of a community might affect the truthfulness of the information on which government itself depends. The quality of any decision, whether you are choosing a pill or invading a country, is affected by biology. The strengths and weaknesses of the brain differ from one person to another, but for nearly everyone, the brain is more receptive to favorable information than unfavorable information and is particularly poor at storing things ambiguous, uncertain, and contrary to current belief. There are limits to the speed of thought and limits as well on the number of choices a person can effectively consider at the same time. Beyond those limits, under the stress of overload and pressured by their peers, individuals come to conclusions before all the facts are considered, often preferring action to truth. And the brain operates in a slowly changing bath of emotions that can block, color, or enhance the accuracy of our perceptions as well as the decisions we reach.

The quality of a decision is affected by the way we interact with others. People often ignore warnings and information they disagree with and they come in time to forget that those messages were ever received. And when they pass the information along to others, they remove uncertainty and ambiguity, unconsciously adding little touches and speculations that will make the narrative more "logical" or attractive. People hate confusion and will often submit to the decisions of others rather than struggle with contradictory facts themselves. Experts and professionals resist information or procedures that challenge their authority—they avoid the fine print, they discourage questioning, and they dismiss with a fine harrumph even the casual doubt. In fact, we all do this.

The quality of a decision is affected by the very tools we use. The information we receive is secretly manipulated by those we have been taught to honor and trust. Computer systems, which we once called "thinking machines," are often as addled as their operators, whom we once called "geniuses." Software glitches result in the misrepresentation of reality, sometimes on a very large scale, and our communications technology often fails in a crisis. The press, in which we are told to place such faith, is more interested in news than in truth, and in every country, to a greater or lesser degree, governments are lying to their people.

THE TRUTHFUL ORGANIZATION

The question Lippmann raised was whether the quality of the decisions we make is also affected by the nature of the organization in which we work or the community where we live. Maybe there is a size beyond which truth just can't keep up. Biologists argue that for every species there is a maximum size; after that the skeletal system, the nervous system, and even the skin begin to fail. Anthropologist Robin Dunbar has suggested that people cannot effectively maintain social relationships with more than one hundred and fifty others—too much time is lost in small talk, mutual grooming, and e-mail.[2] Others have suggested that there is even a limit to the number of people who can speak the same language. When communities grow beyond a certain size, subgroups create idioms and slang as a way of reasserting their identity, and in some cases these dialects emerge as new languages. So it is entirely plausible, and certainly consistent with experience, that those in large organizations with many layers of reporting must struggle harder to stay accurately informed. Lippmann thought that America's representative democracy might work better if more decisions were shifted to the states. But there is more to the problem than decentralization.

Structure, too, can affect the quality of information being exchanged. How the group is organized and run can have a big impact on whether the decisions a group makes are successful or not. In 1965 the US Department of Defense studied the productivity of research labs it had funded over the previous decade. It wanted to know why some labs were more productive than others. Was it the quality of the staff, the nature of the task, the availability of funds, or the urgency of the issue? And to find the answer, it examined the characteristics of one hundred research and development teams that had produced successful innovations in the past.

What the DoD found is that the attribute with the highest correlation to success was the way the team was organized. Some labs revolved around a brilliant individual who made all the decisions and personally determined the accuracy of any information being used. Others were governed by a set of procedures that minimized confrontation and provided unambiguous guidance. The group made rules and everyone followed them. But the most successful research labs, by far, had little apparent structure and no installed authority. Decisions were made in a collegial system in which the alternatives were considered and selected by the group based on evidence that they all shared. Sometimes more than one "truth" was accepted and tested. The direction of research shifted with the findings, and the labs that were organized this way were notorious for missing deadlines. But in the end, these were the groups that were most successful in producing significant new technologies.[3]

In addition to size and structure, there is a third element affecting the success of a group's decision, the organization's truth system. Most groups function primarily as information-processing societies. They have standards for determining what is true (inspiration, reason, and consensus). They have a specialized language including acronyms, buzzwords, and unique phrases that make some things easier to say than others. They have a process for sharing information: sometimes it is very hierarchical, as in the military or in a corporation; sometimes it is very collegial, as in a club, a committee, or a project team. Groups have concepts—existing descriptions of reality on which all the members agree but which may or may not be true. And they have values—goals, biases, and shared visions of the future. Finally, there is usually a commitment to speak truthfully to each other in the name of some greater objective. Those who corrupt the system through lies, fraud, embezzlement, cheating, or misrepresentation are usually shunned or expelled.

A group seems to integrate new information with its accepted concepts and values the way an individual does. And when there is a conflict, it has a tendency to choose the interpretation most likely to ensure its own survival. Startup companies are keenly alert to competing technology or changes in the market and, in their struggle to survive, they are smarter, quicker on their feet, and more realistic. But just as often an older, well-established group will lose track of its original purpose. New facts are optimistically misinterpreted; the group's virtual truth drifts further and further from reality.

Seven years after the failure of Enron, the value of Bear Stearns, the fifth-largest investment bank on Wall Street, collapsed from $57 a share on Friday morning to $2 on Monday, as its risky mortgage-backed investments were examined by potential buyers. No information was updated, no assets changed hands during the weekend, no secrets were revealed. The only thing that happened was that the facts were viewed for the first time by analysts with a different set of concepts and values.[4]

> The demise of the firm . . . was a collective failure of the governing five-man executive committee that over the years became so fixated on increasing the firm's book value—and expecting the stock price to follow—that it lost sight of the concentrated, underhedged exposure to the home mortgage market that left Bear vulnerable.[5]

When the group's truth system is healthy and working well, it provides high-quality information and efficient communications, which in turn free individual members to think and act effectively. We turn to the family, the work team, members of a church, or old friends because the language they use, the beliefs they share, and their standard for truth provide the best framework for judging new facts. These groups have a broader and more developed conceptual platform for thinking about an issue. They offer a vocabulary and style of discussion that allow us to express our thoughts more clearly. They have procedures for confirming doubtful data and a process for resolving contradiction that is consistent with our deepest convictions. Whether in a club, a new collaboration, a startup company, or a political movement, we have all at one time or another had the liberating experience of joining a group where everyone else speaks the way we do, shares our values (and prejudices), judges information against the same standard and laughs at the same jokes.

It is not overly simplistic to say that such truth systems give meaning to people's lives, guiding individual decisions and providing a context for their behavior. In *Ideology and Utopia*,[6] Karl Mannheim, a Hungarian sociologist and contemporary of Lippmann, used the phrase "sphere of truth" to describe a local body of knowledge that its followers have accepted and that inevitably reflects their own biases. He thought a group's way of thinking reflected its sociology and history, and that in some cases the ideology might overwhelm the facts.

But Mannheim may not have gone far enough. People join groups not just for *what they think* but for *how they think*. Edward O. Wilson observed in his essay *On Human Nature* that we are almost compulsively drawn to a group whose way of thinking matches our own, sometimes leaving old teams, families, and careers behind.[7] It is not just the ideology; it is often the richness and efficiency of the discussion that draws new members in, allowing them to discover and develop their own thoughts. As we have already seen, individuals in a strong truth system (nuclear engineers, NASA, the Dana-Farber medical team, the neocons) had a greater loyalty to their group than to facts or, for that matter, to the safety of others. And real truth was lost in the process.

Whatever their ideological origins, the principal problem faced by most groups is how to stay productive in a new world. What does a group do when the world changes but the group's map of the world does not? To operate most effectively, a group has to minimize dissenting descriptions and hew closely to its core beliefs. But to innovate and grow, it must occasionally do the opposite: change its concept of the world and suffer the confusion that results. The members realize that the way the group has been describing the world is wrong; it doesn't work that way any longer, and a new description must be found. Productivity is lost in experimentation and error. But out of this ferment will come the new ideas that the group can steady itself against and become productive once again.

Changing the group's understanding of the world is always difficult. History provides evidence of at least four ways by which it can be done: the leader can change the rules; the group can change the leader; the group can keep a small team looking for new truth; or the whole group can stop from time to time and ask whether its truth systems are sound.

Change the Rules. The simplest but rarest method of revising the group's basic ideas is to have the leader announce the change himself. Management theorists are fond of encouraging this, correctly observing the tremendous power an organization can tap when a goal is surpassingly clear and meaningful. But this is not easy. Ambiguity, confusion, and dissent are anathema to a leader. He or she is the keeper of the truth system, and his continued power depends upon the group's loyal allegiance to the concepts and values he or she represents. In the past we have selected leaders for their singleness of purpose and their refusal to take no for an answer, even when it is the right answer. The lesson of history is that when new truths emerge, even the best and most flexible old leader has difficulty changing. He or she is just swept away. Remember this when bringing a revolutionary idea to the king: kings hate revolutionary ideas.

Change the Leader. In ancient cultures, we are told, a leader who lost too many battles was taken out to the edge of the village and hit on the head with a rock. Although the process of succession has improved somewhat, the idea remains that when the group's virtual truth diverges too much from reality, the leader must be changed. Installing new leaders for the purpose of getting a better administration of the group's agenda is both popular and successful in a democratic organization, and the transition goes forward in a more or less predictable, if noisy, fashion. But in businesses, bureaucracies, scientific communities, religions, and other less democratic organizations, the process of leaving one well-established truth for another, even with a new leader, sometimes casts the group adrift in a weakened state of ambivalence from which the original members slowly and quietly withdraw.

Organize for Change. To renew the truth system from within, an organization needs to allow new ideas to be developed and discussed, even though the process may detract from productivity. Successful organizations—particularly in high-technology industries—permit a small subgroup to do this, assigning to a few the task of testing new descriptions of the world. After World War II, Lockheed Aircraft famously invented the skunk works, a rogue team of brilliant inventors, free of bureaucracy and supervision, who worked fast and usually in secret to produce a succession of aviation's most important innovations. Task forces, a research department, or a long-range planning committee are genuinely useful ways to keep the group from becoming dependent on a single set of ideas. But such institutional truth seekers are always at risk. Their insights range from petty and irrelevant to bold and disruptive. They challenge the leader to explain his position while the rest of the group is demanding that he make progress on it. As Socrates said in his own (unsuccessful) defense: critics are extremely annoying. But they are less annoying than extinction.

Take Time for Change. A group can also institutionalize dissent and truth seeking through a regularly scheduled review. Whether this takes the form of New Year's resolutions, an annual planning retreat, a national election, or a midlife crisis, the most successful method for conducting an organized examination of one's fundamental ideas and information is to isolate the activity in time and enter deeply into the exercise. It is frightening for leaders to watch their basic beliefs and authority treated with such vigorous disrespect; many limit the scope of such reviews rather than run the risk of losing control. Remember the enormous amount of intellectual effort required for an individual to revise a fundamental concept? It is proportionately even more difficult for a group to grapple with a description of the future that challenges its feeling of competence, its sense of shared values, and its current allocation of power.

TRUTH SYSTEMS CRUMBLE

People rarely seem to leave a group over a decision, but they do leave when the truth system in which the group operates becomes broadly inconsistent with their own experience and ideas. In the aftermath of the Iraq propaganda campaign, several senior analysts publicly quit the CIA and State Department. John Brady Kiesling, John Brown, and Mary Wright left the diplomatic service in protest against the events.[8] Greg Thielmann left the State Department after twenty years; Richard Clarke and Rand Beers left the White House counterterrorism effort. Paul Pillar, the CIA's senior analyst who wrote the sanitized version of the Iraq NIE left in 2005, saying "[O]fficial intelligence was not relied on in making even the most significant national security decisions. . . . The administration used intelligence not to inform decision making but to justify a decision already made."[9] When deputy director of the CIA, John McLaughlin, resigned after thirty-two years, a senior official said, "It's the worst roiling I've ever heard of. . . . There's confusion throughout the ranks and an extraordinary loss of morale and incentive."[10] Michael Scheuer resigned as chief of the CIA's Osama bin Laden unit, saying, "I have concluded that there has not been adequate national debate over the nature of the threat posed by Osama bin Laden and the force he leads and inspires."[11] Scott Ritter, chief UN weapons inspector resigned, stating, "My government is making a case for war against Iraq that is built upon fear and ignorance, as opposed to the reality of truth and fact."[12] They left their friends and careers behind.

After several years of war in Iraq, the US Army has started to lose its midlevel officers at an alarming rate. In spite of generous reenlistment bonuses, the men and women who manage boots on the ground are criticizing senior leadership, saying that the generals have lost touch with reality. "There are some great captains and majors who have great insight into this type of warfare. They are not leaving because they don't have enough money; they are leaving because no one is listening to them. They don't trust the people above them," said an army officer who served two tours in Iraq.[13]

The decline of a truth system is a dangerous and fertile time. As the group loses momentum, subgroups form and skirmish among themselves. Individuals lose interest, become estranged, and search elsewhere for descriptions of the world more in line with their own observations. The allocation of responsibility breaks down, and with it goes the group's ability to act efficiently. The great prescriptive ideas that once led the community into action are reduced to smaller plans that everyone understands but no one cares about. Everyone in the group seems to have a hobby.

Émile Durkheim, the nineteenth-century French sociologist, contributed extraordinary insights to our understanding of the relationship between the ideas of a group and the identity of the individual—and then proceeded to make of his life a demonstration. As a philosophy student at the École Normale, he was restless and dissatisfied with the emphasis on traditional theories of social behavior and he sought instead to construct a "science" of sociology based on more rigorous analysis. With other young scholars, he forged a more quantitative approach, which at first offended the established academic community and then converted it to his practical, activist, research-oriented ways. But he lived too long. At the end of his career, his organizing vision of sociology as a new science was challenged, and he was personally attacked by the members of his own professional group for being "too German." After the heartbreak of his son's death in World War I, he withdrew from all activities and died a few months later at the age of fifty-nine.

The group, said Durkheim, offers its members the intellectual scaffolding they require for growth and fulfillment. The bonds that hold society together are a common set of "representations" (truths) that prescribe certain types of behavior.[14] Max Weber, Durkheim's contemporary, added that organizations provide the individual with the "enchantment" of answers to the major problems of his life, as well as an opportunity to take action in cooperation with others.[15] The traditional functions of a society such as predictable justice, allocation of work, an integrated marketplace, and a moral code, have at their core a common body of ideas and descriptions that are taken to be accurate. They have a process for determining truth. But when a member is attacked by the group or abandoned by it, he not only loses the "moral respect" of his position within the structure but is bereft as well of communion with the ideas that emboldened him to act. Often, Durkheim wrote, he chooses to die.

According to Edward O. Wilson, the larger the group is, the weaker are the bonds it has with its members.[16] For the leader of a large group, there is enormous power and latitude of action, and these benefits increase as the group expands. For its members, though, the group's ideas become of necessity more general, less actionable, and therefore less useful, like broad concepts that have grown in time into pointless generalities. One by one, the members become alienated. They hear other voices and leave to create splinter groups that focus on more relevant issues. A new religion, a radical new school of art, or a startup company begins with single-minded enthusiasm that carries the group to the extraordinary accomplishments for which it will be remembered. But as growth continues, the energy begins to dissipate. Members disengage and finally disappear. The formal information channels lose their usefulness as gossip takes over. While the leaders vigorously deny that anything is wrong, information to the contrary seeps out to every member of the group like a midnight message of fear or doubt. You don't have to be in the chain of command to get the news; in fact, if you rely on formal communications for your information, you'll be the last to know.

Within the system, antitruth statements begin: "We don't seem to have an accurate understanding of the world we live in, and when we act we aren't as successful as we used to be." Such questions sound like an attack; the leaders of the group become obsessed with preserving the old way. Membership dwindles as individuals give up on the structure that once empowered them and wander out into a formless community of free speech and mindless chatter.

Living outside the truth system means living without guidelines. Opportunities are everywhere, but there is no way to test them. The information floods in, but there are no ideas; there is lots of freedom but no direction. Everything is aimless. The desire is there to belong again, but all groups seem equally ridiculous.

Durkheim referred to this as "anomie," society's most terrible moment when the laws break down and the truths that define a culture are lost in a babble of doubt and self-interest. In his case, the Second Empire was collapsing, and with it the moral and philosophical code of nineteenth-century Europe. Technology was drawing people away from crafts toward an industrial society in which individuals could no longer see the results of their work but had to labor on without reward like part of the machinery itself. Across Europe from 1870 to 1880, the suicide rate nearly doubled, and the level of crime and mental illness increased dramatically.[17]

In the end, the ideas that unify the group are not destroyed by some new external truth; they collapse from within, nibbled to death by the facts. Small supporting descriptions are proven false, and then larger, more fundamental beliefs are questioned, until the whole structure crumbles slowly into a heap of overwrought philosophies and irrelevant ritual.

The process of creating a new truth system seems to begin most often with an individual who presents a provocative new account of nature or human affairs. It is often a single person at the edge of the group, slightly alienated from the established concepts with little or nothing to lose. He or she goes forward, grappling with contradiction and ambiguity, choosing the pleasure of learning over the companionship of the group's dogma.

Moreover, the initial element of a new truth system is often a simple one, and the success of the idea seems to be as frequently the result of a strong conviction as of deep insight. One by one the wanderers make eye contact. They agree on a new description of the situation and then on a remedy. Small groups emerge, recognize each other, compromise, and combine—struggling to preserve what they can of their own identity. People begin to gather. A voice is given to the new order, leaders rise, and a philosophy is written providing a structure for future truth testing—the rules by which this system, too, will one day collapse. Finally a meeting is called and the new doctrine is distributed. Sign up or get out, the leaders explain. An organization is created, choosing as its first act to silence any further dissent.

It is useful from time to time for a group to review the health of its truth system. Is the market opportunity still the one you saw at the beginning? Is the technology you pioneered still the best solution to the problem? Is your country still the best educated and most prosperous in the world? Does the community still need the arts center you started, or the committee on beautification that once seemed so vital to the town? Is the group you joined five years ago still your best source of timely and accurate information on its subject, or do you increasingly rely on other friends, newsletters, or gossip. Do new ideas get discussed as vigorously as they did at the beginning? Do you stay up all night arguing with each other the way you once loved to do? Are more members leaving than joining? Are your products and services succeeding less in the real world? Are you speaking the truth to each other? Consider the possibility that some of what you believe is wrong. That the virtual truth in which you operate now includes so much embedded false knowledge, so constantly reinforced, that the members seem to be on another planet. Maybe the only reason you stay is because these are your friends.

Information systems have a way of turning strange. In a study of how high-tech corporations keep up with rapidly changing technology, my colleagues and I visited the main library of one of the biggest computer companies in the world, perched serenely on top of a beautifully groomed hill. We asked how the company's scientists gained access to the latest discoveries in this fast-changing, highly competitive industry, and the librarian explained that abstracts of virtually all the world's technical journals are indexed and put up on the corporation's worldwide online reference system, which is available at every desk. How quickly? Well, the man said, although we often get the abstracts a month or so in advance, we usually wait to put them online until after the actual journals have arrived and been catalogued and shelved. Otherwise the scientists see the abstract online and ask for the journal, and when they can't get it they complain that the library isn't doing its job.

Some years ago I reviewed the US State Department's process for handling diplomatic messages coming in from embassies around the world. At that time the standard practice was to make 114 copies of each incoming document—this delayed delivery three days—so that all the relevant departments and cross-filing systems could get a copy with equal speed. No one was permitted an early look.

I was involved in the design of a new system for managing the classified and unclassified documents flooding into the International Atomic Energy Agency in Vienna, and when we presented our plan to the director general, he asked us to make it less secure. The IAEA, he said, is a nest of nuclear spies, and they depend for their work on being able to steal copies of incoming papers from the current, very traditional, document registry. If you make the new system too secure, he said, they will destroy it, and then we will be worse off than we are now.

Information systems evolve, sometimes in the wrong direction, and a group needs to ask from time to time whether its connection to information from the real world is as tight and quick as it needs to be. Does communication within the community work as well as you wish? Are the members of your group getting the truth?

CAN DEMOCRACY SURVIVE?

The truth system in greatest danger of failing at this point seems to be America's democracy. According to Nobel economist Joseph Stiglitz and his colleague Linda Bilmes, the decision to launch a war in Iraq will cost the United States more than $3 trillion, directly or indirectly crowding out investments that would have increased America's productivity in the future.[18] In more human terms, thousands of American soldiers have died violently in the morning of their lives. Tens of thousands more have been variously maimed: arms and legs blasted to the bone, faces and hands furiously burned. *Lancet*, the British medical journal, estimates with ghoulish precision that by the end of 2006, 601,027 Iraqi men, women, and children had been killed: 56 percent shot, 13 percent bombed, 14 percent dead in other explosions, 13 percent dead in air strikes, and 2 percent dead of other war-related causes. And the death rate is still rising.[19] The ancient city of Baghdad lies in ashes, and America's ability to make successful decisions is in danger.

Whether or not one agrees with the need for war, whether or not one believes that the effort was competently undertaken, it is now clear that the process by which the nation made that deadly decision was a subversion of America's traditional form of government. Through skillful propaganda and deception, a handful of men and women in the second Bush administration manipulated the information available to voters and legislators in order to achieve the goal of war, and in doing so they deeply injured the democracy they claimed to be advancing. The number of people who say they trust the government in Washington to do what is right, always or most of the time, dropped from 55 percent in October 2001 to 24 percent in July 2007.[20] The number of Americans who thought the war in Iraq was worth fighting dropped from 70 percent in April 2002 to 36 percent in July 2007.[21] In the spring of 2008, a *New York Times*/CBS poll found that 81 percent of Americans believed that the country has "pretty seriously gotten off on the wrong track," up from 69 percent in 2007 and 35 percent in early 2002.[22] A Pew Research poll done in mid-2007 reported that the majority of Americans found the news media to be inaccurate, politically biased, and uncaring.[23] That loss of faith is equally strong across the full political spectrum. This is not just disaffection with the government's policies and performance. It seems to be a response to a genuinely different view of democracy being pushed by a small group of policy makers in the United States, taking us back to the argument between Voltaire and Rousseau. Politicians and political commentators are raising again the fundamental question of whether the important decisions should be made by the few or the many, whether people can reason for themselves, and whether representative democracy can really work in a country as large and diverse as the United States.

If government by the few has a modern ideological foundation, it lies in the writings of Leo Strauss, a minor philosophy professor at the University of Chicago, who is often cited by conservative political theorists as their basic text. Strauss was born in Germany at the turn of the century and grew up as the Weimar Republic came to power after World War I. The experience must have made a terrible impression on him. Germany, freshly freed from a monarchy, was financially strained by the reparations requirements of the Versailles Treaty. Quarrelsome, weak, and ineffective, the new democratic government was buffeted on the left by the socialist workers party, eager for benefits even during their seemingly perpetual strikes. On the right was the old officer corps, nostalgic for the discipline and efficiency of Kaiser Wilhelm's empire. The country wandered into the cabaret culture of relativism and self-indulgence, and then its government failed completely in 1933 as the Nazis stormed onto the stage of history.

So it is understandable that, having experienced this firsthand, Strauss would come to question traditional ideas of political philosophy, particularly those of liberals, who, in his opinion, had followed the Enlightenment to its logical nihilistic extreme. The "crisis of the west," he wrote, was that reliance on reason alone does not include in its calculations the force of moral and subjective judgments—the same question Shakespeare was raising in *Othello*. Strauss believed that reason, untempered by morality, faith, or patriotism, had opened the way to a soulless arithmetic of pleasure and self-interest, empty of the larger passions that inspire a nation. The tyranny of reason, Strauss said, was the disease of modernity.[24]

The solution he offered was peculiar. A great studier of Plato, Strauss believed that the masses were too ignorant and self-absorbed to participate effectively in a democracy—an observation Voltaire had made before—and that they should be led by a few enlightened leaders who were, in turn, secretly advised by philosophers like himself. It was a model of the world that owed less to Plato's *Republic* than to the 1930s comic book hero Flash Gordon, who zoomed about in space, saving the galaxy from the evil Ming the Merciless. Flash was aided by Dr. Zarkov, the brilliant Germanic scientist who saw spies everywhere, and by the plucky and callipygian news reporter, Dale Arden, who followed them cheerfully from the ice kingdom of Frigia to the jungles of Tropica, wearing little more than a silver T-shirt and cutoff shorts. In Strauss's vision of how the world should work, there would be three levels of society, the wise, the gentlemen, and the vulgar (Strauss's terms), but only the wise men would know the real secrets of the universe. Here was a scheme that put the philosopher (Zarkov) at last at the levers of power, whispering to a dim but dashing leader (Flash), who, with patriotic lies and phony derring-do, would rally the simple people and lead them out of danger. This was an idea with serious nerd appeal, and it gained a great following among those who wanted to play Zarkov. Shadia Drury, the leading scholarly critic of Strauss, describes his philosophy:

The real Platonic solution as understood by Strauss is the *covert rule of the wise*. This covert rule is facilitated by the overwhelming stupidity of the gentlemen. The more gullible and unperceptive they are, the easier it is for the wise to control and manipulate them.

For Strauss, the rule of the wise is not about classic conservative values like order, stability, justice, or respect for authority. The rule of the wise is intended as an antidote to modernity. Modernity is the age in which the vulgar many have triumphed. It is the age in which they have come closest to having exactly what their hearts desire—wealth, pleasure, and endless entertainment. But in getting just what they desire, they have unwittingly been reduced to beasts.

Nowhere [according to Strauss] is this state of affairs more advanced than in America. And the global reach of American culture threatens to trivialize life and turn it into entertainment.[25]

The key to making this work, Strauss says, is that everyone is supposed to lie to everyone else. The philosophers lie to the leaders because only the philosophers can stare into the perfidy of man and see the truth. The leaders tell "noble lies" to the people and keep their deliberations secret because the people are too stupid to understand the reality. The great tyrants of the world are masters of deception, so America, too, must deceive the world to compete. Strauss says that even Plato is hiding his real message in text that seems to say the opposite, though why he would do so is not clear.

Wolfowitz studied with Strauss in Chicago and admired him enormously, but he calls the idea that Strauss influenced public policy through a small fraternity of powerful followers "laughable."[26] Yet the Bush administration—particularly Wolfowitz and the Office of Special Plans—perfectly exemplified Strauss's tactics. There may have been a rational and patriotic argument for invading Iraq, and if there was it should have been presented truthfully. But instead, these men advanced their position through propaganda and Straussian deception, mounting a full-scale assault on the process of democracy itself.

The original idea of the founding fathers was that the actions of government should conform to the wishes and opinions of the many, not the few. And in order to make that practical, the yeoman farmer—a man without schooling or an understanding of the issues at hand—would choose a representative whose education, reasoning skills, and opinions equipped him to decide what was good for his constituency. If he failed to do that, he would be replaced. The authors of the Constitution had no illusions. They did not expect every man to have an informed opinion on matters of government. But they believed that even uneducated and emotional people can choose someone whose concepts and values are similar to their own. Democracy isn't perfect. It does not, for example, always protect the rights of minorities who rarely prevail in the selection of the representative and whose voice is therefore dimly heard. Representative democracy is also a complex form of government that can be slowed or manipulated by the party in power. Good bills die. Votes are cast in a quid pro quo that often has little to do with what is best for the country. The high cost of running for office in a media-intensive world is increasingly borne by corporations and special interests who expect favorable legislation and earmarks in return. But none of these criticisms address the more difficult contemporary issue. Democracy is based on information, and if that information is false—particularly if it has been deliberately corrupted and concealed by special interests, by the media and by our own political leaders—then it is a government of smoke and mirrors. Its purpose—to protect the welfare, opportunity, and security of its citizens—is in danger.

THE MACHINERY OF KNOWLEDGE

Walter Lippmann and Leo Strauss started with the same problem, but they came to different solutions. They both believed that voters are rarely able to understand all the facts available, nor do they seem much interested in trying. How then can the masses be trusted with the complex decisions of government? The solution, they thought, was to assign the analysis of information to a few who have the skills, the education, and the temperament for the task. But they went further still. The truth detecting business, so vulnerable to self-interest, should be held at arm's length from those in power. Those who struggle to determine what is really true (not what should be done about it) should be immune to influence and safe from retribution. Strauss thought the task should be given to those he called the "wise," and because the truth of human affairs is dispiriting and arcane, he would caution his philosophers to lie, even to the "gentlemen" they advised. But Lippmann believed in "experts." He separated them from power and said that in a world where information is remote from reality and corrupted by emotions, decision making should be a two-step process. Experts would analyze and prepare the information. Then the men of action, as Lippmann called them, would make the decision.

But then Lippmann began to dream. At the end of *Public Opinion*, he wrote about "intelligence bureaus," independent analysts affiliated with universities who were trained to handle complex information impartially, who could call for data from all the relevant government departments and prepare the alternatives to be considered. Would this reduce the influence of bias, self-interest, and emotion on the decisions of government? It might. The government uses private and not-for-profit think tanks and research contractors to good effect today across the entire spectrum of its activities. And although we hear occasionally about false results, the problems usually lie in the way the contract was awarded, not in how the work was done. Would it remove false knowledge and propaganda entirely from the system? No.

Lippmann ends up crying from the heart that citizens must take responsibility for truth, and in the last pages of the book he has fallen into a lugubrious funk. Information will never be free of lies and distortions. We will never escape the emotions and experience that color our interpretations. Propaganda and false knowledge will continue to dominate our "pseudo-environment," and we will go on, helpless in its grip. Even the "machinery of knowledge," as he called his intelligence bureaus, could not save us.

He should have seen the Internet.

Just when it seems that the world is awash with lies, out of the noisy, rambunctious, and irresponsible ferment of the Internet has risen the blog. Blogs were the first to examine the CBS story on Bush's military service and pronounce the documents fake.[27] It was a blogger (talkingpointsmemo.com) who caught Senator Trent Lott making the disparaging racial remark that led to his resignation from the office of Senate Majority leader.[28] It was a blog that examined Senator Kerry's claim that he spent Christmas in Cambodia and found it false.[29] In January 2007, Talking Points Memo (TPM) spotted a story about a US attorney who had been fired in Arkansas, and the editors dogged it for months, driving the issue of political firings in the Justice Department into the mainstream media and onto the Senate agenda.[30] At one point, when the Department of Justice put three thousand pages of related documents up on the Web, TPM readers were invited to move in like ants and index every page.[31] There are several blogs tracking the rise of the avian flu with greater precision than the World Health Organization.[32] There are dozens of sites debating the viability of democracy in America. Hundreds of blog sites are devoted to the subject of bloggery itself.

Counting blogs is like counting the stars in the sky. According to Technorati.com there are 100 million worldwide, with 175,000 new blog sites launched every day.[33] Half of these die within the first three months and only 15 percent are still active a year later.[34] It takes at least a year of consistent daily posting to gain a regular audience. Visitors post messages that are often irrelevant and obscene, and there is no money in it yet, except for the dozen or so most popular sites.[35] Thirty-six percent of the world's blogs are in Japanese (spoken by 2 percent of the world); 33 percent are in English (spoken by 7 percent of the world).

Farsi, the language of Iran, became the tenth-most popular blogging language in 2006.[36] Half of all Iranians are under thirty, and in spite of the government blocking as many as a third of all Web sites, the country supports nearly one million blogs for a population of sixty-five million, or about one blog for every five literate adults. One of the hottest topics on Farsi blogs in mid-2008 was the run-up to the American presidential election. In the future: Blogistan. A virtual "nation" of active young people in the Middle East is likely to emerge, forming new concepts about their world that may or may not be consistent with what either the United States or their own governments want them to believe. They are communicating many-to-many, learning together like a vast, self-organizing mob, and their ability to master detail, breadth and timeliness is beyond any other knowledge management regime in human history. An unregulated printing press was the wild sword by which nineteenth-century Europe was jabbed and harried into an entirely new political structure, beginning with the French Revolution. The fax machine was the instrument by which the Tiananmen Square rebellion was organized (and later eulogized). How long will it be before the blog becomes the new *vox populi*?

There is a moment in the first *Star Wars* movie when, with a mighty swoop, Darth Vader cuts Obi-Wan Kenobi in half with his light saber. But Obi-Wan does not die. He is transformed instead into a virtual warrior, free from the pesky bonds of corporeal existence, and "more powerful than you could possibly imagine." The same thing has happened to al Qaeda, which now communicates with its worldwide forces over the worldwide web. According to Craig Whitlock of the *Washington Post*, Ayman al-Zawahiri and his cadre of bloggers, armed with the latest Sony ultralight laptops, webcams and digital editing equipment, smuggle videos out of Pakistan on memory sticks and post them onto password-protected Web sites from cyber cafes in neighboring countries. As-Sahab (meaning "the cloud" in Arabic), the propaganda arm of the al Qaeda movement, launched ninety-seven original videos last year, five times as many as in 2005, including an eighty-minute documentary called "The Power of Truth." Whitlock quotes Defense Secretary Robert M. Gates in a 2007 speech:

> It is just plain embarrassing that al Qaeda is better at communicating its message on the internet than America. As one foreign diplomat asked a couple of years ago, "How has one man in a cave managed to outcommunicate the world's greatest communication society?"[37]

In December, 2007, al-Zawahiri, who has a $25 million bounty on his head, participated in a Web forum for the faithful and received 1,888 questions, patiently answering nearly four hundred of them. One expert says: "In many, many ways, the damage has already been done. It certainly would have been a lot easier if the U.S. government had taken this seriously back in 2004." Information war has broken out in Blogistan, while America sleeps.

The Huffington Post (www.huffingtonpostcom), the Daily Kos (www.dailykos.com), Talking Points Memo (www.talkingpoints memo.com), Instapundit (www.instapundit.com), and Eschaton (www.atrios.blogspot.com) together get more than three million visits a day. It is difficult to compare the reach and impact of online media with their print counterparts, but as a newspaper, the *New York Times*, for example, has a daily paid circulation of 1.1 million, while its online site reaches 21 million unique visitors a month.[38] More to the point, the number of visitors coming to the major news blogs every month grew 40 percent from 2006 to 2008, while daily circulation of morning and evening newspapers in the United States dropped about 6 percent during the same period.

The blogosphere is not just a ranting contest. Several open forums dedicated to narrow subjects have evolved into trustworthy repositories of knowledge that are genuinely useful to readers and researchers. The nonprofit Cooperative Research Project (cooperativeresearch.org), which went live in 2002, has since developed a database of more than six thousand recent events related primarily to terrorism and the war on Iraq. Each event briefly describes the occurrence, assigns it to the time line, and indexes it according to subject and persons involved. Viewers can contribute new events or edit existing ones, and there seems to be no overriding political or ideological agenda.

Wikipedia has become the universal model for online knowledge banks of the future. Launched in 2001, it now maintains nearly nine million articles, written and edited by seventy-five thousand contributors in more than two hundred and fifty languages. Articles can be on subjects as narrow as an individual, a book, or a word, or as broad as the history of art, profusely linked to other Wikipedia articles or external Internet resources.

And the blogs are fast. When Tim Russert died in June 2008, executives at NBC blocked publication of the story for more than an hour while the members of his family were being notified. But the news was already flashing around the Internet. Thirty-eight minutes after the newscaster had been pronounced dead, forty minutes before the network released the story, Russert's page on Wikipedia was updated by a volunteer employed by an Internet services company that provides Web hosting for some of the NBC stations. Eleven minutes later another volunteer working for another NBC contractor reversed the updates, removing all references to the man's death. The person who made the original changes was apparently identified and fired. Minutes later, when the network announcement was made, the changes were re-instated.[39] Comparable events are now routinely reported on the Web within minutes, sometimes accompanied by cell phone videos.

In the future, these tools will begin to address specifically the issue of government. Sites have already been created that focus on individual politicians, examining the truthfulness of every utterance. While this may be used in the short-term as a platform for yet more misrepresentation, the possibility remains that as we learn to do this right, contributors on all sides can converge on a more truthful understanding of what the candidate represents. Issues, too, are the subject of this citizen research. In the spirit of Lippmann's experts, some Internet sites share out the task of reading every page of the government's latest publication. They gather and annotate every media message and knowledgeably explore the legal and economic details of every proposal or event.

Advocates say that blogs are like a town meeting, but they aren't that organized. They burst into rhetorical flames and irrelevant hollering on a regular basis. Like the brain, the blogosphere has no metastructure; everything is connected to everything else. And like the brain, access is governed by "availability": the site easiest to get to is the site most people have visited before. Search engines of the future will present results in a self-organizing matrix that structures the choices along multiple axes of content, time, popularity, type of document, and complexity. And maybe then there will be the machine equivalent of concepts and values—established patterns and personal preferences that help us find what we need more quickly, even if it is not what we were looking for. Documents read online will be linked behind the scenes to independently produced materials, contrary opinions, and challenges of fact, making it slightly more difficult to float a completely untruthful assertion. More important, blogs may help readers understand that these modern, multidimensional representations of the world are not always true.

The Internet today is a swirling soup of data that is not yet information, and information that is not yet knowledge. Today there is no control over quality and little concern for truth. And yet, there may be a new kind of truth in the blogosphere based on consensus and convergence. The ideas of Nobel economist Friedrich Hayek, widely admired by those who advocate greater reliance on free enterprise, have an interesting application in this case. Hayek claims that people have too much information to be effectively governed the way they might have been two centuries ago. And central governments have too little information to do the job well.[40] Just as free markets are able to determine the "true value" of an enterprise at any moment by voting with their dollars, he says, some policy decisions formerly made by a central government might in the future be better made nationally or regionally by a comparably informed public. Good information, openly shared, might not only make government more responsive to people's needs, it might make some traditional functions of centralized government obsolete. The Internet provides a new mechanism by which those policy matters can be decided.

If we could measure it, we might detect in its millions upon millions of Web pages, constantly changing, the palpable pulse of a sentient world: raw data from chicken farms in China; dissenting opinions from nuclear engineers; independent evaluations of doctors, hospitals, and prescription drugs; cell phone videos of the latest official misbehavior. In November 2007, when General Musharraf imposed martial law on Pakistan, the media treated opposition leader Benazir Bhutto as the classic political opponent, returning from exile to rally her oppressed people. But on its Web site, the *New York Times* opened a public forum and called for photos, videos, and commentary from Pakistanis themselves. The result was a startlingly different portrait of Bhutto. Allegations were made that her apparent "opposition" was more likely part of a secret power-sharing deal with Musharraf, intended to fool the Americans into continuing their support for his regime.[41] The next day, the front page of the *New York Times* took a new tone: "Bhutto's Persona Raises Distrust, as Well as Hope."[42] Maybe this kind of citizen journalism will grow to shape the mainstream media fifty years from now.[43]

SO?

The condition of democracy in the United States today can only be described as fragile. In 2004, 30 percent of eligible Americans said they always vote in state and national elections and would certainly vote in the future. Another 20 percent of registered Americans voted in 2004 but said they don't vote on a regular basis.[44] Not that it seems to make much difference. Congress is significantly disconnected from the will of the people. A careful study by the Chicago Council on Foreign Relations and the Program on International Policy Attitudes recently compared what the public wants with how the House and Senate actually voted on key issues. It showed that Congress deeply misunderstands the public's wishes, particularly on foreign affairs.[45] Specifically, the study found that:

- Seventy-six percent of Americans are in favor of participating in the International Criminal Court, but only 41 percent of congressmen voted that way.
- Seventy-one percent of Americans want the United States to join the Kyoto treaty to reduce greenhouse gasses that are causing global warming. Only 44 percent of Congress voted for it.
- Eighty-seven percent want America to participate in the Comprehensive Nuclear Test Ban Treaty, but only 48 percent of Congress agreed.
- Sixty-two percent of Americans want to halt further development of missile defense systems until the current prototypes and proposed technologies have been successfully tested. Only 38 percent of Congress voted that way.
- Sixty-nine percent of Americans are opposed to any increase in defense spending. But in the last ten years, defense spending has doubled in real dollars and is now greater than all defense spending by all the other countries in the world combined. The United States annually spends about $2,000 per capita on defense, about twenty times the average of all the other countries in the world.[46]
- Seventy-four percent believe that America should take no

sides in the Israeli-Palestinian conflict, but Congress has cast all but 1 percent of its votes resolutely in favor of Israel.

- In a different poll taken by CBS News in October 2007, 81 percent of those responding, including 70 percent of Republicans, said they favored expanding the S-CHIP program to provide health insurance for more poor and middle-class children. Most of these respondents said they would support the expansion even if it meant an increase in taxes.[47] Two days after the poll was reported in all the major newspapers and on network television news, Congress voted against the expansion.

In the Chicago Council poll, 60 percent to 70 percent of those interviewed said they thought that their representative in Congress was voting the way they would on these issues.[48] The truth is, they probably didn't know what their congressman was doing.

And the confusion goes the other way as well. Sixty-four percent of the public said they were willing to go along with the majority of the UN, even if its decisions are contrary to the US position. But two-thirds of Congress and its staff think the public is either indifferent or opposed to the UN.[49]

Congress gets two hundred million e-mail messages a year, every representative has a Web site, thousands of well-established political blogs are being published, and thousands more special-interest groups post issue explanations and advocacy. But communication between citizens and their government has declined. Representatives do not listen to their constituents, and constituents have stopped asking why. In a Reuters/Zogby poll taken in May 2008, only 11 percent of Americans said they thought Congress was doing a good job, the lowest approval rate ever recorded. "There is a real question among Americans now about how relevant this government is to them," reported John Zogby. "They tell us they want action on health care, education, the war and immigration, but they don't believe they are going to get it."[50]

This disconnect extends to the White House. When ABC's correspondent reminded Vice President Cheney in early 2008 that only a third of Americans believe the Iraq invasion was justified, Cheney dismissed the voters' views as irrelevant:

VP CHENEY: So?
ABC'S WHITE HOUSE CORRESPONDENT MARTHA RADDATZ: So? You don't care what the American people think?
VP CHENEY: No. I think you cannot be blown off course by the fluctuations in the public opinion polls.[51]

Democratic governments routinely and systematically lie to the press and to the people, concealing, distorting, and in some cases fabricating the information on which citizens are expected to vote. And although such manipulation of public opinion may be as old as government itself, this behavior seems to have risen dramatically in recent years. In the United States, freedom of information requests are now largely ignored.[52] Congressional requests and even contempt citations are greeted with brassy refusals. Even the courts seem unable to bring candor and clarity to government. We have been misled.

In a poll taken in 2004, when overall approval of Congress was 43 percent, two-thirds of the voters polled said they thought congressmen were voting for friends and special interests and not for the people back home.[53] More people probably believe that today. Congress is the gearbox of democracy where, through research and debate, the will of the people is supposed to be translated efficiently into purpose and direction. But it is seen by many today as little more than a mangle of false knowledge and special interests. We might be better off replacing all our 535 senators and congressmen with a jury pool of regular voters chosen at random from hardware stores, beauty parlors, and baseball games around the country. Move them to Washington for a year, give them home leave one week a month, and require of them only that they read their mail, work hard, tell the truth, and return quietly to their former lives with a medal and the thanks of a grateful nation. The most serious students of American democracy have proposed solutions no less radical. Robert Dahl, past president of the American Political Science Association, has suggested the creation of a "minipopulus" of a thousand citizens randomly selected to deliberate on a single issue. They would be supported by researchers and experts, and their conclusions would advise the Congress.[54] Hannah Arendt, respected political theorist, has recommended a "council state" in which many government decisions are made by concentric circles of citizens' groups.[55] What we have now is not working.

Will the Internet generation of information-savvy young voters save democracy? Early indications are not promising. A recent study of Internet users eighteen to twenty-five years old showed, surprisingly, that while their tools have changed, their underlying information habits are not very different from those of their elders. Eighty percent say they are interested in news about national affairs, essentially the same as fifteen years ago. They are slightly more optimistic about government: only 24 percent of young Internet users think that Washington has lost touch with the people, compared with 35 percent of people over twenty-five. But only 40 percent of young people feel that it is "my duty as a citizen to always vote."[56] It is a generation amused but not engaged.

Warning. Truth systems rise, they flourish in a time of miracles, they decay, and then they fail, replaced after a while by new systems. We deal with the real world and with each other less through direct contact than through information. And when that information grows increasingly false—distorted, misunderstood, incorrectly reported, or hidden behind a wall of privilege—then, if history repeats itself, the group will lose the loyalty of its members and it will fail. Democracy in America today has the hallmarks of such a declining system. Congress fails to understand—or at least to follow—the public will. The public in turn has a poor understanding of what Congress is doing. Half of the eligible adults don't vote, even in a presidential election, and nine out of ten people think their government is doing a poor job. The United States intelligence community was not able to effectively prevent a terrorist attack, the administration led the nation into a long and costly war for the wrong reasons, and the bureaucracy at the federal and state level could not help thousands of people driven from their homes by Katrina. Nor does it appear prepared for a global pandemic that might kill millions. Whether one believes that government should be large or small, whether it should help those in need or promote free enterprise, it must have truthful information systems to be effective. And currently the United States does not. Although it continues to be a comfortable home for many highly successful global corporations, the most likely future for American citizens now is declining economic competitiveness, declining influence in the world, and a declining standard of living.

THE FUTURE ISN'T WHAT IT USED TO BE

I am optimistic. Information is just the way we talk to each other, and we can learn to do it better. As individuals, we can study the tricks that reason plays and be less vulnerable to the sly and beguiling mind. Warnings, ambiguity, and dissonant evidence are particularly difficult to deal with, but we can learn to be more skeptical.

As members of a group, we can look more carefully at how information is altered as it is exchanged. We can be wary of the omissions, inventions, and distortions that come so naturally to everyone, without losing hope in the miracle of shared knowledge. Executives can train themselves in the new information literacy, and professional schools can require their students to study information assessment as a primary skill. Families, work groups, and communities are joined together in truth systems, and through them we can learn to hear, reconcile, test, and act on information in a more coordinated and trustworthy way.

As consumers who depend on information for our productivity, prosperity, and sometimes our lives, we can expect the truth. We can be more demanding of professionals, government, and the media. We can hold our sources accountable. Ask the question, and don't stop until you understand the answer. Challenge the doctor, cancel your subscription, change the channel, dump the politician, call out the lie, and continue to demand that truth be taken seriously.

Twenty thousand years ago our ancestors learned that they needed to work together in order to bring down the big game. The whole village was involved tracking the herd, preparing the weapons, making the kill, cutting the meat, and dressing the hide. Cooperation became the new imperative, and the idea of a lone hunter stalking his prey faded into myth. But the evolution from lone hunter to group hunting has only gone part way. For several thousand years the model for organizing work was simple and productive: one person decided what many others would do. A hundred backs, one brain. Then, as the world became more complex, it grew harder for one person to keep up with the information necessary to make the right decision. Responsibility had to be distributed, and decisions were made, in fact if not in name, by a like-minded and subordinate priesthood. The back/brain ratio shifted to a hundred backs/one brain and his deputies.

But now we're having trouble. Our modern decision structure is failing us. There are conflicts in experience, concepts, values, and self-interest. And these are compounded by instincts for territoriality, struggles for self-esteem, latent rivalry and the constant haunting of desire. Individual fallibility and group behavior further distort the process. New technology draws us into a faster and more intimate dependence on information instead of direct experience. We don't even have good rules for talking truthfully to each other. And in work teams, companies, communities, and nations, deadly decisions have too often been the result.

We are at a new juncture in human history, when the decisions that matter are less likely to be made successfully by a single person. We need to approach modern knowledge in groups, and to be successful—in fact, to survive—we must find a new structure for decision making that allows broader and more diverse participation, and holds everyone accountable. A hundred brains, one back. We must learn to think together.

We are at the beginning of a new age when information—not land, labor, or capital—will be the primary economic engine in the world, but that information must be true to be useful. The description of reality on which we are gambling so much of our health, prosperity, and progress must be more accurate. In science, medicine, finance, and global relations, we no longer navigate in a world we can touch and see but in a truth system of ideas and information that we, together, have assembled. And those who can learn to do that work effectively will thrive. If we train more people in critical thinking and analysis skills, we can safely go where science and technology now offer to take us. But this means grappling with a more detailed and confusing model of the world; suffering criticism, dissent, and uncertainty with greater confidence; building communications systems that are reliable and true; and treating the facts with more respect. We are on the verge of managing the world around us at a remarkable level of complexity and we can be successful if we will just take the truth of information more seriously.

The possibility that a new world can be discovered through information is what inspires us to question, to argue, and to dream. We need not stumble about, mired in flawed process and self-interest. Thinking together, we can succeed in those extraordinary endeavors that are the promise of the new Information Age.

ENDNOTES

INTRODUCTION

1. William James, *The Meaning of Truth* (Amherst, NY: Prometheus Books, 1997).

CHAPTER 1: FALSE KNOWLEDGE

1. Michael Davie, *Titanic: The Death and Life of a Legend* (New York: Alfred A. Knopf, 1987), p. 132.

2. Ibid., p. 43.

3. Walter Lord, *The Night Lives On* (New York: William Morrow, 1986), p. 169.

4. Davie, *Titanic*, p. 103.

5. Barbara Starfield, "Is US Health Really the Best in the World?" *JAMA* (July 26, 2000): 483–85.

6. Mitchell Adams et al., *Saving Lives, Saving Money: The Imperative for Computerized Physician Order Entry in Massachusetts Hospitals* (Boston: Massachusetts Technology Collaborative and the New England Healthcare Institute, February 2008), p. 9.

7. Associated Press, "Study Recommends Program to Cut Rate of Cancer Deaths," *New York Times*, October 29, 1986.

8. Dolores Kong, "Heart Attacks Were Avoidable," *Boston Globe*, May 6, 1991.

9. Chun Wei Choo, *The Knowing Organization* (New York: Oxford University Press, 1998), p. 168.

10. Alfred Harrison, Statement to the United States Senate Committee on Commerce, Science and Transportation, Subcommittee on Consumer Affairs, Foreign Commerce and Tourism, May 16, 2002.

11. "A Policy of Evasion and Deception," *Washington Post*, February 6, 2003.

12. Judith Miller and Julia Preston, "Threats and Responses: The Inspector; Blix Says He Saw Nothing to Prompt a War," *New York Times*, January 31, 2003.

13. Peter Beaumont, Antony Barnett, and Gaby Hinsliff, "Iraqi Mobile Labs Nothing to Do with Germ Warfare, Report Finds," *Observer*, June 15, 2003.

14. "Tape Urges Muslim Fight against U.S.," CNN, February 12, 2003, http://www.cnn.com/2003/ALLPOLITICS/02/11/powell.binladen/index.html. Also: Firas Al-Atraqchi, "Misleading the Public: Osama Wants Saddam Dead," *Dissident Voice*, October 12, 2003, http://www.dissidentvoice.org/Articles/Al-Atraqchi_Osama-Saddam.htm.

15. Richard Sales, "The Niger Forgeries," Sic Semper Tyrannis, October 26, 2005, http://turcopolier.typepad.com/sic_semper_tyrannis/richard_sale/index.html.

16. Joby Warrick, "U.S. Claim on Iraqi Nuclear Program Is Called into Question," *Washington Post*, January 24, 2003.

17. Walter Isaacson, "GQ Icon: Colin Powell," *Gentleman's Quarterly*, October 2007, http://men.style.com/gq/features/landing?id=content_5900.

18. *Jeppesen v. Brocklesby*, US Supreme Court (1985).

19. Allen Kent, James G. Williams, Rosalind Kent, and Carolyn M. Hall, *Encyclopedia of Microcomputers*, vol. 9 (New York: Marcel Dekker, 1987), p. 35.

CHAPTER 2: VIRTUAL TRUTH

1. Throughout the discussion of Three Mile Island, I am drawing in part on Daniel Ford's book *Three Mile Island: Thirty Minutes to Meltdown* (New York: Penguin Books, 1982), a comprehensive and widely accepted account of these events.

2. Ford, *Three Mile Island*, p. 89.

3. Ibid., p. 111.

4. Ibid., p. 43.

5. Ibid., p. 110.

6. *Report of the President's Commission on the Accident at Three Mile Island* (Washington, DC: Government Printing Office, 1979), p. 111.

7. Ibid., p. 127.

8. Ford, *Three Mile Island*, p. 210.

9. *Report of the President's Commission*, p. 139.

10. Ford, *Three Mile Island*, p. 210.

11. *Report of the President's Commission*, p. 138.

12. Ford, *Three Mile Island*, p. 230.

13. *Report of the President's Commission*, pp. 224–25.

14. Ford, *Three Mile Island*, pp. 90–91.

15. Frederic Charles Bartlett, *Remembering* (London: Cambridge University Press, 1932).

16. Ford, *Three Mile Island*, p. 126.

17. Seymour M. Hersh, *The Target Is Destroyed* (New York: Random House, 1986), p. 200.

18. *Report of the Presidential Commission on the Space Shuttle* Challenger *Accident* (Washington, DC: US Government Printing Office, June 6, 1986).

19. Ibid., p. 125.

20. Ibid., p. 126.

21. *Report of the Presidential Commission*, pp. I–142–44, II–H3.

22. Malcolm McConnell, *Challenger: A Major Malfunction* (Garden City, NY: Doubleday, 1987), p. 123.

23. Throughout this description of the conference, I am indebted to Malcolm McConnell's lucid discussion in ibid., pp. 191–98, as well as to the *Report of the Presidential Commission*.

24. McConnell, *Challenger*, p. 55.

25. Ibid., p. 7.

26. Ibid., pp. 196–98.

27. *Report of the Presidential Commission*, p. 92.

28. McConnell, *Challenger*, p. 194.

29. Ibid., p. 200.

30. *Report of the Presidential Commission*, p. 88.

31. Ibid., p. 98.

32. Ibid., p. 101.

33. Ibid., p. 103.

34. Albert O. Hirshman, *Exit, Voice and Loyalty* (Cambridge, MA: Harvard University Press, 1970), pp. 92–93.

35. Ted Tweitmeyer, "*Challenger* 20 Years Later—The Rest of the Story," rense.com, http://www.rense.com/general69/chall.htm. Also: Chris Bergin, "Remembering the Mistakes of *Challenger*," NASAspaceflight.com, January 28, 2007.

36. Associated Press, "Ex-Shuttle Rocket Chief Quits Space Agency," *New York Times*, July 17, 1986.

37. *Report of the Columbia Accident Investigation Board* (Washington, DC: Government Printing Office, 2003), p. 9.

CHAPTER 3: MEMBERS OF THE MIND

1. The diagram of the brain included here is intended only to identify the major functions, and it is not anatomically correct. For an accurate description, I refer the reader to Charles Hampden-Turner, *Maps of the Mind: Charts and Concepts of the Mind and Its Labyrinths* (London: Collier/Macmillan, 1982).

2. Robert Ornstein and Richard F. Thompson, *The Amazing Brain* (Boston: Houghton Mifflin, 1984), pp. 21ff.

3. Robert Ornstein and David Sobel, *The Healing Brain* (New York: Simon & Schuster, 1987), p. 36.

4. Wilder Penfield and T. Rasmussen, *The Cerebral Cortex of Man* (New York: Macmillan, 1957).

5. Richard Restak, *The Brain* (New York: Bantam, 1984), p. 12.

6. Marvin Minsky, *The Society of Mind* (New York: Simon & Schuster, 1986), pp. 89–92.

7. Michael Gazzaniga, *The Social Brain* (New York: Basic Books, 1987).

8. James Grier Miller, *Living Systems* (New York: McGraw-Hill, 1978), p. 384.

9. E. H. Hess and J. M. Polt, "Pupil Size as Related to Interest Value of Visual Stimuli," *Science* 132 (1960): 349–50.

10. Quoted by K. R. Popper in Philip N. Johnson-Laird and P. C. Wason, *Thinking* (London: Cambridge University Press, 1977), p. 268.

11. E. Foulke and A. A. Broadbeck, "Transmission of Morse Code by Electrocutaneous Stimulation," *Psychology Record* 18 (1968): 617–22.

12. Miller, *Living Systems*, p. 105.

13. Ibid.

14. Charles B. Nemeroff and Garth Bisette, "Neuropeptides in Psychiatric Disorders," *American Handbook of Psychiatry* (New York: Basic Books, 1986), pp. 64–110.

15. Jean-Pierre Changeux, *The Neuronal Man* (New York: Oxford University Press, 1985), pp. 134–39.

16. Ibid., p. 101.

17. Johannes Kepler, *A New Astronomy* (1609). A good account of his discovery of the ellipse is available at http://www.schillerinstitute.org/fid_97-01/982_orbit_ceres_chaps/982_chap_6-9.pdf.

18. There may be significant cultural differences in how much uncertainty an individual can tolerate. Geert Hofstede, a Dutch scientist who has studied team behavior among airline crews in many different countries, argues from his experimental data that in the "collectivist" cultures of Greece, Korea, and many Latin American countries where emphasis is placed on the group's goals rather than the individual's, there is a high degree of "uncertainty avoidance." In the United States, by contrast, Hofstede reports that airline pilots and other team leaders are more comfortable working in a situation where not all the answers are clear. They are more willing to depart from procedure, improvise, and "go it alone." The Dutch psychologist notes that this may explain why American pilots so often ignore checklists and why they often take a simple do-it-my-way approach to crew relations. See Geert Hofstede, *Cultures and Organizations: Software of the Mind* (New York: McGraw-Hill, 2004).

19. David Evans, "*Vincennes*, A Case Study." This excellent but apparently unpublished analysis was written by a retired marine lieutenant colonel and appears on the Hampton Roads Navy ROTC training site at http://www.odu.edu/ao/hrnrotc/students/ns_courses/302/vincennes.pdf.

20. Ted Koppel, "The USS *Vincennes*: Public War, Secret War," *Nightline*, ABC News, July 1, 1992.

21. "Sea of Lies," *Newsweek*, July 13, 1992, pp. 29–39, http://alt-f4 .org/img/seaoflies.html.

22. *Investigation Report: Formal Investigation into the Circumstances Surrounding the Downing of Iran Air Flight 655 on 3 July 1988* (Washington, DC: Office of the US Secretary of Defense, August 18, 1988), http:// homepage.ntlworld.com/jksonc/docs/ir655-dod-report.html.

23. "Sea of Lies," pp. 29–39.

24. *Investigation Report*, p. 5.

25. Ibid., p. 4.

26. In January 2008, the Iranian Revolutionary Guards were at it again, harassing American warships in the Straits of Hormuz by buzzing around them in open boats. But the language has not changed. The Americans shouted through their bullhorns: "You are straying into danger and may be subject to defensive measures. . . . Request you alter course immediately to remain clear." And the Iranians responded with bracing candor: "I am coming to you. You will explode after a few minutes." No shots were actually fired.

27. Evans, "*Vincennes*," p. 9.

28. "Protector of the American Fleet," *New York Times Magazine*, October 6, 1985, pp. 34–37.

29. *Investigation Report*, p. 51.

30. Ibid., p. 43.

31. Ibid., p. 42.

32. Will Rogers, Sharon Rogers, and Gene Gregston, *Storm Center: The USS* Vincennes *and Iran Air Flight 655: A Personal Account of Tragedy and Terrorism* (Annapolis, MS: US Naval Institute Press, 1992).

33. Evans, "*Vincennes*," p. 12.

34. Miller, *Living Systems*, p. 139.

35. George A. Miller, "The Magical Number Seven, Plus or Minus Two," *Psychological Review* 63 (1956): 81–97.

36. Paul C. Nystrom and William H. Starbuck, *Handbook of Organizational Design* (New York: Oxford University Press, 1981), pp. 21ff.

37. Miller, *Living Systems*, pp. 121–202.

38. Miller, *"The Magical Number Seven,"* pp. 92–95.

39. B. M. Gross, *The Managing of Organizations*, vol. 2 (New York: Macmillan, 1964), p. 771.

CHAPTER 4: CHALLENGING TRUTH

1. Lawrence K. Altman, "Big Doses of Chemotherapy Drug Killed Patient, Hurt 2nd," *New York Times*, March 24, 1995.

2. "Initial Misstep Goes Undetected," *Boston Globe*, March 23, 1995.

3. Richard A. Knox, "Doctor's Orders Killed Cancer Patient. Dana-Farber Admits Drug Overdose Caused Death of Globe Columnist, Damage to Second Woman," *Boston Globe*, March 23, 1995.

4. Richard A. Knox, "Response Is Slow to Deadly Mixups; Too Little Done to Avert Cancer Drug Errors," *Boston Globe*, June 26, 1995.

5. Ibid.

6. Richard A. Knox, "Drug Dosage Was Questioned, Dana-Farber Pharmacist Sent Order Back to Doctor in Breast Cancer Case," *Boston Globe*, June 19, 1995.

7. Philip Aspden, *Patient Safety: Achieving a New Standard for Care* (Washington, DC: National Academies Press, 2004), p. 43.

8. "Johns Hopkins Settles in 2-year-old's Death," *USA Today*, February 3, 2004.

9. Maria Kotula, "Transplant Patient Nearly Killed by Prescription Error," WCNC-TV, Charlotte, NC, May 8, 2007, http://www.wcnc.com/news/local/stories/wcnc-050807-krg-prescription_error.4e424690 .html.

10. Emma Jane Kirby, "Cancer Patients' Battle for Justice," BBC News, October 18, 2007.

11. In the years since the death of Betsy Lehman, Dana-Farber has broken from the tradition of ignore, deny, forget by publicly and persistently focusing on the events of 1994. All new employees at the cancer hospital receive training in how to reduce the risk of medical error, using the Betsy Lehman case as an example. More computer checks have

been put in place, the authority of one doctor to write such dangerous prescriptions has been reduced, and Dana-Farber executives have waged a continued campaign, at the hospital and within the profession, to emphasize the responsibility that everyone on a medical team bears in getting the information right. Scott Allen, "With Work, Dana-Farber Learns from '94 Mistakes," *Boston Globe*, November 30, 2004, http://www.boston.com/news/local/articles/2004/11/30/with_work_dana_farber_learns_from_94_mistakes/?page=1.

12. Liz Kowalczyk, "Surgical Mistakes Persist in Bay State," *Boston Globe*, October 26, 2007.

13. Geert Hofstede, *Culture's Consequences, Comparing Values, Behaviors, Institutions, and Organizations Across Nations* (Thousand Oaks, CA: Sage Publications, 2001).

14. James Wallace, "Aerospace Notebook: Machismo Cockpit Culture Puts Safety in Jeopardy," *Seattle Post-Intelligencer*, November 20, 2007.

15. These five assertiveness steps are attributed to a CRM consultant named Todd Bishop. The original material has not been located.

16. Dr. Gerald B. Healy, "Ending Medical Errors with Airline Industry's Help," *Boston Globe*, January 8, 2008.

17. Hamilton Jordan, *No Such Thing as a Bad Day* (Atlanta: Longstreet, 2001).

18. William James, "Lecture II: What Pragmatism Means," *William James: Writings 1902–1910* (New York: Library of America, 1988).

19. Witter Bynner, *The Way of Life, According to Lau Tzu* (New York: Perigee, 1986).

20. Yu-lan Fung, *A Short History of Chinese Philosophy* (New York: Free Press, 1997). An excellent overview.

21. Edith Hamilton, ed., *The Collected Dialogues of Plato* (Princeton, NJ: Princeton University Press, 2005).

22. *Hippocrates, Volume 2*, trans. W. H. S. Jones (Cambridge, MA: Harvard University Press, 1923).

23. Will Durant and Ariel Durant, *The Age of Reason Begins* (New York: Simon & Schuster, 1961), p. 623.

24. Brian Vickers, ed., *Francis Bacon: The Major Works* (New York: Oxford University Press, 2002). The four idols (the cave, the tribe, the marketplace and the theater) are described in Bacon's essay "The New

Organon, or True Directions Concerning the Interpretation of Nature," published in 1620.

25. Durant and Durant, *The Age of Reason Begins*, p. 95.

26. John Locke, *An Essay Concerning Human Understanding* (London: Oxford University Press, 1894).

27. Ben Ray Redman, *The Portable Voltaire* (New York: Penguin, 1977). A good introduction and sampler.

28. Durant and Durant, *The Age of Reason Begins*, p. 19.

29. Jean-Jacques Rousseau, *The Social Contract and Discourses by Jean-Jacques Rousseau*, trans. G. D. H. Cole (Toronto: J. M. Dent and Sons, 1923). From the "Discourse on the Arts and Sciences," http://oll.liberty fund.org/?option=com_staticxt&staticfile=show.php%3Ftitle=638&chap ter=71081&layout=html&Itemid=27.

30. Will Durant and Ariel Durant, *Rousseau and Revolution* (New York: Simon & Schuster, 1967), p. 880.

CHAPTER 5: THE INFORMATION WAR

1. In constructing this overview of the 9/11 attack, I am greatly indebted to the work of Paul Thompson and the open source Cooperative Research Project, which has attempted heroically to maintain an accurate time line of these events on its Web site, www.cooperative research.org. But unfortunately, the public record, including the *9/11 Commission Report*, is riddled with inaccuracies and elisions, and when all the available accounts are compared, there remain many inconsistencies and contradictions.

2. George W. Bush, "Remarks by the President upon Arrival," White House news release, September 16, 2001, http://www.whitehouse.gov/news/releases/2001/09/20010916-2.html.

3. Don Van Natta Jr., "Democrats Raise Questions over Remarks on Warnings," *New York Times*, May 18, 2002.

4. Richard S. Dunham, "Five Questions Bush Must Answer," *Business Week*, May 20, 2002.

5. Kathleen T. Rhem, "Myers and Sept. 11: We Hadn't Thought about This," Armed Forces Press Service, October 23, 2001.

6. John Ashcroft, "Press Briefing with FBI Director Robert Mueller," US Department of Justice, September 17, 2001.

7. Michael V. Hayden, "Statement for the Record before the Joint Inquiry of the Senate Select Committee on Intelligence," US Congress, October 17, 2002, http://www.fas.org/irp/congress/2002_hr/101702 hayden.html.

8. Walter Pincus and Dan Eggen, "White House Says Declassification of Pre-9/11 Document Will Be Delayed," *Washington Post*, April 10, 2004.

9. Mitch Lipka, "Multiple Identities of Hijack Suspects Confound FBI," *Sun-Sentinel*, September 28, 2001.

10. *Final Report of the National Commission on Terrorist Attacks upon the United States*, July 22, 2004, p. 168, http://www.9-11commission.gov.

11. Dan Eggen and Kathleen Day, "U.S. Ties Hijackers' Money to Al Qaeda; Investigators See Cash Trail as Key," *Washington Post*, October 7, 2001.

12. Paul Beckett, Carrick Mollencamp, and Michael Phillips, "Withdrawal Pains: In the Financial Fight against Terrorism, Leads Are Hard Won," *Wall Street Journal*, October 10, 2001.

13. *Final Report of the National Commission on Terrorist Attacks*, p. 457.

14. Joby Warrick and Joe Stephens, "Before Attack, U.S. Expected Different Hit; Chemical, Germ Agents Focus of Preparations," *Washington Post*, October 2, 2001.

15. Ralph Blumenthal, "Tapes Depict Proposal to Thwart Bomb Used in Trade Center Blast," *New York Times*, October 28, 1993.

16. Peter Lance, *Triple Cross* (New York: HarperCollins Publishers, 2006), p. 143.

17. Lindsay Murdoch, "Pact of Blood" *Advertiser* (Adelaide), June 3, 1995.

18. Ashton Carter, John Deutch, and Philip Zelikow, "Catastrophic Terrorism: Tackling the New Danger," *Foreign Affairs* 77, no. 6 (November 1998).

19. James Risen, "US Failed to Act on Warnings in '98 of a Plane Attack," *New York Times*, September 18, 2002.

20. Nicholas Rufford, "MI6 Warned US of Al-Qaeda Attacks," *Sunday Times* (London), June 9, 2002.

21. Douglas Waller, "Inside the Hunt for Osama," *Time*, December 21, 1998.

22. James Risen and Eric Lichtblau, "CIA Was Given Data on Hijacker Long Before 9/11," *New York Times*, February 24, 2004.

23. House Permanent Select Committee on Intelligence and the Senate Select Committee on Intelligence, *Report of the Joint Inquiry into the Terrorist Attacks of September 11, 2001*, 108th Cong., 1st sess., 2003, 135.

24. House Permanent Select Committee on Intelligence and the Senate Select Committee on Intelligence, *Final Report, Part Three; Topics—The Attacks of September 11, 2001*, 108th Cong., 1st sess., 2003.

25. For a fuller treatment of this interesting problem, see Brian Skyrms, *The Stag Hunt and the Evolution of Social Structure* (Cambridge: Cambridge University Press, 2003).

26. Gregg Gordon, "600 File Sept. 11 Suit," *(Minneapolis) Star Tribune*, August 16, 2002. See also Bob McKeown, interview with Jean-Charles Brisard, *Fifth Estate*, Canadian Broadcasting Corporation, October 29, 2003, http://www.cbc.ca/fifth/conspiracytheories/brisard.pdf.

27. Mark Bowden, "US Had Capability But Lacked Will to Act against Bin Laden, Critics Say," *Philadelphia Inquirer*, September 16, 2001.

28. Barton Gellman, "The Covert Hunt for bin Laden: Broad Effort Launched after '98 Attacks," *Washington Post*, December 19, 2001.

29. Michael Scheuer, *Imperial Hubris: Why the West Is Losing the War on Terror* (Dulles, VA: Potomac Books, 2005), pp. 263–64.

30. Richard A. Clarke, *Against All Enemies: Inside America's War on Terror* (New York: Basic Books, 2004), p. 195.

31. James V. Grimaldi and John Mintz, "Agent Alleges FBI Ignored Hamas Activities," *Washington Post*, May 11, 2002.

32. Barton Gellman, "US Was Foiled Multiple Times in Efforts to Capture Bin Laden or Have Him Killed," *Washington Post*, October 3, 2001.

33. James Goodwin, "Inside Able Danger: The Secret Birth, Extraordinary Life and Untimely Death of a US Military Intelligence Program," Government Security News, September 2005.

34. Ibid.

35. Mark Zaid, testimony before the Senate Judiciary Committee, "Able Danger and Intelligence Information Sharing," US Congress,

Senate Committee on Judiciary, 109th Cong., 1st sess., September 21, 2005, http://judiciary.senate.gov/testimony.cfm?id=1606&wit_id=4668. Also: "Joint Hearing on the Able Danger Program," House Armed Services Committee: Subcommittee on Strategic Forces and Subcommittee on Terrorism, Unconventional Threats and Capabilities, February 15, 2006, http://www.floppingaces.net/wp-content/hearing.pdf.

36. Sarah Lai Stirland, "DoD Employees Barred from Testifying about Terrorist Data-Mining Effort," *National Journal's Technology Daily*, September 21, 2005, http://www.govexec.com/dailyfed/0905/092150 tdpm1.htm.

37. "Pentagon Probes Able Danger Claims," Fox News, August 19, 2005.

38. James Rosen, "A 9/11 Tip-Off: Fact or Fancy? Debate Still Swirls around Claims that Secret Military Program ID'd Hijackers a Year before Attacks," *Sacramento Bee*, November 24, 2005.

39. Kie Fallis, Testimony to the Joint House and Senate Select Intelligence Committee, October 8, 2002, http://www.thememoryhole.org/911/hearings/911hearing-trans-oct08.htm.

40. Eric Rosenberg, "Official: Attack on Cole Foreseen," Hearst Newspapers, November 10, 2005.

41. "Curt Weldon, interview on *Lou Dobbs Tonight*, CNN, February 16, 2006, http://transcripts.cnn.com/TRANSCRIPTS/0602/16/ldt.01.html.

42. Anthony Shaffer, prepared statement to House, Armed Service Committee, Congress of the United States, 109th Cong., 2d sess., February 15, 2006, http://www.abledangerblog.com/2006/02/lt-col-shaffers-written-testimony.html.

43. Ibid.

44. Curt Weldon, Congressional Record: June 27, 2005, H5243-H5250, http://www.fas.org/irp/congress/2005_cr/s062705.html.

45. Thomas H. Kean and Lee H. Hamilton, "Kean-Hamilton Statement on Able Danger," 9/11 Public Discourse Project, August 12, 2005, p. 4, http://www.freerepublic.com/focus/f-news/1464859/posts.

46. Louis Freeh, "An Incomplete Investigation: Why Did the 9/11 Commission Ignore Able Danger?" *Wall Street Journal*, November 17, 2005.

47. Josh White, "Hijackers Were Not Identified Before 9/11, Investigation Says," Washington Post, September 22, 2006.

48. Steve Coll, *Ghost Wars: The Secret History of the CIA, Afghanistan, and Bin Laden, From the Soviet Invasion to September 10, 2001* (New York: Penguin, 2004), p. 482.

49. James Risen, "CIA's Inquiry on Qaeda Aide Seen as Flawed," *New York Times*, September 22, 2002.

50. Antony Barnett, Lee Hannon, and Martin Bright, "UK Spymasters Shrugged off al-Qaeda Recruit's Warning," *Observer*, June 6, 2004.

51. House Permanent Select Committee on Intelligence and the Senate Select Committee on Intelligence, *Joint Inquiry Staff Statement, Part I*, 107th Cong., 2d sess., 2002, http://www.fas.org/irp/congress/2002_hr/091802hill.html.

52. Greg Palast, *Best Democracy Money Can Buy: An Investigative Reporter Exposes the Truth about Globalization, Corporate Cons, and High-Finance Fraudsters* (New York: Plume Books, 2002), p. 102.

53. James Bamford, *A Pretext for War* (New York: Doubleday, 2004), p. 267.

54. Bryan Burrough, Evgenia Peretz, David Rose, and David Wise, "The Rush to Invade Iraq: The Ultimate Inside Account," *Vanity Fair*, May 2004, p. 234.

55. Clarke, *Against All Enemies*, p. 232.

56. Ibid., p. 30.

57. "Bremer Criticized Bush on Terrorism before Attacks," Associated Press, April 29, 2004.

58. Jim Garamone, "Intelligence Chief Details Threats Facing America," American Forces Press Service, February 22, 2001.

59. Robert Burns, "CIA Chief Calls bin Laden Biggest Threat to US Security," Associated Press, February 7, 2001.

60. *Final Report of the National Commission on Terrorist Attacks*, p. 255.

61. Condoleezza Rice, interview of the National Security Advisor by Network Correspondents, White House news release, March 24, 2004, http://www.whitehouse.gov/news/releases/2004/03/20040324-3.html.

62. "Why Was Russia's Intelligence on Al-Qaeda Ignored?" *Jane's Intelligence Review* (October 5, 2001).

63. Condoleezza Rice, testimony to Hearing of the National Com-

mission on Terrorist Attacks upon the United States, April 8, 2004, news.findlaw.com/hdocs/docs/terrorism/911comm40804tran.pdf.

64. Ned Stafford, "Echelon Gave Authorities Warning of Attacks," *Washington Post*, September 14, 2001.

65. Stephen Push, Kristin Breitweiser, and Eleanor Hill, Testimonies to the House Permanent Select Committee on Intelligence and the Senate Select Committee on Intelligence, 107th Cong., 2d sess., 2002.

66. Ibid.

67. Paul Haven, "Before Sept. 11, There Were Hints from Overseas that Something Was Afoot," Associated Press, May 19, 2002.

68. John K. Cooley, "The US Ignored Foreign Warnings, Too," *International Herald Tribune*, May 21, 2002.

69. Clarke, *Against All Enemies*, p. 236.

70. House Permanent Select Committee on Intelligence and the Senate Select Committee on Intelligence, *Final Report, Part Three*.

71. Bob Woodward, "Two Months Before 9/11, an Urgent Warning to Rice," *Washington Post*, October 1, 2006.

72. Ibid.

73. George Tenet, *At the Center of the Storm: My Years at the CIA* (New York: HarperCollins, 2007), p. 154.

74. Nina Burleigh, "Bush, Oil and the Taliban," Salon.com, February 8, 2002, http://dir.salon.com/story/politics/feature/2002/02/08/forbidden/index.html.

75. Final Report of the National Commission on Terrorist Attacks, p. 260.

76. Harry Samit, testimony in the Zacarias Moussaoui trial, US District Court for the Eastern District of Virginia, Alexandria Division, March 9, 2006. The law has changed since 2001. In July 2006, the Ninth Circuit Court of Appeals in California upheld the right of customs officials to search, and sometimes confiscate, laptops of all persons crossing the border into the United States, including American citizens, without a warrant or probable cause. Martha L. Arias, "Laptops Content May be Subject to Inspection upon Entering the United States," Internet Business Law Services, March 7, 2007, http://www.ibls.com/internet_law_news_portal_view.aspx?s=latestnews&id=1584.

77. Greg B. Smith, "Some Got Warning: Don't Go Downtown on Sept. 11, Feds Say Mid-Easterners Knew of the Coming Danger," *New*

York Daily News, October 12, 2001. This story is no longer available on *New York Daily News* Web site.

78. Allen M. Poteshman, "Unusual Option Market Activity and the Terrorist Attacks of September 11, 2001," *Journal of Business* 79 (2006): 1703–26.

79. Evan Thomas and Mark Hosenball, "Bush: We're at War," *Newsweek*, September 24, 2001.

80. Herbert A. Simon, *Administrative Behavior* (New York: Simon & Schuster, 1945), p. 55.

81. Twelfth Public Hearing, National Commission on Terrorist Attacks upon the United States (Washington: US Congress, June 17, 2004), http://www.9-11commission.gov/archive/hearing12/9-11Commission_Hearing_2004-06-17.htm.

82. Gail Sheehy, "9/11 Tapes Reveal Ground Personnel Muffled Attacks," *New York Observer*, June 17, 2004.

83. *Final Report of the National Commission on Terrorist Attacks*, pp. 17–20.

84. Glen Johnson, "Probe Reconstructs Horror, Calculated Attacks on Planes," *Boston Globe*, November 23, 2001.

85. William B. Scott, "F-16 Pilots Considered Ramming Flight 93," *Aviation Week & Space Technology*, September 9, 2002.

86. William Langley, "Revealed: What Really Went on During Bush's Missing Hours," *Daily Telegraph* (London), December 16, 2001.

87. *Final Report of the National Commission on Terrorist Attacks*, p. 42.

88. Ibid., p. 36.

89. Clarke, *Against All Enemies*, pp. 1–2.

90. Ibid., p. 3.

91. Dan Balz and Bob Woodward, "America's Chaotic Road to War (Part 1: Sept. 11)," *Washington Post*, January 27, 2002. Also Clarke, *Against All Enemies*, p. 18.

92. *Final Report of the National Commission on Terrorist Attacks*, p. 41.

93. Ibid., p. 42.

94. Ibid., p. 43.

95. Ibid., p. 45.

96. Barton Gellman and Jo Becker, "A Different Understanding with the President," *Washington Post*, June 24, 2007.

97. The original plan for establishing an emergency government had been developed in 1980 by Dick Cheney, then the congressman from Wyoming, and Donald Rumsfeld, former secretary of defense and CEO of G. D. Searle & Co. The action officer on the project was Lt. Colonel Oliver North, and within a few years the budget for this highly classified project had reached a billion dollars a year. Although the plan remains secret, it is said to include provisions for warrantless eavesdropping, widespread detention of legal and illegal Americans, and the imposition of martial law. James Mann, "The Armageddon Plan," *Atlantic*, March 2004.

98. Barton Gellman and Susan Schmidt, "Shadow Government Is at Work in Secret," *Washington Post*, March 1, 2002.

99. George W. Bush, remarks on United States Financial Sanctions against Foreign Terrorists and Their Supporters and an Exchange with Reporters, White House news release, September 24, 2001, http://www.whitehouse.gov/news/releases/2001/09/20010924-4.html.

100. "Increasing FDNY's Preparedness," New York City Fire Department, August 19, 2002, http://www.nyc.gov/html/fdny/html/mck_report/toc.html.

101. "World Trade Center Disaster: Initial Response," Fire Engineering, September 2002, http://www.fireengineering.com/articles/article_display.html?id=158382.

102. *Final Report of the National Commission on Terrorist Attacks*, p. 304, http://www.firehouse.com/terrorist/wtcaudio/wtcaudio9.html.

103. Wayne Barrett and Dan Collins, "Rudy's Grand Illusion," *Village Voice*, August 29, 2006.

104. Ibid.

105. John Peruggia, transcript of World Trade Center Task Force Interview, City of New York, October 25, 2001, http://graphics8.nytimes.com/packages/pdf/nyregion/20050812_WTC_GRAPHIC/9110160.PDF.

106. Joseph Fortis, transcript of World Trade Center Task Force Interview, City of New York, November 9, 2001, http://graphics8.nytimes.com/packages/pdf/nyregion/20050812_WTC_GRAPHIC/9110200.PDF.

107. Jim Dwyer and Michelle O'Donnell, "9/11 Firefighters Told of Isolation Amid Disaster," *New York Times*, September 9, 2005.

108. Ibid.

109. Jere Longman, *Among the Heroes: United Flight 93 and the Passengers and Crew Who Fought Back* (New York: Harper Paperbacks, 2002), pp. 107–108.

110. Mike Wagner and Ken McCall, "Passengers Thwarted Hijackers," Pittsburgh: WPXI 11, September 13, 2001.

111. Ian Christopher McCaleb, "Bush: U.S. Feels 'Quiet, Unyielding Anger,'" *CNN Breaking News*, September 12, 2001, http://archives.cnn.com/2001/US/09/11/white.house.

112. Bamford, *A Pretext for War*, p. 285.

113. Richard A. Clarke, "Clarke's Take on Terror; What Bush's Ex-Adviser Says about Efforts to Stop War on Terror," *60 Minutes*, March 21, 2004, http://www.cbsnews.com/stories/2004/03/19/60minutes/main607356.shtml.

114. Laurie Mylroie, "The World Trade Center Bomb: Who Is Ramzi Yousef? And Why It Matters," *National Interest*, Winter 1995/96.

115. Mylroie's book *Saddam Hussein's Unfinished War against America* has apparently been removed from the market and replaced by *The War against America: Saddam Hussein and the World Trade Center Attacks: A Study of Revenge* (New York: Harper Paperbacks, 2001).

116. George Wright, "Wolfowitz: Iraq War Was about Oil," *Guardian Unlimited*, June 4, 2003.

117. "The Taliban Guy the CIA Won't Question," *Time*, February 25, 2002.

118. Ron Suskind, *The One Percent Doctrine; Deep Inside America's Pursuit of Its Enemies Since 9/11* (New York: Simon & Schuster, 2006), p. 58.

119. Peter Bergen, "The Battle of Tora Bora: What Really Happened?" PeterBergen.com, October 28, 2004, http://www.peterbergen.com/bergen/articles/details.aspx?id=198.

120. Murray Waas, "Key Bush Intelligence Briefing Kept from Hill Panel," *National Journal*, November 22, 2005.

121. Robert Scheer, "The 9/11 Secret in the CIA's Back Pocket," *Los Angeles Times*, October 19, 2004.

122. Eric Lichtblau, "9/11 Report Cites Many Warnings about Hijackings," *New York Times*, February 10, 2005.

123. Office of Inspector General, "A Review of the FBI's Handling

of Intelligence Information Related to the September 11 Attacks," US Department of Justice, November 2004.

124. Eric Lichtblau, "Report Details F.B.I.'s Failure on 2 Hijackers," *New York Times*, June 10, 2005.

125. Andrew Card, "What If You Had to Tell the President?" *San Francisco Chronicle*, September 11, 2002, http://sfgate.com/cgi-bin/article.cgi?f=/c/a/2002/09/11/MN911voice03.DTL.

126. Seymour M. Hersh, "King's Ransom: How Vulnerable Are the Saudi Royals?" *New Yorker*, October 22, 2001.

127. In his book *The Commission: The Uncensored History of the 9/11 Commission* (New York: Twelve, 2008), *New York Times* reporter Philip Shenon disclosed that the commission's executive director, Philip Zelikow, engaged in extensive and "surreptitious" communications with Karl Rove and others in the White House throughout the commission's twenty-month investigation. Shenon asserts that Zelikow suppressed information about his own previous involvement in the White House post-9/11 actions, including his role in demoting Richard Clarke. Shenon concludes, based on extensive interviews with members of the commission and its staff, that Zelikow used his position as executive director to remove from the report any criticism of the Bush administration for failing to prevent the attacks.

128. David Ray Griffin, *The 9/11 Commission Report* (Northampton, MA: Olive Branch Press, 2005), pp. 90–91.

129. Ibid., pp. 91–94.

130. Ibid., pp. 25–32.

131. Ibid., 32–39.

132. Craig Unger, "Saving the Saudis," *Vanity Fair*, October 2003, http://www.wesjones.com/saudi1.htm.

133. *Final Report of the National Commission on Terrorist Attacks*, p. 346, http://www.faqs.org/docs/911/911Report-346.html.

134. "Why the 9/11 Conspiracy Theories Won't Go Away," *Time*, September 3, 2006.

135. The Harris Poll, February 6–12, 2007, http://www.pollingreport.com/institut.htm.

CHAPTER 6: DEADLY DECISIONS

1. Walter Laqueur, *A World of Secrets: The Uses and Limits of Intelligence* (New York: Basic Books, 1985), p. 175.

2. Evan Thomas, "How Bush Blew It," *Newsweek*, September 19, 2005.

3. Doris Kearns Goodwin, *Team of Rivals: The Political Genius of Abraham Lincoln* (New York: Simon & Schuster, 2005), p. 275.

4. Matthew Continetti, "*Scheuer v. Clarke,*" *Daily Standard*, November 22, 2004.

5. Richard A. Clarke, *Against All Enemies: Inside America's War on Terror* (New York: Basic Books, 2004),

6. Office of Inspector General, "A Review of the FBI's Handling of Intelligence Information Related to the September 11 Attacks," US Department of Justice, November 2004, pp. 128–32.

7. Ibid., pp. 139–60.

8. Ibid., p. 151.

9. John Riley, "Agent: Suspicions of Plot Ignored," *Newsday*, March 21, 2006.

10. "Coleen Rowley's Memo to FBI Director Robert Mueller: An Edited Version of the Agent's 13-Page Letter," *Time*, May 21, 2002.

11. Bethany McLean, interview, JournalismJobs.com, June 2005, http://www.journalismjobs.com/bethany_mclean.cfm.

12. Michael Grunwald and Manuel Roig-Franzia, "Awaiting Ivan in the Big Uneasy," *Washington Post*, September 15, 2004.

13. Joel K. Bourne, "Gone with the Water," *National Geographic*, October 2004, http://magma.nationalgeographic.com/ngm/0410/feature5/?fs=www3.nationalgeographic.com&fs=plasma.nationalgeographic.com.

14. Michael Behar, "Hurricanes," *Popular Science*, April 2005, http://www.popsci.com/popsci/science/22040b4511b84010vgnvcm1000004eecbccdrcrd.html.

15. Mark Schleifstein, "Home Is Where the Flood Is; 1 in 3 Stay Put in Big Hurricane," *(New Orleans) Times Picayune*, November 22, 2003, http://hurricane.lsu.edu/_in_the_news/1103tp.htm.

16. Mark Schleifstein, "In Case of Emergency: Officials Hope Eight

Days of Intense Training for a Catastrophic Hurricane Will Aid Recovery Efforts If the Real Thing Ever Hits," *Times-Picayune*, July 20, 2004, http://www.ohsep.louisiana.gov/newsrelated/incaseofemrgencyexercise.htm.

17. Susan B. Glasser and Michael Grunwald, "The Steady Buildup to a City's Chaos," *Washington Post*, September 11, 2005.

18. "Katrina: Failure at Every Turn," Knight Ridder, September 11, 2005.

19. Bertrand Russell, a philosopher who thought a great deal about truth and had a habit of saying things concisely, said: "A stupid man's report of what a clever man says can never be accurate, because he unconsciously translates what he hears into something he can understand" (*History of Western Philosophy*).

20. Horst Faas and Peter Arnett, "Civilians Fear My Lai is U.S.' Achilles Heel," *Cleveland Plain Dealer*, December 8, 1969.

21. *Final Report of the National Commission on Terrorist Attacks upon the United States*, July 22, 2004, p. 43.

22. Michael Massing, "Now They Tell Us," *New York Review of Books*, February 26, 2004.

23. Voltaire (Francois-Marie Arouet), Letter to Friedrich William, Crown Prince of Prussia, November 28, 1770.

24. Walter Cronkite, *CBS Evening News*, February 27, 1968.

25. Jonathan Van Meter, "Unanchored," *New York Magazine*, September 19, 2005.

26. Peter Wyden, *Bay of Pigs* (New York: Simon & Schuster, 1979), pp. 136–38.

27. This lovely observation is from an early Internet posting by Phil Gibbs, on the Usenet, Physics, FAQ (Frequently Asked Questions), September 1996, updated by Sugihara Hiroshi in July 1997, http://math.ucr.edu/home/baez/physics/General/occam.html

28. Associated Press, "Military Aides Still Carry the President's Nuclear 'Football,'" *USA Today*, May 5, 2005. http://www.usatoday.com/news/washington/2005-05-05-nuclear-football_x.htm.

29. Roberto Aron and Jonathan L. Rosner, *How to Prepare Witnesses for Trial* (New York: McGraw-Hill, 1985), pp. 86–87.

30. Alfred North Whitehead, *Adventures of Ideas* (New York: Macmillan, 1956), p. 313.

31. "Big Dig Epoxy, Who Blew It?" *Design News*, July 11, 2007, http:// www.designnews.com/article/CA6459232.html.

32. *Achieving Justice: Freeing the Innocent, Convicting the Guilty; Report of the ABA Criminal Justice Section's Ad Hoc Innocence Committee to Ensure the Integrity of the Criminal Process* (Chicago: American Bar Association, 2006), pp. xvii–xviii.

CHAPTER 7: THE COMING EPIDEMIC

1. Laurie Garrett, "The Next Pandemic?" *Foreign Affairs*, July/August 2005.

2. Grattan Woodson, *Bird Flu Manual* (Charleston, SC: Book-surge.com, 2006), p. 60.

3. "Were Bird Flu Fears Overblown? H5N1 Virus 'Extremely' Stable, Says Animal Health Chief," MSNBC News, January 10, 2008, http://www.msnbc.msn.com/id/22590623/from/ET/.

4. *HHS Pandemic Influenza Plan* (Washington, DC: Department of Health and Human Services, 2005), http://www.hhs.gov/pandemicflu/plan/pdf/HHSPandemicInfluenzaPlan.pdf.

5. D. Scott Parson, Testimony to the Committee on Financial Services Subcommittee on Oversight and Investigations Protection and Compliance Policy, US House of Representatives, June 29, 2006, http://www.ustreas.gov/press/releases/js4342.htm.

6. Larry H. Altshuler, *Bird-Flu Primer* (New York: Sterling and Ross, 2006), p. 38.

7. *Pandemic Flu and the Potential for U.S. Economic Recession* (Washington, DC: Trust for America's Health, December 2007), http://healthyamericans.org/reports/flurecession/FluRecession.pdf.

8. *HHS Pandemic Influenza Plan*, p. 153.

9. "Epidemic and Pandemic Alert and Response," World Health Organization, 2006, http://www.who.int/csr/en.

10. "Were Bird Flu Fears Overblown?"

11. "WHO Bird Flu Expert Says 300 Dead in China, Government Hiding the Truth," *Frankfurter Allgemeine Zeitung*, November 20, 2005, http://www.curevents.com/vb/showthread.php?t=28953.

12. Harriet A. Washington, "Why Africa Fears Western Medicine," *New York Times*, July 31, 2007.

13. Woodson, *Bird Flu Manual*, p. 19.

14. *Pandemic Influenza Preparedness and Response Plan* (New York: New York City Department of Health and Mental Hygiene, July 2006), http://www.nyc.gov/html/doh/downloads/pdf/cd/cd-panflu-plan.pdf.

15. *Pandemic Influenza Preparedness and Response Plan* (California Department of Health Services, September 8, 2006), http://www.dhs.ca.gov/ps/dcdc/izgroup/pdf/pandemic.pdf.

16. Woodson, *Bird Flu Manual*, pp. 41ff.

17. "Were Bird Flu Fears Overblown?"

18. Dorothy Porter, *Health, Civilization, and the State* (New York: Routledge, 1999), pp. 36ff.

19. Christopher Lee, "Ex-Surgeon General Says White House Hushed Him," *Washington Post*, July 11, 2007.

20. "Avian Flu: Current Situation," CDC.gov, July 2007. http://www.cdc.gov/flu/avian/outbreaks/current.htm.

21. Brian G. Southwell, Yoori Hwang, and Alicia Torres, "Avian Influenza and US TV News," *CDC EID Journal* 12, no. 11, November 2006. http://www.cdc.gov/ncidod/EID/vol12no11/06-0672.htm.

22. Daniel Kahneman and Amos Tversky, "Prospect Theory: An Analysis of Decision under Risk," *Econometrica* (March 1979): 263–91.

CHAPTER 8: WALTZING INTO WAR

1. "Online Papers Modestly Boost Newspaper Readership," Pew Research Center for the People & the Press, July 30, 2006, http://pewresearch.org/pubs/238/online-papers-modestly-boost-newspaper-readership.

2. Blake Morrison, Rita Rubin, and Michael Hiestand, "Kelley Issues Apology as More Fabrications Emerge," *USA Today*, April 22, 2004.

3. Lou Dobbs, *Lou Dobbs Tonight*, CNN, April 14, 2005, http://transcripts.cnn.com/TRANSCRIPTS/0504/14/ldt.01.html.

4. "Lou Dobbs, Advocacy Journalist?" *60 Minutes*, CBS News, May 6, 2007.

5. Madeleine Pelner Cosman, "Illegal Aliens and American Medicine," *Journal of American Physicians and Surgeons* 10, no. 1 (Spring 2005).

6. "CBS Contributor Dobbs Defends False Leprosy Claim after Confrontation by CBS' Stahl," Media Matters for America, May 11, 2007, http://mediamatters.org/items/200705110004.

7. "*Wash. Post*'s Criticism of Sensationalist Katrina Coverage Focused on CNN, Ignored Fox," Media Matters for America, October 6, 2005, http://mediamatters.org/items/200510060009.

8. Sridhar Pappu, "Being Geraldo," *Atlantic Monthly*, June 2005.

9. Howard Kurtz, "Geraldo Rivera, In the Heat of Battle," *Washington Post*, December 24, 2001.

10. Bill O'Reilly, "Lessons of the New JonBenet Ramsey Information," *FoxNews Talking Points*, August 18, 2006, http://www.foxnews.com/story/0,2933,209229,00.html.

11. "Tobacco-Industry Sponsored Research Misled Public on Secondhand Smoke Issue, Study Finds," *Mayo Clinic*, September 2001. http://www.mayoclinic.org/news2001-rst/893.html.

12. "Interview: Famous Cancer Researcher's Secret Ties to Industry," *Families Against Cancer & Toxics*, December 2006. http://www.familiesagainstcancer.org/?id=412.

13. David Barstow, "Behind TV Analysts, Pentagon's Hidden Hand," *New York Times*, April 20, 2008.

14. Ibid.

15. Tom Fenton, *Bad News* (New York: Regan Books, 2005), p. 32.

16. Brian Stelter, "Reporters Say Networks Put Wars on Back Burner," *New York Times*, June 23, 2008.

17. Sherry Ricchiardi, "Whatever Happened to Iraq?," *American Journalism Review*, June/July 2008. http://www.ajr.org/Article.asp?id=4515.

18. Edward S. Herman and Noam Chomsky, *Manufacturing Consent* (New York: Pantheon Books, 1988), pp. 1–35.

19. In late 2007, Dan Rather, former anchorman at CBS News, claimed that CBS News president Andrew Heyward and senior vice president Betsy West blocked him from airing the story of Abu Ghraib, where US military and CIA officials were accused of torturing their Iraqi prisoners. In a breach-of-contract lawsuit against his former employer, Rather said that executives of CBS and its parent company, Viacom,

were yielding to pressure from the White House not to run the story. He himself received a phone call from General Richard B. Myers, chairman of the Joint Chiefs of Staff, asking that they not air the story because of the PR damage it would do. Rather claimed that the network finally agreed to broadcast the story but insisted that the item, which was a major CBS scoop, should receive no on-air promotion, that it would not be referred to elsewhere in the CBS Evening News, and that it be aired only once. Rather said that Sumner Redstone, chairman of Viacom, considered it to be "in his corporate interest to curry favor with the Bush administration." CBS said that Rather's claims were "without merit." From the Associated Press, September 21, 2007.

20. Herman, p. 17.

21. Liz Cox Barrett, "Yellin: News Execs Pushed For Positive Bush Stories," *Columbia Journalism Review.org*, May 29, 2008. http://www.cjr.org/the_kicker/yellin_news_execs_pushed_for_p.php.

22. Paul Myron Anthony Linebarger, *Psychological Warfare* (Washington, DC: Combat Forces Press, 1954), p. 39.

23. "President Participates in Social Security Conversation in New York," White House press release, May 24, 2005, http://www.whitehouse.gov/news/releases/2005/05/20050524-3.html.

24. Jill Kimball, "R. J. Reynolds Spends $4.5 Million on Anti-Measure 50 Advertisements," *Oregon Daily Emerald*, September 8, 2007. Also: "Big Tobacco Defeats Sick Kids," *New York Times*, November 8, 2007.

25. Mark Griffiths and Jonathan Parke, "The Psychology of Music in Gambling Environments," *Journal of Gambling Issues*, March 2005, http://www.camh.net/egambling/archive/pdf/JGI-issue13/JGI-Issue13-griffiths_2.pdf.

26. Sharon Rorem, "Fragrance-Free Nation: Malls and Scents; How Retail Stores Use Ambient Aromas," Suite 101.com, February 2, 2003, http://www.suite101.com/article.cfm/fragrance_free_nation/101247.

27. George Lakoff, "Inside the Frame," interview with Alternet.com, January 15, 2004, http://www.alternet.org/story/17574.

28. Jim Rutenberg, "McCain Tries to Define Obama as Out of Touch," *New York Times*, July 31, 2008.

29. Larry Freed, "Customer Reviews Drive Online Satisfaction, Recommendation and Loyalty," ForeSee Results, Spring 2007 report,

http://www.foreseeresults.com/_downloads/researchcommentary/Top
-100-Customer-Reviews-Spring-07.pdf.

30. Jim Robbins, "Climate Talk's Cancellation Splits a Town," *New York Times*, January 17, 2008.

31. Attributed to Hitler by Sir Hartley Shawcross, chief prosecutor at the Nuremburg Trials, in his opening address to the International Military Tribunal on December 4, 1945, http://www.courttv.com/archive/casefiles/nuremberg/shawcross.html.

32. William Branigan and Dana Priest, "Senate Report Blasts Intelligence Agencies' Flaws," Washington Post, July 9, 2004. See also "Report of the Select Committee on Intelligence on the US Intelligence Community's Prewar Intelligence Assessments on Iraq," http://www.fas.org/irp/congress/2006_rpt/srpt109-360.html.

33. In March 2008, the Department of Defense reported that thousands of hours of interrogations and an exhaustive analysis of six hundred thousand Iraq documents captured during the invasion showed no direct connection between Saddam's Iraq and al Qaeda. Because the material was considered "politically sensitive," however, the DoD announced that the full text of the report would be made available only on CD to those who mailed in a written request. The report would not be made available to the media. ABC News and others, posing as citizens, acquired the report and put it online within twenty-four hours, http://a.abcnews.com/images/pdf/Pentagon_Report_V1.pdf.

34. George J. Tenet, *At the Center of the Storm: My Years at the CIA* (New York: HarperCollins, 2007).

35. The Center for Public Integrity has documented nine hundred and thirty-five false statements related to Iraq made by President Bush, Secretary Powell, Secretary Rumsfeld, and the senior members of the administration in the two years beginning on September 11, 2001. The center provided transcripts and videos of the most important. The report is available at http://www.publicintegrity.org/WarCard/. In responding to this report, the White House said that the United States was part of "a broad coalition of nations," and that the intelligence underlying the statements had come from "multiple countries." White House Press Secretary Dana Perino further called the study "flawed" because it looked only at statements by members of the administration and not at

statements from congressmen and others around the world. "Study: Bush, Aides Made 935 False Statements in Run-Up to War," CNN, January 25, 2008, http://www.cnn.com/2008/POLITICS/01/23/bush.iraq/?imw=Y&iref=mpstoryemail.

36. Pat Roberts, remarks on the WMD Commission Report, US Senate press release, March 31, 2005, http://intelligence.senate.gov/050331.htm.

37. *Crude Oil: Uncertainty about Future Oil Supply Makes It Important to Develop a Strategy for Addressing a Peak and Decline in Oil Production* (Washington, DC: Government Accountability Office, February 2007), http://www.gao.gov/new.items/d07283.pdf.

38. Ritt Goldstein, "Oil Wars Pentagon's Policy Since 1999," *Sidney Morning Herald*, May 20, 2003.

39. Bill Clinton, televised statement to the American people, December 19, 1998, http://www.freerepublic.com/focus/f-news/1073519/posts.

40. "Arab American Publisher Says Bush Told Him in May 2000 He Planned to 'Take Out' Iraq," *Democracy Now!* March 11, 2005, http://www.democracynow.org/article.pl?sid=05/03/11/1449253.

41. Kim Cobb, "Writer Says Bush Talked about War in 1999," *Houston Chronicle*, October 31, 2004.

42. James Bamford, "The Man Who Sold the War," *Rolling Stone*, November 17, 2005.

43. Ibid.

44. Sheldon Rampton and John Stauber, *The Best War Ever: Lies, Damned Lies, and the Mess in Iraq* (New York: Jeremy Tarcher/Penguin, 2006), pp. 102ff.

45. Jane Mayer, "The Manipulator," *New Yorker*, June 7, 2004.

46. Mark Hosenball, "Intel: The Hunt for the Iranians' Informer," *Newsweek*, June 14, 2004.

47. Mayer, "The Manipulator."

48. Jonathan S. Landay and Tish Wells, "Global Misinformation Campaign Was Used to Build Case for War," Knight Ridder, March 16, 2004.

49. Nicholas Rufford, "Revealed: How MI6 Sold the Iraq War," *Times Sunday* (London), December 28, 2003.

50. Ibid.

51. Ibid.

52. Tommy R. Franks, *American Soldier* (New York: HarperCollins, 2004), p. 362.

53. Donald H. Rumsfeld, interview with the Associated Press, August 3, 2003, http://www.defenselink.mil/transcripts/transcript.aspx?transcriptid=2490.

54. Thomas E. Ricks, *Fiasco: The American Military Adventure in Iraq* (New York: Penguin, 2007), p. 77.

55. James Naughtie, *The Accidental American: Tony Blair and the Presidency* (New York: Public Affairs, 2004).

56. Patrick Tyler, "U.S. Strategy Plan Calls for Ensuring No Rivals Develop," *New York Times*, March 8, 1002.

57. *Rebuilding America's Defenses: Strategies, Forces, and Resources for a New Century* (Washington, DC: Project for the New American Century, 2000), http://www.newamericancentury.org/RebuildingAmericasDefenses.pdf.

58. Laurie Mylroie and Judith Miller, *Saddam Hussein and the Crisis in the Gulf* (New York: Ballantine Books, 1990).

59. Franklin Foer, "The Source of the Trouble," *New York Magazine*, June 7, 2004.

60. Howard Kurtz, "Reporter, Times Are Criticized for Missteps," *Washington Post*, October 17, 2005.

61. Karen Gullo, "Criminal Charges Filed in Probe," Associated Press (September 18, 2001). See also Edward J. Epstein, "Prague Revisited: The Evidence of an Iraq/al-Qaida Connection Hasn't Gone Away," Slate, November 19, 2003, http://www.slate.com/id/2091354/.

62. George W. Bush, during a question-and-answer period with the press, following a meeting with Colombian president Alvaro Uribe, September 25, 2001.

63. Warren P. Strobel, Jonathan S. Landay, and John Walcott, "Dissent over Going to War Grows among US Government Officials," Knight Ridder, October 7, 2002.

64. John Pilger, "This War of Lies Goes On," *Daily Mirror* (London), November 18, 2001, http://www.chss.montclair.edu/english/furr/pol/wtc/pilgerwaroflies111801.html.

65. George W. Bush, interview with the news media, March 13, 2001, http://www.whitehouse.gov/news/releases/2002/03/text/20020313-8.html.

66. *Report on the US Intelligence Community's Prewar Intelligence Assessments on Iraq* (Washington, DC: Select Committee on Intelligence, US Senate, July 7, 2004), http://www.globalsecurity.org/intell/library/congress/2004_rpt/iraq-wmd_intell_09jul2004_report2.pdf.

67. "Spinning the Tubes," *Four Corners*, Australia Broadcasting Corporation, October 27, 2003, http://www.abc.net.au/4corners/content/2003/transcripts/s976015.htm.

68. Ibid.

69. When the American army arrived in Iraq, it found an explanation for the extra thickness of the tube wall. The propellant used in these rockets had been purchased from a friend of Saddam's brother and was substandard. But rather than expose this corruption and switch to a different supplier, the military built the rocket casings a little tougher, used more propellant, and achieved the same goal.

70. *Report on the US Intelligence Community's Prewar Intelligence Assessments on Iraq*, p. 93.

71. "Impeachable Crimes Highlighted at UDC Forum," *Executive Intelligence Review* (May 25, 2007, http://www.larouchepub.com/other/2007/3421udc_forum_cheney.html.

72. David Johnston, "The Reach of War: Conclusions; Powell's 'Solid' C.I.A. Tips Were Soft, Committee Says," *New York Times*, July 11, 2004.

73. Bryan Burrough, Evgenia Peretz, David Rose, and David Wise, "The Rush to Invade Iraq: The Ultimate Inside Account," *Vanity Fair*, May 2004.

74. Ibid.

75. David Barstow, William J. Broad, and Jeff Gerth, "Skewed Intelligence Data in March to War in Iraq," *New York Times*, October 3, 2004.

76. Ibid.

77. Cheney is probably referring to Jeffrey Goldberg, "The Great Terror," *New Yorker*, March 25, 2002.

78. Dick Cheney, interview with Wolf Blitzer, *CNN Late Edition*, March 24, 2002, http://www.whitehouse.gov/vicepresident/news-speeches/speeches/vp20020324-2.html.

79. Bamford, *The Man Who Sold the War*.

80. McCollam Douglas, "How Chalabi Played the Press," *Columbia Journalism Review*, July/August 2004.

81. Stephen Pelletiére, "A War Crime or Act of War?" *New York Times*, January 31, 2003.

82. Elizabeth Bumiller, "Traces of Terror: The Strategy: Bush Aides Set Strategy to Sell Policy on Iraq," *New York Times*, September 7, 2002.

83. Michael R. Gordon and Judith Miller, "US Says Hussein Intensifies Quest for A-Bomb Parts," *New York Times*, September 8, 2002.

84. Colin Powell, press briefing after the OAS Meeting, US State Department, September 8, 2002, http://www.state.gov/secretary/former/powell/remarks/2003/21348.htm.

85. Dick Cheney, interview on *Meet the Press*, NBC News, September 8, 2002, http://www.mtholyoke.edu/acad/intrel/bush/meet.htm.

86. Condoleezza Rice, interview on *CNN Late Edition*, CNN, September 8, 2002. http://transcripts.cnn.com/TRANSCRIPTS/0209/08/le.00.html.

87. Michael Isikoff and David Corn, *Hubris: The Inside Story of Spin, Scandal, and the Selling of the Iraq War* (New York: Three Rivers Press, 2006), p. 35.

88. David Albright, *Iraq's Aluminum Tubes: Separating Fact from Fiction* (Washington, DC: Institute for International Security, December 5, 2003), http://www.isis-online.org/publications/iraq.

89. "Spinning the Tubes."

90. Ibid.

91. Isikoff and Corn, *Hubris*, p. 124.

92. Ibid., p. 145.

93. Nancy Gibbs and John F. Dickerson, "Inside the Mind of George W. Bush," *Time*, September 6, 2004.

94. Gary Langer, "Support for Iraq Attack Drops," ABC News, September 27, 2002, http://abcnews.go.com/sections/us/DailyNews/Iraqpoll020927.html.

95. Isikoff and Corn, *Hubris*, pp. 124–126.

96. Walter Pincus, "Report Cast Doubt on Iraq-Al Qaeda Connection," *Washington Post*, June 22, 2003.

97. *Report on the US Intelligence Community's Prewar Intelligence Assessments on Iraq*, p. 84.

98. *Report of the Commission on the Intelligence Capabilities of the United States Regarding Weapons of Mass Destruction* (Washington, DC, March 31, 2005), p. 202, http://www.wmd.gov/report/wmd_report.pdf.

99. "CIA Admits Lack of Specifics on Iraqi Weapons before Invasion," Agence France-Presse, November 30, 2003.

100. Isikoff and Corn, *Hubris*, pp. 133–34.

101. Dana Milbank and Mike Allen, "Iraq Flap Shakes Rice's Image," *Washington Post*, July 27, 2003.

102. Isikoff and Corn, *Hubris*, pp. 138–39.

103. Walter Pincus, "Prewar Findings Worried Analysts," *Washington Post*, May 22, 2005. See also *Report on the US Intelligence Community's Prewar Intelligence Assessments on Iraq.*

104. Isikoff and Corn, *Hubris*, pp. 140–41.

105. Ibid.

106. George W. Bush, speech, October 7, 2002, http://www.white house.gov/news/releases/2002/10/20021007-8.html.

107. "Threats and Responses: Excerpts from House Debate on the Use of Military Force against Iraq," *New York Times*, October 10, 2002.

108. Senators Joseph Biden (D-DE), Hillary Clinton (D-NY), Tom Daschle (D-SD), Christopher Dodd (D-CT), John Edwards (D-NC), Chuck Hagel (D-NE), and Charles Schumer (D-NY) all voted in favor of the resolution, claiming later that they were really opposed to the war.

CHAPTER 9: TRUTH SYSTEMS

1. Walter Lippmann, *Public Opinion* (New York: Simon & Schuster, 1922).

2. R. I. M. Dunbar, "Coevolution of Neocortical Size, Group Size and Language in Humans," *Behavioral and Brain Sciences* 16, no. 4 (1993): 681–735.

3. *Management Factors Affecting Research and Exploratory Development*, DoD Contract SD 235, April 1965. This research was conducted by Arthur D. Little, Inc., Cambridge, MA.

4. Joe Bel Bruno and Madlen Read, "After Bear Stearns Rescue, Who's Next?" Associated Press, March 18, 2008.

5. Landon Thomas Jr., "Bear's Family Feud: Quarrel Erupts Between the Bank's Elder Statesmen," *New York Times*, May 7, 2008.

6. Karl Mannheim, *Ideology and Utopia* (New York: Harcourt Brace, 1936), pp. 262–75.

7. Edward O. Wilson, *On Human Nature* (Cambridge, MA: Harvard University Press, 1978).

8. "Third U.S. Diplomat Resigns over Iraq Policy," Reuters, March 21, 2003.

9. Sheldon Rampton and John Stauber, *The Best War Ever: Lies, Damned Lies, and the Mess in Iraq* (New York: Jeremy Tarcher/Penguin, 2006), p. 147.

10. Dana Priest and Walter Pincus, "Agency Is Said to Be in Turmoil under New Director Goss," *Washington Post*, November 13, 2004.

11. Dana Priest, "Former Chief of CIA's Bin Laden Unit Leaves," *Washington Post*, November 12, 2004.

12. "Scott Ritter Addresses Iraqi Parliament," BBC, September 8, 2002. http://news.bbc.co.uk/2/hi/not_in_website/syndication/monitoring/media_reports/2244614.stm.

13. Ann Scott Tyson, "Petraeus Helping Pick New Generals; Army Says Innovation Will Be Rewarded," *Washington Post*, November 17, 2007.

14. Emile Durkheim, *The Division of Labor in Society* (Glencoe, IL: Free Press, 1947), pp. 226–29.

15. Max Weber, *The Theory of Social and Economic Organization* (Glencoe, IL: Free Press, 1947), pp. 124–35.

16. Edward O. Wilson, *On Human Nature* (Cambridge, MA: Harvard University Press, 2004), p. 163.

17. Émile Durkheim, *Suicide* (Glencoe, IL: Free Press, 1951).

18. Joseph E. Stiglitz, "War at Any Cost? The Total Economic Costs of the War Beyond the Federal Budget," testimony before the Joint Economic Committee, US Senate, February 28, 2008, http://www2.gsb.columbia.edu/faculty/jstiglitz/download/papers/Stiglitz_testimony.pdf. See also Joseph E. Stiglitz and Linda Bilmes, *The Three Trillion Dollar War* (New York: W. W. Norton, 2008). A lower estimate of $1.7 trillion through 2017 was made by the Congressional Budget Office in its October 2007 report, http://www.cbo.gov/ftpdocs/86xx/doc8690/10-24-CostOfWar_Testimony.pdf.

19. Gilbert Burnham, Riyadh Lafta, Shannon Doocy, and Les Roberts, "Mortality after the 2003 Invasion of Iraq: a Cross-Sectional Cluster Sample Survey," *Lancet*, October 11, 2006. http://www.zmag .org/lancet.pdf. This report has attracted questions and criticism over the methods used. See Neil Munro and Carl M. Cannon, "Data Bomb," *National Journal*, January 4, 2008. http://nationaljournal.com/njcover.htm. Linda Bilmes reports that, in addition to the dead, one-third of the seven hundred and eighty thousand troops discharged since the beginning of the Iraq war have required hospital treatment, including one hundred and twenty thousand treated for mental health conditions. Linda Bilmes, "Another Year, Another $300 Billion," *Boston Globe*, March 16, 2008.

20. "Major Institutions; CBS/New York Times Poll, July 19–17, 2007," Polling Report.com., http://www.pollingreport.com/institut.htm.

21. ABC News/Washington Post Poll, July 18–21, 2007, Washington-post.com., July 30, 2007, http://media.washingtonpost.com/wp-srv/politics/ssi/polls/postpoll_072307.html.

22. David Leonhardt and Marjorie Connelly, "Nation Is Headed on the Wrong Track," *New York Times*, April 2, 2008.

23. "Internet News Audience Highly Critical of News Organizations," Pew Research, August 9, 2007, http://people-press.org/reports/display.php3?ReportID=348.

24. Leo Strauss, *The City and Man* (Chicago: Rand McNally, 1964), pp. 1–4.

25. Danny Postel, "Noble Lies and Perpetual War: Leo Strauss, the Neo-Cons, and Iraq," openDemocracy, October 18, 2003, http://www .opendemocracy.net/faith-iraqwarphiloshophy/article_1542.jsp.

26. Paul Wolfowitz, interview with *Vanity Fair*, May 9, 2003, http://www.defenselink.mil/transcripts/transcript.aspx?transcriptid=2594.

27. Howard Kurtz, "After Blogs Got Hits, CBS Got a Black Eye," *Washington Post*, September 20, 2004.

28. Jay Rosen, "The Legend of Trent Lott and the Weblogs," *Press-Think*, March 15, 2004, http://journalism.nyu.edu/pubzone/weblogs/pressthink/2004/03/15/lott_case.html.

29. Jonathan V. Last, "The Not-So-Swift Mainstream Media," *Weekly Standard*, September 6, 2004, http://www.weeklystandard.com/Utilities/printer_preview.asp?idArticle=4517&R=ECD5DE.

30. In February 2008, Talkingpointsmemo.com received the prestigious Polk Award for Legal Reporting, the first blog to do so. According to the citation, TPM.com "led the news media in coverage of the politically motivated dismissals of United States attorneys across the country. Noting a similarity between firings in Arkansas and California, Marshall and his staff (with his staff reporter-bloggers Paul Kiel and Justin Rood) connected the dots and found a pattern of federal prosecutors being forced from office for failing to do the Bush Administration's bidding. Marshall's tenacious investigative reporting sparked interest by the traditional news media and led to the resignation of Attorney General Alberto Gonzales."

31. Robert Smith, "TalkingPoints Site Kept Attorneys Story Alive," *All Things Considered*, National Public Radio, March 22, 2007, http://www.npr.org/templates/story/story.php?storyId=9083501.

32. The best overall site on the issue of avian flu is http://www.fluwikie.com.

33. David Sifry, "State of the Blogosphere, August 2006," *Sifry's Alerts*, August 7, 2006, http://www.sifry.com/alerts/archives/000436.html.

34. Peter Hirshberg, "Discovery, News and Blogs on the New Technorati.com," *Technorati.com*, December 4, 2007, http://technorati.com/weblog/2007/12/405.html. Also David Sifry, "State of the Blogosphere, August 2006," *Sifry's Alerts*, August 7, 2006. http://www.sifry.com/alerts/archives/000436.html.

35. "Blog Growth Stalling: Some Reasons Why I Nearly Quit Blogging," *Webomatica*, April 27, 2007, http://www.webomatica.com/wordpress/2007/04/27/blog-growth-stalling-some-reasons-why-i-nearly-quit-blogging/.

36. Dave Sifry, "The State of the Live Web," *Technorati*, April 5, 2007, http://technorati.com/weblog/2007/04/328.html.

37. Craig Whitlock, "Al-Qaeda's Growing Online Offensive," *Washington Post*, June 24, 2008.

38. Richard Pérez-Peña, "*Times* to Stop Charging for Parts of Its Web Site," *New York Times*, September 18, 2007.

39. Noam Cohen, "Delaying News in the Era of the Internet," *New York Times*, June 23, 2008.

40. F. A. Hayek, *The Road to Serfdom* (Chicago: University of Chicago Press, 1994).

41. Robert Mackey, "A Call for Eyewitness Photos, Video and Text from Pakistan," *New York Times*, November 9, 2007, http://thelede.blogs.nytimes.com/2007/11/09/a-call-for-eyewitness-photos-video-and-text-from-pakistan/.

42. Jane Perlez, "Bhutto's Persona Raises Distrust, as Well as Hope," *New York Times*, November 10, 2007.

43. Whatever level of mutual support the "secret deal" involved, it did not extend to security. In spite of her urgent pleas for greater police protection, Bhutto was assassinated on December 28, 2007, while three of Musharraf's military guards stood by. The government claimed that security was not at fault; they said Bhutto died from injuries sustained when she struck her head on the edge of the car roof, ducking from the blast. To block any further speculation, the doctors who treated her were silenced, the police chief prohibited an autopsy, and all medical records were immediately confiscated. But an amateur video taken of the scene quickly circulated on the Internet. It appeared to show the assassin, three pistol shots, and Bhutto's hair and scarf being lifted by the force of the bullets as they struck her in the back of the head.

44. In 2002, the International Institute for Democracy and Electoral Assistance published an analysis of voting behavior around the world since 1945, and it ranked the United States 138 out of 169 nations that practice democracy in some form. Compared to Italy (92 percent), Australia (84.2 percent) and Canada (82.6 percent), for example, an average of 47.7 percent of Americans eligible to vote actually participated in the twenty-eight national elections analyzed, comparable to Mexico (48.1 percent), Nigeria (47.6 percent) and Chile (45.9 percent). Rafael López Pintor and Maria Gratschew, "Voter Turnout since 1945," Stockholm: International Institute for Democracy and Electoral Assistance (2002), 84. http://www.idea.int/publications/vt/index.cfm.

45. "The Hall of Mirrors: Perceptions and Misperceptions in the Congressional Foreign Policy Process," Chicago Council on Foreign Relations and the Program on International Policy Attitudes, October 1, 2004.

46. *SIPRI Yearbook 2006, Armaments, Disarmament and International Security*, chap. 8 (Stockholm: Stockholm International Peace Research Institute, 2006).

47. "The Debate Over S-CHIP and the War in Iraq," *CBS News Poll*, October 17, 2007, http://www.cbsnews.com/htdocs/pdf/CBS_news_poll _101707.pdf.

48. "The Hall of Mirrors," p. 19.

49. Ibid., p. 21.

50. John Whitesides, "Voters Unhappy with Bush and Congress," Reuters, October 11, 2007.

51. Dan Froomkin, "Cheney Doesn't Care What You Think," *Washington Post*, March 20, 2008, http://www.washingtonpost.com/wp-dyn/ content/blog/2008/03/20/BL2008032001868.html.

52. Michael J. Sniffen, "Audit: Bush Barely Trims FOIA Backlog," Associated Press, March 17, 2008, http://news.yahoo.com/s/ap/20080317/ ap_on_go_pr_wh/sunshine_week_bush_foia.

53. Edward G. Carmines, Jessica C. Gerrity, and Michael W. Wagner, "How the American Public Views Congress; a Report Based on the Center on Congress' 2004 Public Opinion Survey," Center on Congress at Indiana University, 2005, www.centeroncongress.org/spanish/pdf/ COC%20Survey%2008_2005.pdf.

54. Robert A. Dahl, *Democracy and Its Critics* (New Haven, CT: Yale University Press, 1989) pp. 340–41.

55. Hannah Arendt, *Crises of the Republic* (San Diego, CA: Harcourt Brace Jovanovich, 1972), pp. 232–33.

56. "How Young People View Their Lives, Futures and Politics," Pew Research Center for the People & the Press, January 9, 2007, p. 26.

SELECTED BIBLIOGRAPHY

Achieving Justice: Freeing the Innocent, Convicting the Guilty; Report of the ABA Criminal Justice Section's Ad Hoc Innocence Committee to Ensure the Integrity of the Criminal Process. Chicago: American Bar Association, 2006.

Albright, David. *Iraq's Aluminum Tubes: Separating Fact from Fiction.* Washington, DC: Institute for International Security, December 5, 2003. http://www.isis-online.org/publications/iraq.

Altshuler, Larry H. *Bird-Flu Primer.* New York: Sterling and Ross, 2006.

Balz, Dan, and Bob Woodward. "America's Chaotic Road to War (Part 1: Sept. 11)." *Washington Post,* January 27, 2002.

Bamford, James. "The Man Who Sold the War." *Rolling Stone,* November 17, 2005.

———. *A Pretext for War.* New York: Doubleday, 2004.

Barstow, David, William J. Broad, and Jeff Gerth. "Skewed Intelligence Data in March to War in Iraq." *New York Times,* October 3, 2004.

Bartlett, Frederic Charles. *Remembering.* London: Cambridge University Press, 1932.

Bateson, Gregory. *Steps to an Ecology of Mind.* New York: Ballantine Books, 1972.

Bergen, Peter. "The Battle of Tora Bora: What Really Happened?" PeterBergen.com, October 28, 2004. http://www.peterbergen.com/bergen/articles/details.aspx?id=198.

Blakemore, Colin. *Mechanics of the Mind*. London: Cambridge University Press, 1977.

Branigan, William, and Dana Priest. "Senate Report Blasts Intelligence Agencies' Flaws." *Washington Post*, July 9, 2004. See also "Report of the Select Committee on Intelligence on the U.S. Intelligence Community's Prewar Intelligence Assessments on Iraq" at http://www.fas.org/irp/congress/2006_rpt/srpt109-360.html.

Burrough, Bryan, Evgenia Peretz, David Rose, and David Wise. "The Rush to Invade Iraq: The Ultimate Inside Account." *Vanity Fair*, May 2004.

Campbell, Jeremy. *Grammatical Man: Information, Entropy, Language and Life*. New York: Simon & Schuster, 1982.

Carmines, Edward G., Jessica C. Gerrity, and Michael W. Wagner. *How the American Public Views Congress: A Report Based on the Center on Congress' 2004 Public Opinion Survey*. Center on Congress at Indiana University, 2005. http://www.centeroncongress.org/spanish/pdf/COC%20Survey%2008_2005.pdf.

Carter, Ashton, John Deutch, and Philip Zelikow. "Catastrophic Terrorism: Tackling the New Danger." *Foreign Affairs* 77, no. 6 (November 1998).

Changeux, Jean-Pierre. *The Neuronal Man*. New York: Oxford University Press, 1985.

Cheney, Dick. Interview, *Meet the Press*. NBC News, September 8, 2002. Transcript available at http://www.mtholyoke.edu/acad/intrel/bush/meet.htm.

Clarke, Richard A. *Against All Enemies: Inside America's War on Terror*. New York: Basic Books, 2004.

———. "Clarke's Take on Terror; What Bush's Ex-Adviser Says about Efforts to Stop War on Terror." *60 Minutes*, March 21, 2004. http://www.cbsnews.com/stories/2004/03/19/60minutes/main607356.shtml.

Coll, Steve. *Ghost Wars: The Secret History of the CIA, Afghanistan, and Bin Laden, from the Soviet Invasion to September 10, 2001*. New York: Penguin, 2004.

Cooley, John K. "The U.S. Ignored Foreign Warnings, Too." *International Herald Tribune*, May 21, 2002.

Crosby, Alfred W. *America's Forgotten Pandemic: The Influenza of 1918*. New York: Cambridge University Press, 2003.

Crude Oil; Uncertainty about Future Oil Supply Makes It Important to Develop a Strategy for Addressing a Peak and Decline in Oil Production. Washington, DC: Government Accounting Office, February 2007. http://www.gao.gov/new.items/d07283.pdf.

Douglas, McCollam. "How Chalabi Played the Press." *Columbia Journalism Review* (July/August 2004).

Dulles, Allen W. *The Craft of Intelligence: America's Legendary Spy Master on the Fundamentals of Intelligence Gathering for a Free World*. Guilford, CT: Lyons Press, 2006.

Dunham, Richard S. "Five Questions Bush Must Answer." *Business Week*, May 20, 2002.

Durkheim, Émile. *The Division of Labor in Society*. Translated by George Simpson. Glencoe, IL: Free Press, 1947.

———. *Suicide*. Translated by John A. Spaulding and George Simpson. Glencoe, IL: Free Press, 1951.

Dwyer, Jim, and Michelle O'Donnell. "9/11 Firefighters Told of Isolation amid Disaster." *New York Times*, September 9, 2005.

Ellul, Jacques. *Propaganda*. New York: Alfred A. Knopf, 1965.

Final Report of the National Commission on Terrorist Attacks upon the United States, July 22, 2004. http://www.9-11commission.gov.

Foer, Franklin. "The Source of the Trouble." *New York Magazine*, June 7, 2004.

Ford, Daniel F. *Three Mile Island: Thirty Minutes to Meltdown*. New York: Penguin Books, 1982.

Freeh, Louis. "An Incomplete Investigation: Why Did the 9/11 Commission Ignore Able Danger?" *Wall Street Journal*, November 17, 2005.

Garrett, Laurie. "The Next Pandemic?" *Foreign Affairs* 84, no. 4 (July/August 2005).

Gazzaniga, Michael. *The Social Brain*. New York: Basic Books, 1987.

Gellman, Barton. "The Covert Hunt for bin Laden: Broad Effort Launched After '98 Attacks." *Washington Post*, December 19, 2001.

———. "US Was Foiled Multiple Times in Efforts to Capture Bin Laden or Have Him Killed." *Washington Post*, October 3, 2001.

Gellman, Barton, and Susan Schmidt. "Shadow Government Is at Work in Secret." *Washington Post*, March 1, 2002.

Glasser, Susan B., and Michael Grunwald. "The Steady Buildup to a City's Chaos." *Washington Post*, September 11, 2005.

Goldstein, Ritt. "Oil Wars Pentagon's Policy Since 1999." *Sidney Morning Herald*, May 20, 2003.

Goodwin, James. "Inside Able Danger: The Secret Birth, Extraordinary Life and Untimely Death of a U.S. Military Intelligence Program." *Government Security News*, September 2005. http://www gsnmagazine .com/sep_05/shaffer_interview.html.

Griffin, David Ray. *The 9/11 Commission Report*. Northampton, MA: Olive Branch Press, 2005.

"The Hall of Mirrors; Perceptions and Misperceptions in the Congressional Foreign Policy Process." *Chicago Council on Foreign Relations and the Program on International Policy Attitudes (PIPA)*, October 1, 2004.

Hayek, F. A. *The Road to Serfdom*. Chicago: University of Chicago Press, 1994.

Herman, Edward S., and Noam Chomsky. *Manufacturing Consent*. New York: Pantheon Books, 1988.

Hersh, Seymour M. "King's Ransom: How Vulnerable Are the Saudi Royals?" *New Yorker*, October 22, 2001.

———. *The Target Is Destroyed*. New York: Random House, 1986.

HHS Pandemic Influenza Plan. Washington, DC: Department of Health and Human Services, 2005. http://www.hhs.gov/pandemicflu/plan/ pdf/HHSPandemicInfluenzaPlan.pdf.

Hirshman, Albert O. *Exit, Voice and Loyalty*. Cambridge, MA: Harvard University Press, 1970.

House Armed Services Committee: Subcommittee on Strategic Forces and Subcommittee on Terrorism, Unconventional Threats and Capabilities, *Joint Hearing on the Able Danger Program*, February 15, 2006. http://www.floppingaces.net/wp-content/hearing.pdf.

"Impeachable Crimes Highlighted at UDC Forum." *Executive Intelligence Review*, May 25, 2007. Transcript available at http://www.larouche pub.com/other/2007/3421udc_forum_cheney.html.

Increasing FDNY's Preparedness. New York: New York City Fire Department, August 19, 2002. http://www.nyc.gov/html/fdny/html/mck _report/toc.html.

Investigation Report: Formal Investigation into the Circumstances Surrounding the Downing of Iran Air Flight 655 on 3 July 1988. Washington, DC: Office of the US Secretary of Defense, August 18, 1988. http://homepage.ntlworld.com/jksonc/docs/ir655-dod-report.html.

Isikoff, Michael, and David Corn. *Hubris: The Inside Story of Spin, Scandal, and the Selling of the Iraq War.* New York: Three Rivers Press, 2006.

Jaynes, Julian. *The Origins of Consciousness and the Breakdown of the Bicameral Mind.* Boston: Houghton Mifflin, 1976.

Johnson, Glen. "Probe Reconstructs Horror, Calculated Attacks on Planes." *Boston Globe,* November 23, 2001.

Kahneman, Daniel, and Amos Tversky. "Prospect Theory: An Analysis of Decision under Risk." *Econometrica* (March 1979): 263–91.

Kean, Thomas H., and Lee H. Hamilton. "Kean-Hamilton Statement on Able Danger." *9/11 Public Discourse Project,* August 12, 2005, p. 4. http://www.freerepublic.com/focus/f-news/1464859/posts.

Knox, Richard A. "Doctor's Orders Killed Cancer Patient; Dana-Farber Admits Drug Overdose Caused Death of Globe Columnist, Damage to Second Woman." *Boston Globe,* March 23, 1995.

Lakoff, George, and Mark Johnson. *Philosophy in the Flesh: The Embodied Mind and Its Challenge to Western Thought.* New York: Basic Books, 1999.

Lance, Peter. *Triple Cross.* New York: HarperCollins Publishers, 2006.

Landay, Jonathan S., and Tish Wells. "Global Misinformation Campaign Was Used to Build Case for War." Knight Ridder, March 16, 2004.

Laqueur, Walter. *A World of Secrets: The Uses and Limits of Intelligence.* New York: Basic Books, 1985.

LeDoux, Joseph. *The Emotional Brain: The Mysterious Underpinnings of Emotional Life.* New York: Simon & Schuster, 1996.

Lichtblau, Eric. "Report Details F.B.I.'s Failure on 2 Hijackers." *New York Times,* June 10, 2005.

Linebarger, Paul Myron Anthony. *Psychological Warfare.* Washington, DC: Combat Forces Press, 1954.

Lippmann, Walter. *Public Opinion.* New York: Simon & Schuster, 1922.

Longman, Jere. *Among the Heroes: United Flight 93 and the Passengers and Crew Who Fought Back*. New York: Harper Paperbacks, 2002.

Lord, Walter. *The Night Lives On*. New York: William Morrow, 1986.

Mannheim, Karl. *Ideology and Utopia*. New York: Harcourt Brace, 1936.

Massing, Michael. "Now They Tell Us." *New York Review of Books*, February 26, 2004.

Mayer, Jane. "The Manipulator." *New Yorker*, June 7, 2004.

McConnell, Malcolm. *Challenger: A Major Malfunction*. Garden City, NY: Doubleday, 1987.

Miller, George A. "The Magical Number Seven, Plus or Minus Two." *Psychology Review*, no. 63 (1956).

Miller, James Grier. *Living Systems*. New York: McGraw-Hill, 1978.

Minsky, Marvin. *The Society of Mind*. New York: Simon & Schuster, 1986.

Mylroie, Laurie. "The World Trade Center Bomb: Who Is Ramzi Yousef? And Why It Matters." *National Interest* (Winter 1995/96).

Naughtie, James. *The Accidental American: Tony Blair and the Presidency*. New York: Public Affairs, 2004.

9/11 Timeline. Cooperative Research Project, 2007. http://www.cooperative research.org.

Ornstein, Robert, and David Sobel. *The Healing Brain*. New York: Simon & Schuster, 1987.

Ornstein, Robert, and Richard F. Thompson. *The Amazing Brain*. Boston: Houghton Mifflin, 1984.

Palast, Greg. *Best Democracy Money Can Buy: An Investigative Reporter Exposes the Truth about Globalization, Corporate Cons, and High-Finance Fraudsters*. New York: Plume Books, 2002.

Pandemic Flu and the Potential for U.S. Economic Recession. Washington, DC: Trust for America's Health, December 2007. http://healthy americans.org/reports/flurecession/FluRecession.pdf.

Pandemic Influenza Preparedness and Response Plan. New York: New York City Department of Health and Mental Hygiene, July 2006. http://www.nyc.gov/html/doh/downloads/pdf/cd/cd-panflu-plan.pdf.

Pandemic Influenza Preparedness and Response Plan. Sacramento: California Department of Health Services, September 8, 2006. http://www.dhs.ca.gov/ps/dcdc/izgroup/pdf/pandemic.pdf.

Pangle, Thomas L. *Leo Strauss: An Introduction to His Thought and Intellectual Legacy.* Baltimore: Johns Hopkins University Press, 2006.

Parson, D. Scott. Testimony to the Committee on Financial Services Subcommittee on Oversight and Investigations Protection and Compliance Policy. US House of Representatives, June 29, 2006. http://www.ustreas.gov/press/releases/js4342.htm.

Pelletière, Stephen. *Iraq and the International Oil System: Why America Went to War in the Gulf.* Westport, CT: Praeger, 2001.

———. "A War Crime or Act of War?" *New York Times,* January 31, 2003.

Penfield, Wilder, and T. Rasmussen. *The Cerebral Cortex of Man.* New York: Macmillan, 1957.

Pilger, John. "This War of Lies Goes On." *Daily Mirror* (London), November 18, 2001.

Porter, Dorothy. *Health, Civilization, and the State.* New York: Routledge, 1999.

Postel, Danny. "Noble Lies and Perpetual War: Leo Strauss, the Neocons, and Iraq." openDemocracy, October 18, 2003. http://www.opendemocracy.net/faith-iraqwarphiloshophy/article_1542.jsp

"Protector of the American Fleet." *New York Times Magazine,* October 6, 1985, pp. 34–37.

Rampton, Sheldon, and John Stauber. *The Best War Ever: Lies, Damned Lies, and the Mess in Iraq.* New York: Jeremy Tarcher/Penguin, 2006.

———. *Weapons of Mass Deception: The Uses of Propaganda in Bush's War on Iraq.* New York: Jeremy Tarcher/Penguin, 2003.

Rebuilding America's Defenses: Strategies, Forces, and Resources for a New Century. Washington, DC: Project for the New American Century, 2000. http://www.newamericancentury.org/RebuildingAmericasDefenses.pdf.

Report of the Commission on the Intelligence Capabilities of the United States Regarding Weapons of Mass Destruction. Washington, DC, March 31, 2005. http://www.wmd.gov/report/wmd_report.pdf.

Report of the Presidential Commission on the Space Shuttle Challenger Accident. Washington: Government Printing Office, June 6, 1986.

Report of the President's Commission on the Accident at Three Mile Island. Washington, DC: Government Printing Office, 1979.

Report on the U.S. Intelligence Community's Prewar Intelligence Assessments on

Iraq. Washington, DC: Select Committee on Intelligence, US Senate, July 7, 2004. http://www.globalsecurity.org/intell/library/congress/2004_rpt/iraq-wmd_intell_09jul2004_report2.pdf.

A Review of the FBI's Handling of Intelligence Information Related to the September 11 Attacks. Washington, DC: Office of Inspector General, US Department of Justice, November 2004.

Rice, Condoleezza. Testimony to Hearing of the National Commission on Terrorist Attacks upon the United States, April 8, 2004. news.findlaw.com/hdocs/docs/terrorism/911comm40804tran.pdf.

Risen, James. "CIA's Inquiry on Qaeda Aide Seen as Flawed." *New York Times*, September 22, 2002.

———. "US Failed to Act on Warnings in '98 of a Plane Attack." *New York Times*, September 18, 2002.

Rosen, James. "A 9/11 Tip-Off: Fact or Fancy? Debate Still Swirls around Claims that Secret Military Program ID'd Hijackers a Year Before Attacks." *Sacramento Bee*, November 24, 2005.

Rufford, Nicholas. "Revealed: How MI6 Sold the Iraq War." *Sunday Times* (London), December 28, 2003.

Samit, Harry. Testimony in the Zacarias Moussaoui Trial, US District Court for the Eastern District of Virginia, Alexandria Division, March 9, 2006.

Scheer, Robert. "The 9/11 Secret in the CIA's Back Pocket." *Los Angeles Times*, October 19, 2004.

Scherer, K., and P. Ekman, eds. *Approaches to Emotion.* Hillsdale, NJ: Lawrence Earlbaum, 1984.

Scheuer, Michael. *Imperial Hubris: Why the West Is Losing the War on Terror.* Dulles, VA: Potomac Books, 2005.

"Sea of Lies." *Newsweek*, July 13, 1992, pp. 29–39.

Shaffer, Anthony. Prepared Statement to House, Armed Service Committee, Congress of the United States, 109th Cong., 2d sess., 2006. http://www.abledangerblog.com/2006/02/lt-col-shaffers-written-testimony.html.

Sifry, Dave. "The State of the Live Web." Technorati, April 5, 2007. http://technorati.com/weblog/2007/04/328.html.

Simon, Herbert. *Administrative Behavior.* New York: Macmillan, 1957.

———. *Models of Man.* New York: John Wiley & Son, 1957.

Skyrms, Brian. *The Stag Hunt and the Evolution of Social Structure*. New York: Cambridge University Press, 2003.

Smith, Adam. *Powers of Mind*. New York: Simon & Schuster, 1975.

Smith, Robert. "TalkingPoints Site Kept Attorneys Story Alive." *All Things Considered*, National Public Radio. March 22, 2007. http://www.npr.org/templates/story/story.php?storyId=9083501.

Snow, Nancy. *The Information War: American Propaganda, Free Speech and Opinion Control Since 9/11*. New York: Seven Stories Press, 2003.

Southwell, Brian G., Yoori Hwang, and Alicia Torres. "Avian Influenza and U.S. TV News." *CDC EID Journal* 12, no. 11 (November 2006). http://www.cdc.gov/ncidod/EID/vol12no11/06-0672.htm.

"Spinning the Tubes." *Four Corners*, Australia Broadcasting Corporation, October 27, 2003. http://www.abc.net.au/4corners/content/2003/transcripts/s976015.htm.

Sunstein, Cass R. *Infotopia: How Many Minds Produce Knowledge*. New York: Oxford University Press, 2006.

Suskind, Ron. *The One Percent Doctrine: Deep Inside America's Pursuit of Its Enemies Since 9/11*. New York: Simon & Schuster, 2006.

Tenet, George. *At the Center of the Storm: My Years at the CIA*. New York: HarperCollins, 2007.

Thomas, Evan. "How Bush Blew It." *Newsweek*, September 19, 2005.

Thomas, Evan, and Mark Hosenball. "Bush: 'We're at War.'" *Newsweek*, September 24, 2001.

Trippi, Joe. *The Revolution Will Not Be Televised: Democracy, the Internet, and the Overthrow of Everything*. New York: HarperCollins, 2004.

Unger, Craig. "Saving the Saudis." *Vanity Fair*, October 2003. http://www.wesjones.com/saudi1.htm.

US Congress. House Permanent Select Committee on Intelligence and the Senate Select Committee on Intelligence. *Final Report, Part Three; Topics—The Attacks of September 11, 2001*. 108th Cong., 1st sess., 2003.

US Congress. House Permanent Select Committee on Intelligence and the Senate Select Committee on Intelligence. *Joint Inquiry Staff Statement, Part I*. 107th Cong., 2d sess., 2002. http://www.fas.org/irp/congress/2002_hr/091802hill.html.

US Congress. House Permanent Select Committee on Intelligence and the Senate Select Committee on Intelligence. *Report of the Joint Inquiry into the Terrorist Attacks of September 11, 2001*, 108th Cong., 1st sess., 2003.

Van Meter, Jonathan. "Unanchored." *New York Magazine*, September 19, 2005.

Waas, Murray. "Key Bush Intelligence Briefing Kept from Hill Panel." *National Journal* (November 22, 2005).

Waller, Douglas. "Inside the Hunt for Osama." *Time*, December 21, 1998.

Warrick, Joby, and Joe Stephens. "Before Attack, U.S. Expected Different Hit; Chemical, Germ Agents Focus of Preparations." *Washington Post*, October 2, 2001.

Watzlawick, Paul. *How Real Is Real?* New York: Vintage, 1977.

Weber, Max. *The Theory of Social and Economic Organization*. Translated by A. M. Henderson and Talcott Parsons. Glencoe, IL: Free Press, 1947.

West, Charles K. *The Social and Psychological Distortion of Information*. Chicago: Nelson-Hall, 1981.

Wilson, Edward O. *On Human Nature*. Cambridge, MA: Harvard University Press, 1978.

Wolfowitz, Paul. Interview with *Vanity Fair*, May 9, 2003. http://www.defenselink.mil/transcripts/transcript.aspx?transcriptid=2594

Woodson, Grattan. *Bird Flu Manual*. Charleston, SC: Booksurge.com, 2006.

———. *The Bird Flu Preparedness Planner; What It Is, How It Spreads, What You Can Do*. Deerfield Beach, FL: Health Communications, 2005.

Wright, George. "Wolfowitz: Iraq War Was about Oil." *Guardian Unlimited*, June 4, 2003.

Wyden, Peter. *Bay of Pigs*. New York: Simon & Schuster, 1979.

Zaid, Mark. Testimony before the Senate Judiciary Committee, Able Danger and Intelligence Information Sharing. Washington, DC: US Congress, Senate Committee on Judiciary, 109th Cong., 1st sess., 2005). http://judiciary.senate.gov/testimony.cfm?id=1606&wit_id=4668.

INDEX